THE INTENT TO KILL

Making Sense of Murder

THE INTENT TO KILL

Making Sense of Murder

Edward Green

Clevedon Books   1993   Baltimore, Maryland

Copyright © 1993 by Edward Green

ISBN: 0-937715-02-6

Library of Congress Catalog Number: 92-82975

Manufactured in the United States of America by the Arcata
Graphics Company

Acknowledgments

Werner J. Einstadter and S. Joseph Fauman read an earlier version of the manuscript and gave thoughtful suggestions. Their advice was indispensable in improving the book; the author takes responsibility for any deficiencies. My publisher has provided helpful editorial guidance. Mr. William Delhey, District Attorney of Washtenaw County, Michigan and Mr. Lynwood Noah, Assistant District Attorney, facilitated my access to the materials on the case of Leo Kelly. Mr. William Waterman, Mr. Kelly's counsel, added to my understanding of the case. My wife who doubles as a word consultant patiently put up with my abandon in bringing forth a book. I also express my indebtedness to the many true crime writers whose books have provided many of the personalities and situations which I use as data in analyzing the intents and purposes of people who kill.

Contents

Preface

This is a book about the many ways we comprehend the moral incongruity of people killing people. My thinking on the subject began more than fifty years when I took my first courses in sociology and psychology and evolved over the forty years that I have taught university courses on the subject of crime. During that period I experienced a growing discomfort with certain customs of criminological thought relative to the causation of crime. The first is the elevation of any trait, condition, or circumstance statistically or clinically associated with crime to the status of *cause*. The second is the scientific dogma that there are *many* causes of crime, and the third is the platitude, that no one cause is decidedly more important than others. In testing these doctrines I limit my inquiry to the crime of homicide. The diversity among the various forms of crime in definition, behavior patterns, and view of their gravity would unduly complicate the task for crime generally. Much of what I shall have to say, however, applies to all forms of violent crime

Criminology texts note literally scores of reputed causes based on the observation of conditions under which homicide is more or less likely to occur. But they offer no generalization on how these conditions transform into the resolve to kill. The job of answering this question in individual cases has been preempted by clinical psychologists and psychiatrists who serve the criminal court in judging the mental states of offenders. The untidy methodology of their diagnoses and their partisanship, for the defense or the prosecution, justify little confidence in their opinions.

Virtually every branch of knowledge has something to say about the impulse to kill. The law, in its own matter of fact idiom, goes directly to the seat of awareness in declaring the *intent to kill* to be the cause of homicide The law has nothing to say, however, about the conditions which give rise to that intent. Fiction writers are free to construct the plot and setting for their killings and to lay out every nuance of thought and feeling experienced by the killer as he moves from the inception of the intent to kill to the aftermath. But they use this license, alas, in the service of sensationalism rather than truth as they think of new angles to titillate jaded readers with gruesome details of killings by psychological monsters.

Science, on the other hand, balks at the question of the intent of the killer with the excuse that, *intent*, like *purpose* or *will*, is a metaphysical concept, uninvestigable by the scientific method. Accordingly, science has restricted the search for the causes of crime to measurable conditions which have a material base. This restraint effectively bars the scientific consideration of *the individual's resolve to kill, the one cause into which any and all other "causes" must converge in order for a killing to take place.*

Nevertheless some theories of the cause of murder are verifiably more efficient than others in identifying the conditions under which homicide occurs. They are the ones which bring us closest sequentially and meaningfully to the intents and purposes of the murderer. By this standard, the natural sciences provide the weakest explanations. They seek the causes of murder in conditions as remote from the schemes and purposes of killers as stormy weather, nutrition, the phases of the moon, defective genes, organic defect, mental disorder, and the Pavlovian conditioning of responses. The social sciences locate the causes of murder much closer to the awareness that mobilizes and directs the energies of the individual. Sociologists and social psychologists delve into the social and cultural environment which nourishes the individual's world of meanings to discover the attitudes, values, sentiments, and beliefs which produce a propensity for homicide. But they stop short of explaining how that propensity gets transformed into the most crucial link in the chain of causation: *the intent to kill.*

The scientific inhibition on probing the intent of the killer has chilled efforts to go directly to the heart of the problem. Theories of violent crime commonly begin with data on the characteristics or situations of offenders, but often conclude with abstraction piled on abstraction. The thinking, feeling, intending person is dissolved in the statistical and theoretical "models" that criminologists construct to impart a scientific gloss to their ruminations.

My mission in this treatise is to restore the killer, as a calculating, adaptive, self-determined actor to the homicidal scenario, from which he or she has been removed by the dictates of law and science or the exaggerations of popular literature. The task pools data and insights from scientific, legal, and literary perspectives to identify the conditions which prompt the homicidal solution to problems of personal adjustment and to clarify the transformation of those conditions into the intent to kill.

To accomplish the job I propose to ascertain the killer's intents and purposes by a method of controlled deduction. This exercise bears a resemblance to the clinical artistry claimed by psychiatrists who testify on the mental states and motivation of criminal offenders. But the data of analysis are quite different, since I find no sound basis for attributing violent crime to organic or psychological states. The technique which I put forth is disciplined by the requirement that inferences concerning the intents and purposes of killers heed the social, cultural, and situational stimulation which inform choice. The material on killings consist of case studies developed from the rich literature of official reports and documentary studies of homicides. The resulting insights will be applied to the evaluation of theories of criminal homicide, the process whereby criminal courts arrive at judgments of intent and motive in murder trials, and to the appraisal of public policies for the suppression of violent crime.

Chapter 1 establishes the frame of reference of the inquiry. Chapters 2-4 identify and evaluate the major factors and variables embodied in theories of the cause of criminal homicide. Chapter 5 sets forth a classification of homicides based on the individual interests served and the group interests violated by killing people. Chapters 6-10, respectively, elaborate on each of the forms of homicide identified in Chapter 5. Chapters 11-15 show how confusion over the causes of homicide distorts the fact-finding and judgmental processes of the murder trial. Chapter 16 confronts the conventional views of the causation of homicide with an existential view of reality. Chapter 17 delivers a critical evaluation of existing policies and programs for the control of violent crime. The easy availability of guns adds to the pessimism. In a more optimistic vein the chapter goes on to specify what needs to be done to obstruct and stifle the intent to kill.

In writing this book I have had a number of readerships in mind. Criminologists will recognize the work as a criminology of homicide that balances the view of a rigidly materialistic determination of violent crime with a humanistic view of self-determination. To the journalist-crime writer, the true crime buff, or the curious citizen, I offer a guide for evaluating the conventional, and some unconventional, wisdom concerning the nature, causes, and control of homicide. Criminal lawyers will find fresh ideas to supplement outworn theories of forensic psychiatry in arguing issues of motive and responsibility. They may also find useful some experimentally validated techniques for influencing the direction of judgments which juries are asked to make in murder trials. Finally, for policy makers, activists, and concerned citizens, I show why existing policies have not dented homicide rates and what should be done to utilize more effectively existing resources for combatting violent crime.

THE INTENT TO KILL

Making Sense of Murder

1

Perspectives On Homicide

Murder as a Social Problem

If we accept the dictum of the nineteenth century French physician Alexander Lacassagne that societies get the criminals they deserve, the massive toll of murder in the United States of America is an acute embarrassment. In the past twenty-five years criminal violence in the United States has claimed more than half a million lives, ten times the number of American battle deaths in the Viet Nam War. Fear of victimization rends the social fabric, implanting suspicion of the stranger and hobbling freedom of movement in crime-ridden localities. A conservative estimate of the material cost of the carnage, including loss of income of both victims and offenders, insurance, legal fees, maintenance of offenders in prison for an average of fifteen years, and welfare assistance to the families of victims and imprisoned killers adds up to an estimated $1.5 million per case; for all cases, a total in one year of $112.25 billion, an amount equal to one-half of the average annual federal budget deficit for the years 1986-1990. No dollar amount, however, can make up for the emotional devastation and dislocation of the lives of survivors, condemned to an unending anguish fed by the constant reminder in photos on the mantel of the incompletely fulfilled lives of loved ones.

The United States has the highest homicide rate of all technologically advanced nations, higher even than most less developed nations. We proclaim ourselves the world's standard bearer in the advancement of human rights, yet fail to indoctrinate large segments of our population with the respect for human life and self-restraint required for participation in an orderly society. We lament the toll of premature death from AIDS, heart disease, or cancer, convinced that a cure can be found if enough resources are devoted to research, yet suffer murder with the same resignation that we endure earthquakes and tornadoes. The near constancy of murder rates over long periods of time reinforces the attitude of inevitability. Sedated by the trivialization of murder resulting from the glut of its coverage in the news and its antiseptic portrayal in the entertainment media, dread yields to apathy.

Homicide and Human Nature

Although homicide threatens the most basic of human values, it also usefully serves human interests. The adaptive functions and prevalence of homicide, plus the diversity in the personal characteristics of killers and the circumstances of killing, bolster the opinion common to legal, scientific, and literary texts that humans share with other animal species a latency for killing their own kind.

Nobel Prize winning biologist Konrad Lorenz has taken exception to this view, observing that of all the carnivorous animals, man and the rat stand alone in having no innate inhibitions on killing their own kind. (Lorenz, 229) In a fight between wolves, for example, the baring of the throat by the loser is an instinctively understood signal to the winner to break off the encounter. Naturalist Boyce Rensberger takes issue with Lorenz. Citing the commonness of intra-species killing among free-living animals—lions, gulls, hyenas, hippopotamuses, langurs, and macaques—he regards the imputation of chivalric courtesy to animals as romantic whimsy. (Rensberger, 121) Miss Jane Goodall's extensive observations of chimpanzees, man's closest animal relations, in their natural habitat includes instances of adult members of one band ganging up on and fatally beating individuals of another band. She also notes instances of adult females killing and cannibalizing other females' young. (Goodall) Fossil finds of the crushed skulls of prehistoric human types with nearby stone objects identified as weapons bear witness to the homicidal, and likely cannibalistic, dispositions of the precursors of modern man.

Refinements of brain anatomy which enlarge the thinking capacity of humans account for qualitative differences between humans and animals in the characteristics of intra-species killing. Among animals, position in a hierarchy of physical dominance depends on sex and the relative size and strength of individuals; in human groupings, intellect and man-made weaponry level the effect of physical inequality. An even wider chasm between man and other animals is the human ability to intuit directly, by means of language, as well as signs, the thoughts and feelings of fellow-beings. Thus killing people presents the paradox that individuals, who have the empathic capability of putting themselves in the place of others, do to others what they would avoid at all costs having done to themselves.

In recognition of the deadly capacities of humans, all societies taboo the killing of members. All civilized nations, historical and contemporary, have enacted harsh penalties for criminal homicide. The origin of the prohibition against life threatening acts has been variously explained in terms of survival instincts, the requirement of social stability, and the empathic faculty indispensable to the inter-dependence required for communal living.

Some legal philosophers and criminologists, however, find no basis in the natural order for moral absolutes and argue that the moral evaluation of murder, like lesser crimes, such as prostitution and vagrancy, is relative to time and place. Thus heinous crimes in one historical or geographical setting may be socially approved conduct in another—a claim supported by accounts of the whoesale slaughter of subject peoples, captives, heretics, or enemies in the name God, folk, or morality. Such atrocities do not, however, prove the provisional character of the prohibition of murder since the ban applies only to those who are regarded as members of in-groups; members of out-groups may be fair prey. The more tightly knit the in-group, the less the restriction on killing outsiders. Anthropological lore contains frequent references to non-literate peoples whose word for members of their own group is the equivalent of "human"; outsiders are denoted by terms that mark them as less than human. In historic civilizations the status of *infidel*, *pagan*, or *barbarian* deprived one of the rights and privileges of humankind.

History repeatedly tells of mass slaughter and the annihilation of whole peoples in struggles over land, wealth, limited resources, and religious truth. The dehumanization of religious or racial minorities has provided oppressor groups with license to proclaim their moral superiority and to scapegoat the subjugated class. Lacking an identifiable minority to domineer, the Puritan clergy in Massachusetts colony created one of menopausal women whose erratic behavior, later labelled *involutional melancholia* in psychiatry, earned them denunciation as witches and death by hanging. In the American pre-Civil War South some preachers pondered from the pulpit whether the Negro possesses a soul. Those who concluded they don't, felt justified in regarding them as animals, suitable for enslavement and ineligible for protection by law. European anti-semitism originated in the theological dogma that the Jews forfeited any claim to the ordinary mercies because they killed the Lord. Belief in the Jews' depravity has generated waves of accusations concerning their involvment in evil schemes. The alleged machinations have changed over the centuries in accordance with the delusive imagery of the times—collaboration with the devil, the use of the blood of Christian children in ritual and the manufacture of matzos, economic voracity, and conspiracy to take over the world. The defamation has continued unabated into the modern period, marked by recurrent massacres and the extermination of millions of Jews in Nazi death camps.

The typification of Jews, Gypsies, political undesirables, sexual deviates, and the mentally diseased in dehumanizing terms validated acts of extreme brutality in World War II extermination camps by German SS officers and camp personnel who in their private lives were esteemed by themselves and others as decent people. Those who supervised the killers were unwilling, however, to submit this validation to the judgment of public opinion or history, but attempted to conceal the slaughter with a cloak of secrecy and stringent security precautions. The mass removal of Jews to death camps was disguised as relocation to labor camps, a deception maintained to the end. As the doomed victims marched into extermination centers, they beheld the slogan over the portals, *Arbeit Macht Frei.* (Work Will Free You.) The camp at Theresienstadt for a period was maintained for display to the International Red Cross as a place where Jews were humanely confined.

Not all governments under German control found it necessary or even desirable to gloss over their deadly intentions. Slovakia began in 1939 to enact anti-Jewish laws similar to Germany's. "In 1942 the Slovakian Parliament legislated a deportation of Jews, paying Germany a fee of 500 Reichsmarks for each man, woman and child sent to their deaths, and confiscating their possessions. No other country under German domination sanctified such actions by law." (*New York Times*, 12/3/91, 5)

The equivocation over whether a deliberate killing, neither in self-defense nor for any other legally sanctioned reason, is necessarily a crime is not confined to totalitarian régimes. The disposition in the case of Lt. William Calley, the American army officer court-martialed for his role in ordering the extermination of civilians in the village of My Lai during the Viet Nam War, illustrates the subordination of the legal and moral significance of killing to political considerations. Few questioned the enormity of the slaying of unarmed men, women, and children. Calley was convicted and sentenced to twenty years. But in the sundered political mood of the time, Calley was viewed by many as a victim: first, as a scapegoat for higher echelons of the military beleaguered by criticism of an unpopular war and, second, as a casualty of the brutalizing influence of a war in which Vietnamese women and children allegedly threw grenades at unsuspecting American soldiers. Political pressure helped to bring about a reduction of the sentence to ten years. After only three years of confinement, not in a federal penitentiary, but on a military base, with full freedom of movement, Calley was paroled. The Secretary of the Army declared that he understood how a person in Calley's position might have construed his orders to mean that it was correct to kill unarmed civilians.

Killing in warfare is legal by national and international law so long as it is directed at military targets. The effectiveness of a military unit depends on how efficiently training procedures wipe out inhibitions on killing people. Not until World War II did systematic research give credence to what previously had been military folklore: the refusal or reluctance of many soldiers to use their weapons with maximum effectiveness. Some soldiers in combat fear that shooting their rifles will give away their position and bring down enemy fire. Others have a moral block against killing which is overcome only in situations where killing is the alternative to being killed. Those who survive learn that staying alive depends on their effectiveness at killing. Those who do not grasp this truth are more likely to become casualties.

Gains from Homicide

Homicide has meaningful functions for the offender and the community. Prudently or imprudently effected, murder is impelled by mundane wishes routinely satisfied non-violently in everyday relationships. Killers seek to eradicate threats and and obstacles to personal goals. Killing facilitates the attainment of material and sensual gratification, novelty, security, power, and admiration in circles that regard killing as a respected vocation or a test of courage. The layers of faulty judgment and the maladroitness of performance characteristic of most killings do not disprove the rationality of the killer's goal or the means for achieving it.

Murder, paradoxically, confers benefits upon the law-abiding population. The awareness of disaster which has befallen victims fuels primal adaptive dynamisms in the human psyche. The facts of a killing inform us vicariously of the horror of sudden death and offer lessons on avoidance. The gawking of motorists passing an auto collision, the conversion of the site of a natural disaster into a tourist attraction, the gathering of a crowd around the blood-stained site of a killing, the witnessing of an execution or a lynching—all express outwardly a universal curiosity over what it's like to get killed and, inwardly a gush of relief at being alive. The outrage directed at the murder and the vengeful mood of the legal ritual attending its suppression invigorate the moral order and fortify social solidarity. The social marginality of a large proportion of homicide offenders and victims accommodates the Malthusian solution to the problem of excess population: society gets rid of unproductive and troublesome elements by death or incarceration.

On the practical side, the theme of murder sustains many vocations. For authors, publishers, and booksellers, the topic of murder, fictional or true, has great commercial value. The literary treatment of the subject reflects intellectual and emotional interests ranging from the intriguing challenge of the classic English manor-weekend murder mystery novel to the vicarious fulfillment of sado-masochistic fantasies in the horror genre of murder fiction. Murder is a main staple of motion picture and television stories. The monotonously repetitive exchange of gunfire between the criminal and the lawman, or opposing gangs of criminals exposes the poverty of imagination of the media hacks. Life imitates the artlessness of the media in the routine accounts in the morning news of last night's killings in the community. Fear of violent crime supports the business of installing and monitoring burglar alarms. The demand for protective weapons helps businesses devoted to the manufacture, distribution, and sale of guns and mace spraying devices.

Mental health agencies employing psychiatrists, clinical psychologists, social workers, and supporting staffs for the study and personality evaluation of criminal offenders comprise a large service industry of state and local government. A large share of the work of correctional personnel—prison and jail workers, probation and parole officers, psychologists and educators—is devoted to the custody, care, and rehabilitation of violent offenders. Governments and private foundations award large sums for research on crime. The academic study of crime occupies an important niche in the curriculum of higher education and provides teaching jobs for a legion of faculty. Instruction in criminology and criminal justice, formerly offered in one or two courses in the sociology department of colleges and universities, has proliferated since the nineteen-seventies into numerous undergraduate and graduate offerings, consolidated in independent departments devoted to instruction on crime and its control. Enrollment in these programs is bolstered by the growing requirement of a degree in criminal justice for career advancement in law enforcement.

Views on Causation

However unexceptional, and serviceable, the violent predisposition may be, it is ascribed by law to a defect of character, and by science, to a pathology of mind or body, or a deficiency in the material conditions of life. Maybe that is the reason that so many scientifically grounded efforts to comprehend or suppress violence don't succeed: they focus on the abnormality rather than the normality of killing.

In many pre-modern societies the question of causation did not arise. The fact that a homicide happened—not what produced it, or whether it was intentional—was paramount. The loss of a member of the community was the critical concern. Legal action was aimed at obtaining material reparations from the killer or his family. In modern societies the fact that the killing happened is less important than what brought it about. When the question of what caused a killing arises, the law, in the interest of dispensing justice, asks *why* the killing occurred; science, in the interest of enlightenment, asks *how* the killing occurred. The difference reflects a deep philosophical division between law and science. *Why* locates the origin of the act in the volition of the actor; *how*, puts it outside of the will of the actor. The criminal law holds the killer morally accountable viewing him as a self-willed, rational, person who intends the consequences of his act. The social and behavioral sciences, by contrast, regard the killer as a passive object driven by internal and external forces over which he has no control.

A. The Law

The criminal law holds that killing, like other forms of violent crime, reflects a flawed moral disposition expressed in a pitiless pursuit of self-interest. For a legally forbidden act to be considered a crime, it must embody a maliciousness of purpose or recklessness of action denoted *mens rea*, which in the Latinized language of law, stands for "guilty mind," a ponderous term meaning that the wrongdoer has not complied with the moral duty to suppress conduct he knows to be wrong and injurious in its consequences. The wilfullness of the wrongful conduct is conveyed by the notion of *intent*, construed in law as the resolve to do the forbidden act.

The legal view of the individual as a self-determined moral agent excludes mind from the totality of things subject to natural causation. The person possesses freedom of will; therefore his intentions control his actions. *Motive*, as conceived in law, is what the individual hopes to gain by the offending behavior, and may be inferred from what the killer says of his reasons for killing or the circumstances under which the killing occurs. A motive is not a legally necessary element of a criminal act. The prosecution is not required to demonstrate a motive in order to obtain a conviction. Whether a premeditated poison-killing charged as first degree murder is induced by greed, to inherit the victim's wealth, or by compassion, to end the suffering of a person in the terminal stage of an incurable disease, is not legally germane to the issue of guilt or innocence. Nevertheless judges and juries frequently soften or harden their judgments based on such distinctions. The question of motive may properly arise, however, if it constitutes a link in the chain of evidence, raises a presumption of mental incompetence, or bears on the legal gravity of the killing.

In the uncomplicated prescientific psychology of the criminal law, *motive* is the engine of the act; *intent* is the pilot, maintaining a course of action in the face of changing circumstances to achieve a targeted goal. *Intention*, as apart from *intent*, is the mental image of the completed act. The law connects motive to intent by regarding it as "that which incites one to form the intention." (Kearney, 80)

The intangibility of *intent* seems to present no problem for the legal fact-finding process. The obviousness of the offender's intent is expressed in the maxim of law: *The facts speak for themselves.* The law takes the commonsense view that the actor intends the fore-seeable consequences of his behavior. Elements of behavior exhibited in a slaying—threats, the procurement of a murder weapon, the hiring of an assassin, the luring of a victim to the place of his death, or the purchase of insurance on the life of the victim shortly before the killing—are some of the plain indications of intent. The determination of an accused's intent rests on the presumption that those who make the evaluation—judge, juror, attorney, or expert witness—and the accused, by virtue of their maturation in a common social environment and the ability to share one another's perspectives, define things with some degree of similitude. This supposition is so compelling, that seldom does the intent set forth in the allegation of a criminal act become an issue in the trial.

B. Science

Scientists resist the appeal of the "obvious." Lacking the instruments to measure such intangibles as *intent* and *purpose*, they simply bypass them. They ascribe killing to material forces outside of the control of the killer and invest them with an import far removed from anything the killer has in mind in planning or inflicting the deadly act. To scientists the individual's sense of self-determination, as conceived in law, is an illusion. They contend that the history of science bears repeated witness to the lesson—so convincingly taught by Newton's gravity, Darwin's evolution, Mendel's genetics, and Einstein's relativity—that things are not what they seem to be.

Some behavioral scientists have zealously advanced this lesson to counter the law's view of the rationality of the homicidal act. They seem to vie in locating the cause as far as possible from the actor's conscious awareness. For psychologists who take pride in their scientific purity, the killer's sense of intending and what he says concerning his reasons for killing are the pale reflection of subterranean mental processes outside of conscious awareness or control. They regard the legal notions of intent and motive as metaphysical concepts outside the scope of scientific investigation. Psychologists disapprovingly characterize the belief that behavior is guided by the will of the actor as *mentalism*, the naive notion that the working of the mind as revealed through introspection explains the action which flows from it.

No material condition is excluded from consideration. Psychologists Nathaniel J. Pallone and James J. Hennessy note statistical relationships between homicide and literally scores of organic, neurologic, and mental states, not to mention external conditions including weather, air pollution, physique, church attendance, marital status, participation of women in the labor force, the academic performance of high school students, the number of thunderstorm days in a year, and cigaret consumption.

The effect of any of these factors is indirect, requiring the mediation of additional factors to achieve some sensible linkage with homicide. For example, Pallone and Henessey attribute the correlation between the frequency of thunderstorms and homicide to the release by storms of vast quantities of nitrogen into the atmosphere. The surfeit of nitrogen, they suggest "...may well trigger episodes of nitrogen narcosis" believed to resemble alcohol intoxication which undoubtedly plays an important role in the causation of homicide. (Lester, 1977; noted in Pallone, 1992, 251; 253) Sober reflection on the difference between the two forms of intoxication invalidates the *nitrogen* hypothesis. Alcohol intoxication affects the minds of only those who drink to excess. The thunderstorms which supposedly produce nitrogen narcosis apply to everybody in the area affected. Since the vast majority of the population remains immune to the homicidal effect, the linkage must lie elsewhere. I suggest a more down-to-earth explanation.

Prolonged confinement indoors increases the probability that violence-prone people and their victims will get on one another's nerves under conditions of heightened provocation and the inhibition numbing effects of alcoholic consumption.

Research on the phases of the moon relative to homicide is another example of the vast causal distance which some scientists place between the awareness of the individual and his conduct. Significant correlations between the lunar cycle and homicide rates have been obtained in studies of Dade County (Miami), Florida, and Cuyahoga County (Cleveland), Ohio. Homicide rates tend to rise during the period of the full moon. The investigators hypothesize that the force that brings about the rise and fall of the ocean's tides may replenish or deplete bodily fluids with homicidal implications. (Lieber et al) I propose an alternative explanation, one that concedes some degree of self-determination to the actor. A lighter sky, prompting less sleep and more nocturnal sociability of a kind involving the consumption of liquor and narcotics, conduces to violent interaction. In support of the latter interpretation, it would seem that the lunar effect has no homicidal effect on the more socially stable elements of the population. As Bensing and Schroeder's study of homicide in one of the areas studied for the effects of the lunar cycle (Cleveland, Ohio) indicates, the killings are almost entirely a product of the underclass propensity for violence. (See Chapter 3)

The conception of *cause* employed by social and behavioral scientists contributes to the unreliability of their explanations of homicide. In rigorous scientific usage the term cause signifies an antecedent factor or complex of factors which must be invariably present when the effect occurs and without which the effect does not occur. By this standard, the causes of homicide, if indeed there are scientific causes, have yet to be discovered. When social behavioral scientists write about the "causes of crime," they have in mind a much softer conception of cause. They mean no more than that a condition deemed causal occurs *significantly* more often among criminals than non-criminals. The criterion of *significance* requires only that differences as large as those observed have, by established statistical custom, no more than a 5 percent chance of occurrrence. Thus in actual practice the hypothesized causes in many or most cases do not accompany murder, and are often absent when murder occurs.

To explain individual killings which may or may not be accompanied by statistically established causes, clinical practitioners in psychiatry and psychology apply their distinctive methodology to the examination of the offender. Clinical diagnosis, as detailed in Chapter 11, is routinely performed and the results are stereotypically stated in a morass of neuropsychiatric and psychological test jargon. One reason for the shortcoming of clinical reports is the limited objective assigned to clinicians by the legal system. The law is concerned with the issue of guilt or innocence, not the cause of the killing or the motive of the killer. The court wishes to know only if disease impairs the competency of accused persons to stand trial or so impaired their volition when they committed the crime, that they are not legally responsible.

A more fundamental reason surfaces in cases where the evaluation of responsibility raises the question of what motivated the killing. The usual response found in the testimony and professional memoirs of clinicians displays a sore lack of a vision of the killer as a calculating agent whose readiness to resort to violence is less a result of some biopsychologic disorder than the experience of growing up in a socio-cultural setting that tolerates, or encourages, the violent resolution of interpersonal differences. The exclusion of such insights from court reports could be blamed on the necessity to conform diagnoses to the restrictive language of legal standards of mental competence or sanity. But when the omission typically carries over into scholarly essays and popular writings of clinicians it bares a narrow understanding of criminal behavior rather than an inherent weakness of the clinical method.

The diversity of scientific explanations of homicide set forth by fields of knowledge so differently focused as meteorology, human biology, medicine, psychology, and the social sciences heightens the confusion. The attempt by practitioners of any of these fields to harmonize the differences by invoking the platitude that each discipline contributes importantly to some ultimate, but yet unrevealed, master blueprint of causation rings more of inter-disciplinary diplomacy than scientific truth.

Demonstrably there are clear differences among the scientific disciplines in the efficiency with which they explain the transformations which provoke deadly assault. This matter will be treated in Chapters 2, 3, and 4, but to give the reader a signpost to where I am headed, I set forth the general rule that the closer the occurrence of a hypothesized cause to the effect it purports to explain, the greater its power of explanation. The application of this standard enables us to rank the scientific disciplines with respect to the cogency of what they have to say about the causes of homicide. I note four levels of explanation in ascending order of relevance.

At the bottom of the hierarchy are the physical sciences. As noted above the correlation between natural phenomena—thunderstorms and lunar cycles, for example—and homicide is causally remote. Next are the biological and medical sciences which look for the causes of violent behavior in organic states and organically grounded mental states. Neurological and glandular conditions may indeed heighten irritability to certain kinds of stimulation. The effect, however, is as applicable to law abiding as law-breaking behavior. To effect a connection between organic or physical factors and homicide requires the introduction of additional intervening "causes."

Psychological processes such as need, drive, learning, motivation, perception, personality development, and the formation of attitude, belief, and judgment are causally much closer to purposeful behavior. But these processes, in themselves, are neutral relative to criminal motivation. To paraphrase criminologist Edwin H. Sutherland, both criminal and non-criminal behavior attain expression through these psychological mechanisms. (Sutherland and Cressey, 82)

Sociology, more efficiently than other disciplines, distinguishes among populations at varying degrees of risk to kill. The attitudes, values, sentiments and beliefs which form the ideational stuff of criminal intentions are social and cultural products. Accordingly it is not surprising that academic criminology is mainly a sociological specialty,

One might think that some felicitous combination of research findings from all of the human sciences might enable us reliably to differentiate killers from non-killers. Unfortunately, that is not the case. Most people whose lives enter the orbit of the variables most closely associated with homicide do not kill; and some people least affected by such forces do kill. The contingencies which control the different outcomes have yet to be pinned down by scientific inquiry.

Apologists for the gaps in explanation plead, as they have for decades, that the science of human affairs is still in its early stages, and that more research is necessary to ferret out the yet unknown factors that enter into the equation of human behavior. When this is accomplished, they submit, it should be possible to program all of the relevant data into the memory of a capacious computer which, upon command, will spew forth nearly perfect correlations. Their excuses get lamer with the passage of time. Recent decades have witnessed advances in the variety of factors examined and in the sophistication of research design and data processing technology, with no notable gain in the comprehension, prediction, or control of criminal violence.

C. A Humanistic View

The scientific pitch on criminal behavior has not played well to its intended audiences. The legal system has maintained a politely unyielding attitude, remaining unconvinced that the feelings, thoughts, and attitudes of people, as revealed to ordinary sensibilities, are other than what they seem to be.

Yet a third voice, humanistic thought on the side of self-determination, considers the natural science conception of causality irrelevant to purposive conduct. In this view the rules of scientific causation apply only to entities which lack *will* or the capacity to strive. For example, the formation of molecules of water by the combination of atoms of hydrogen and oxygen, cellular generation and degeneration, microbial infection, and gravitational attraction are not volitional. Only those structures and processes of human nature which are imbedded in the natural order—genetic, physiological, and anatomical—are suitable matters for scientific analysis. These organic conditions, to be sure, set limits to self-determination—the human, no matter how hard he waves his arms, cannot fly like a bird nor can he breathe in the water like a fish. But within the range of what is humanly possible, organic states do not determine choices.

Purposive behavior, in this humanistic view, is not a product of insensate cause and effect relationships, but rather of the judgment by an individual of the best fit between his wants and the means available for their gratification. Scientists, pointing to the uniformities in goal directed behavior revealed by scientific research as a vindication of material determinism, risk the absurdity of denying the obvious: that many people respond similarly to the same kind of stimulation because it makes sense to them to do so, no matter how unfounded the premises of their reasoning may appear to the critical observer, or even to the actor upon sober retrospection.

That most people abide by culturally expected patterns of moral or legal conduct is not an irresistible requirement of material forces. Because the socially prescribed way of doing things has the merit of considerable pre-testing, demonstrated utility, and social acceptance, it is advantageous to conform. Indeed, no matter how deviant people may be in certain areas of conduct, they conform in most regards. When, however, the achievement of cherished desires and goals cannot be accomplished by conventional means, the logic of self-interest spurs at least the consideration of non-conformity with its attendant risks and incentives.

There is yet no efficient means to test the issue of free will versus determinism. One's preference in the matter reflects ideological or esthetic preferences. We can, however, accord both positions their due by recognizing that the person's sense of purpose, whether grounded in reality or illusion, operates within boundaries fixed by one's organic makeup, experience, and the received social and cultural heritage. Within these bounds awareness presents the individual with a succession of choices. The richer one's natural and acquired endowments, the greater the ability to perceive opportunities and to manipulate people and things in pursuing personal interests; hence the broader the range of choices. Thus, in making choices, some individuals are freer than others. People limited by a poverty of mind or spirit are more likely to resort to homicide to remove human barriers to the gratification of wants. People of intellect and means seldom engage in violent assault, a fact obscured by the overrepresentation of middle and upper class murderers in the media coverage and in true crime novels. They hardly need to because they have so many more options for getting what they want; but when they do kill, they are more deliberate and calculating. In the most egregious cases, as in corporate actions known to pose the risk of serious injury to large populations, decision-making executives manage to interpose several transactional levels between themselves and the victims.

Exploring the Mind of the Murderer

To understand in concrete cases the discharge of energy into violent pathways requires an appreciation of the thoughts and feelings of the offender—the penetration, as it were, of the mind of the killer. The novelist, unlike the scientist or investigative reporter, has the enviable power of entering into the immediate awareness of his characters to account for their choices. We have no difficulty, for example, in grasping the motives of the penniless student Raskolnikov in Feodor Dostoevsky's *Crime and Punishment* for his carefully planned robbery and murder of an elderly pawnbroker woman with whom he had prior business dealings. Nor are we puzzled by his murder of the victim's sister when she returned to find him stuffing jewels and money into his pockets. Both women were witnesses who, if left alive, could identify him.

We see through the young man's sophomoric pretenses, his disavowal of the importance of the loot from the robbery and his boast that he planned the killing to test the theory that crime is what little people get punished for doing. By not getting caught he would join the big people—the Napoleons, the mass-murderers—who go down in history as great men. The old lady, with no significance in the larger scheme of things, would deserve her fate because her usury has reduced her to the moral level of a common thief. We readily comprehend the transparency of Raskolnikov's rationalizations from his inability to quiet the cries of an outraged conscience which, in the absence of any danger of his being detected, drives him eventually to confess to the police and submit to punishment.

The considerations which drive Clyde Griffiths in Theodore Dreiser's enduring novel, *An American Tragedy*, to kill are equally clear. Dreiser uses the events in the life of his protagonist to expose the seamy side of the American dream. Clyde's weakness of character and mediocrity are the mirror image of the egoism and moral corruption seeded by the materialistic values of mass society. He details the emergence in Clyde of desires that prime the resolve to kill and the circumstance that triggers the performance of the deadly act. The setting of the novel is a middle American city in the 1920's. Clyde, from a humble background has prospects for a life of wealth

The popularity of these books is attested by the increasing volume of their publication and the millions of dollars expended annually in hardcover and paperback book sales. Television producers have entered the true crime writers' market bidding as high as $125,000 for story rights. (*New York Times*, 6/19/92, D1)

To hold the interest of readers, the writers of true crime books mimic the literary style of fiction, and strive, at risk of bending the facts, to achieve the plot outline of a novel. The sacrifice of objectivity appears in subtle and crude ways. The writer may embroider the physical facts in the interest of imposing a favored theory of murder on them. More boldly the author may assume the prescience of a novelist by taking the license to read the mind of the subject.

A critical reading of the true crime documentary often requires sifting out the melodrama from the facts. The inflation of the essential facts of a routine murder to a book length narrative often entails the injection of doubtfully relevant information concerning minor characters, gossip, and large doses of local history and color. To flavor their work with the excitement and suspense of a novel, some authors recreate dialog, not always with complete fidelity, to fit conversations related by informants and to describe imaginatively the emotions of the persons whose words they recount. Truman Capote, whose book *In Cold Blood* is one of the most notable works in this medium, claimed he could carry on an extended interview and afterward, record it word for word.

The close involvment of true crime writers in the lives of their characters may generate sympathies which detract from objectivity. Capote displays a liking for one of the two murderers in his book. Joe McGinniss's best selling *Fatal Vision* reveals a repugnance for the moral character of his subject. True crime books written by participants in the investigation and trial—defense attorneys, prosecutors, or detectives, often with the assistance of a professional writer—emit an air of self-congratulation for their role in bringing a vicious killer to justice or getting an acquittal in the face of damning evidence. When authors have been dependent on participants in the investigation or the trial for information, there is a tendency to embellish their patron's achievements.

Janet Malcolm's engrossing essay, *The Journalist and the Murderer*, brings to light the potential for bias in the writing of true crime novels. Her book concerns the law suit for fraud and breach of contract filed by convicted murderer Captain Jeffrey MacDonald, the subject of *Fatal Vision*, against author Joe McGinness. In 1970 MacDonald, a United States Army medical officer, was tried and acquitted by a court martial for the murder of his pregnant wife and two small daughters. He claimed that he was awakened in the middle of the night by four intruders—hippy types, three men and a woman—who shouting, "acid is groovy," stabbed his wife and children to death but inflicted only minor injury on him. Doubts about MacDonald's innocence, raised by the stepfather of his late wife, resulted in the reopening of his case by the United States Department of Justice and his retrial eight years later. Before the trial was scheduled to begin, the journalist and the alleged murderer met socially and launched a mutually beneficial relationship. MacDonald wanted a sympathetic chronicler and McGiniss wanted the inside track in a potentially highly profitable writing enterprise which could enhance an already well established reputation and give him an advantage over any other journalist who might undertake to write about the case. They signed a contract which promised the writer exclusivity and release from legal liability. In return MacDonald would get a substantial portion of any royalties from the book and the $300,000 advance that a publisher agreed to in a book contract. MacDonald agreed not to sue for defamation provided that nothing in the book violate the essential integrity of his life story. The relationship ripened into more than a business arrangement. McGinniss' status changed from disinterested observer to close friend of MacDonald and member of the defense team.

In the course of the trial and in the aftermath of the sentencing and appeal, McGinniss came to believe in MacDonald's guilt, but he couldn't let on because he needed his subject's complete confidence to get information required to finish the book. McGinniss maintained his relationship with MacDonald giving repeated reassurance, documented in forty letters to MacDonald, of his belief in the wrongness of the verdict and continuing support. While he was feigning loyalty to MacDonald's cause, he resided in MacDonald's condominium for days searching MacDonald's copious files and records for information he could use to construct a motive for the killings.

While this subversion was going on, McGinniss visited MacDonald in prison and said nothing to disabuse him of his unconditional loyalty. McGinniss denied MacDonald's repeated requests to see pre-publication copies of what he had written by excuses that were less than candid. Others had obtained copies, including Mike Wallace of the television news show *Sixty Minutes,* which he used to prepare for an interview with MacDonald. The revelation of betrayal came when Wallace confronted MacDonald with passages from the book in which McGinniss portrayed his subject as a psychopathic killer. MacDonald sued on the ground that McGinniss had violated the contractual condition that he maintain the essential integrity of the subject's life story.

The lawsuit was argued on the issue of whether a journalist is ethically or legally bound to be totally honest with his subject, and whether some misinformation, or even a lie, if regarded as necessary to get the story, is permissible. McGinniss's case was suported by testimony of other celebrity writers, including William F. Buckley and Joseph Wambaugh who had written about notorious criminals. The suit resulted in a hung jury: only one of the six-person jury held out for McGinniss. Rather than go to a retrial, McGinniss agreed to a settlement that awarded a substantial sum of money to MacDonald.

McGinniss's deceit might be justified on the basis that it enabled him to write a more interesting story, but it was a story which went far beyond a description of events to develop added proof of MacDonald's guilt. From his examination of MacDonald's private papers, McGinniss found out that MacDonald, a physical fitness buff, had been controlling his weight by Eskatrol, a drug thought to produce a psychotic reaction when taken in large doses. McGinniss assumes from records stating that MacDonald took three to five pills, that this was a daily dosage. He attributes the deadly outburst to the accumulated effects of the drug, a state of extreme fatigue due to a lack of sleep, and a repressed anger against women exacerbated by threatening insights his wife had acquired in a psychology course she was taking at a local college.

McGinniss was left with the question of why MacDonald, unlike other men, wasn't able to keep his anger within reasonable limits of expression. To respond, he relied, as Ms. Malcolm suggests, on an uncritical reading of three moral tracts parading as science—Otto Kernberg's *Borderline Conditions and Pathological Narcissism,* Christopher Lasch's *The Culture of Narcissism,* and Hervey Cleckley's *The Mask of Sanity*—from which McGinniss deduced that

MacDonald is a "pathological narcissist," a conclusion, which Ms. Malcolm regards as no more than a restatement of the problem, not a solution.

Despite its limited objectives of entertainment and profit, the true crime documentary often, serendipitously, provides a more complete picture of the circumstances of killing than any other source of information. Corrected for embellishment to promote literary appeal, the better examples of the true crime documentary provide a fullness and fidelity of account unavailable in other forms of inquiry. The authors report the details of the crime as revealed by police investigation, transcripts of trial testimony, and a wealth of behind-the-scenes information not found in official records or current newspaper accounts. The last may include off-the-record interviews with witnesses, police, attorneys, members and friends of the victim and offender, and even the murderer.

True crime writers do not always comprehend that the remarks of the expert witnesses whose testimony or interview comments they report are more in the nature of speculation than of verified scientific truth. Taking their cues from what these experts say, augmented perhaps by some reading on the subject, some venture a diagnosis on their own, and after the second or third book, bring forth their own equally hackneyed "expert" views of the motive of the murderer.

Charting the Course

There is an ironic whimsy, in designating killing a "preventable" cause of death, as denoted in United States Public Health Service reports, since no policy measures have effectively reduced rates of homicide over the years in which they have been tracked. The failure of policy reflects fundamental misunderstandings about what prompts people to kill. The law pays no attention to the social and cultural baggage that the killer brings to his act, and science zeroes in on peripheral matters more or less removed from the core meanings and sentiments expressed by people in killing one another.

The only unifying theme coursing through all of the scientific theories is the working assumption, hardened into doctrine, that the cause of homicide cannot be understood in terms of the will of the offender, but must be sought in conditions outside of the awareness of the killer.

I submit the converse, that the taking of human life cannot be understood without regard to the intents and purposes of the killer. I propose that the conditions associated with crime in scientific research attain their effect only as they influence choice. The resolve to kill and what the killer hopes to achieve by eliminating his victim are the crucial links in the chain of causation. The scores of background factors which comprise the grist of statistical and clinical studies comprise no more than the setting for murder, not the script. They acquire vital significance only as they enter into the meanings which incite the passions and frame homicidal intentions. The next three chapters identify these background factors and accord them their proper place in the total picture of causation. The question of how these factors are transformed into homicidal desires and acts does not lend itself to any existing scientific methodology. We therefore resort to a humanistic analysis which occupies much of the remainder of the book.

2

The Killer Within

I am surprised by the number of well educated people who take for
granted that some organic or mental defect is the primary cause of
homicide. Evidently the advocates of individualistic theories have
done an effective job of propagating their views. Explanations of
violent behavior based on neurological impairment, personality
disorder, glandular malfunction, chromosomal aberration, or low
intelligence have little direct relevance to murder since they are
derived from studies of samples of the general run of adult and
juvenile offenders, very few or none of whom were accused or convicted of homicide, and many of whom were not convicted of
serious crimes of violence. Nevertheless, despite serious flaws in
research design—the lack of an adequate control group, findings
based on very small numbers of cases, haphazard sampling, woolly
definition of *defect*, unreliability of measurement, and a disregard for
logic—presumptions of some inherent abnormality color popular
thought and policy judgments about the motivation of serious violent crime.

The Biology of Murder

The search for a distinctly criminal type based on some organic trait
has energized criminology for the one hundred years of its history.
The hunt has yet to turn up a verifiable example of the genus
criminal man. The notion that killers are *bad seeds*, a breed apart,

endows murder with an aura of fateful inevitability, but also inspires the hope that somehow the dangerous class can be isolated and neutralized by some prophylaxis. Some of the dashed hopes are the use of lobotomy and conditioned reflex theory to pacify violent offenders.

The quest for a biological cause of violent crime began in the late nineteenth century with the pioneer studies of the Italian physician Cesare Lombroso, credited with originating modern criminology. His conviction that the criminal is born, a throwback to a prior stage of physical and social evolution, obtained its theoretical inspiration from Darwin's evolution and its facts from physical measurements of known homicidal brigands. Lombroso ascribed the inferiority of the criminal to physical traits which he presumed to be characteristic of pre-modern man—low brow, receding chin, scanty facial hair, and the large toe separated from the other toes. A systematic evaluation of Lombroso's theory conducted early in this century by the English physician, Charles Goring (1913), comparing the physical measurements of convicts with those of non-convicts, turned up no momentous difference between the two groups. Later writings by Lombroso conceded the crucial importance of environmental factors, but these are seldom cited in critiques of his work.

The perennial research finding that delinquency runs in families keeps alive the claims of advocates of the biological inheritance of criminal behavior. Nineteenth century genealogical studies of "degenerate" families, the disreputable Jukes (Dugdale) and Kallikaks (Goddard), which show that mental defects, prostitution, and crime are passed from one generation to the next, were regarded as conclusive evidence of hereditary transmission. More recent genetically based studies of the inheritance of a criminal propensity have looked at the correlation of criminality between fathers and sons (Goring) or between identical twins compared to fraternal twins. The investigators presume the transmission of criminality from father to son by means of heredity rather than social interaction notwithstanding that no geneticist has succeeded in isolating a gene for criminality.

Scandinavian countries are deemed an ideal setting for studying the effect of genetic factors on human dispositions because their cultural homogeneity presumably minimizes the contamination of the results by cultural factors. The studies are doubtfully relevant to the crime of murder, however, since few of the cases involve violent crime and Scandinavian countries have extremely low murder rates. They have value, however, in exhibiting the assumptions and methods of the research from which some observers generalize to argue for an organic basis of violent crime.

Inquiry involving the comparison of identical twins with fraternal twins offers an appealing design as a test of the genetic origins of any trait. Identical twins, resulting from the split of one fertilized egg have identical heredities. Fraternal twins, developed out of the fertilization of separate eggs, have unidentical heredities. If crime is genetic there should be virtually a complete concordance in crime between identical twins and a less than complete concordance between fraternal twins. A review of ten of these studies by Norwegian researchers Dalgard and Kringlen, shows that the concordance in criminality betwen identical twins is hardly complete, ranging from 26 percent to 100 percent. (The sample size of identicals in the study with 100 percent concordance is 4) The corresponding range for fraternal twins is from 11 percent to 54 percent. The degree of concordance between the identicals in criminality is far less than the resemblance in physical traits, so striking in one-egg twins. Dalgard and Kringlen conclude from their rigorous critique of the research design and methods of determining identicality in these studies "...that *the significance of hereditary factors in registered crime is non-existent.*" (in Savitz and Johnston, 302. emphasis in the original) Nevertheless the belief that twin studies support the theory of a genetic contribution to crime persists. (Wilson and Herrnstein, 90-95) The devotees of this view apparently fail to accord sufficient weight to the obvious: that the greater similarity in conduct between identical compared to non-identical twins results from the greater similarity in the way others perceive and respond to them,

Norwegian researchers O.S. Dalgard and E. Kringlen take account of the social implications of growing up as twins in their rigorously designed research. They examined birth records from 1900 to 1935, obtaining the names and dates of birth of 66,000 individuals comprising 33,000 pairs of twins. A check of the national criminal register yielded a useable sample of 139 pairs, of which one or both had been convicted. The results showed a higher concordance in criminality between identical compared to fraternal twins, but to a much smaller degree than in more loosely designed studies. Employing a strict concept of criminality based on conviction of more serious crimes, Dalgard and Kringlen found a 25.8 percent agreement between one-egg twins and a 14.9 percent agreement between two-egg twins. They conclude that the difference dwindles to insignificance when account is taken that identical twins are brought up and responded to more similarly than fraternals.

What the twin studies prove has nothing to do with the causes of crime. Rather they show that the the more alike siblings are in their genetic makeup and the way they are brought up, the more likely they are to respond similarly to the same stimulation. The fact that a criminal response in one is not accompanied by a criminal response in the other in a large proportion of the pairs shows that forces other than heredity are operative. From a sociological perspective, the stimulation, whether supportive of obedience or disobedience to law, makes the difference between the lawful and unlawful responses.

A Danish study probing for a genetic factor in the transmission of violent behavior crime compares the criminal records of 14,427 adoptees with those of their biological parents. Violent crime in Denmark is unusual, comprising less than 2 percent of the total. Murder is extremely rare. The results show "...a slight but not statistically significant tendency for the violence of the adoptees to be greater if the parents have been convicted of crime." The investigators conclude that the evidence does not support the hypothesis that genetic factors cause violent crime. (Mednick et al, 28) The detrimental effect noted could be a result of whatever meaningful contact the child may have had with the biological parents prior to adoption or the emotional neglect from the interim period of institutionalization or foster placement pending adoption.

Yet every decade brings forth anew researchers who discover some ingrained personal trait by which to explain criminality. The belief that the predisposition to violent crime is largely congenital— "already determined at conception or in utero," as psychologist Joel Norris puts it in a recent publication titled *Serial Killers: The Growing Menace*—implies that the genetic code with which the individual is imprinted at conception contains the criminal code of the jurisdiction in which the infant is born. Norris' reference to research by psychiatrist Robert Cloninger that "individuals whose biological parents are criminal are four times as likely to become criminal than individuals whose biological parents are not criminals," approvingly notes that "...[a]lthough Cloninger has not definitively isolated the actual genes that predispose one to criminal tendencies," he believes that certain types of brain dysfunctions and neurological and hormonal birth defects associated with criminal behavior are congenital.

It has yet to be demonstrated in studies meeting reasonable standards of scientific rigor that genetically determined mental or physical abnormalities have any direct bearing on homicidal violence. There is no proof that these conditions occur proportionately more often among killers compared with non-killers. A very small proportion of people thus afflicted kill; the preponderance of killings are committed by unafflicted people. The evidence on the transmission of criminality from parents to offspring, as will be shown in Chapter 4, more cogently supports the theory that criminal propensities are conveyed socially, not genetically.

The continuing failure of behavioral scientists to grasp fully the environmental context of violent crime appears in a recent *New York Times News Service* story reporting research by Dr. Allen Beck, with the United States Bureau of Justice Statistics. His results showing that half of all juveniles and one third of all adults in state penal institutions have immediate family members who have also been incarcerated were greeted triumphantly by partisans of the genetic interpretation of crime. One of the foremost protagonists, psychologist Richard Herrnstein, observed, "These are stunning statistics...the more chronic the criminal, [particularly the violent criminal] the more likely it is to find criminality in his or her relatives." The findings are indeed valid, but they are hardly "stunning," as studies going back to the fabled Jukes and Kallikaks testify. Another psychologist, Professor Terrie Moffitt proclaims in the same article that the statistics "contradict the popular view that delinquents learn crime from their friends." The statistics do no such thing; they simply allow that parents, who themselves were reared under conditions of social instability, as well as friends, have an influence on the transmission of criminal attitudes—the parents, more often by the example of precarious lives; the friends, more often by precept as well as example. The ascription of the delinquency to some aspect of the relationship between the individual and a family member reflects the failure of analysts to see the broader social context of delinquency. For if the researchers had looked at a sample of non-incarcerated males of the same social background as those they studied, they would have found among them equally a pattern of having a family member who at one time or another had been incarcerated. In fact they would find that most of these non-incarcerated males, by the time they reached an age of eligibilty for imprisonment, would have a criminal record. As criminologist Marvin E. Wolfgang observed in clarifying the meaning of the findings, "...you should remember that most of these people come from low socioeconomic backgrounds, disadvantaged neighborhoods, where a high proportion of people will be sent to jail whether they are related or not." (*Sarasota Herald Tribune*, Jan 31, 1992, p. 6A)

A similar confusion of reasoning marks the medical theory that nutritional deficiencies, for example excessive consumption of refined sugars, cause crime. (Hoffer, 218) The proportion of persons with some form of nutritional imbalance among groups of offenders is likely to be no greater than that found in the lower class populations which furnish the preponderance of criminal offenders. In the absence of studies with suitable control groups, we can't be sure. If there is a connection between diet and crime, it is indirect. The cultural orientation that makes for ignorance concerning healthful diet also underlies the proclivity for crime. Observers on the British scene frequently note the excessive consumption of sweets beginning in childhood. Yet the British have lower rates of violent crime than Americans, and very seldom kill one other.

The quest for an organic trait by which to distinguish criminals from non-criminals has a venerable history and a meager pay-off. The physical anthropologist Earnest Hooton (1939) found minor differences between a sample of prison inmates and a haphazard sample of non-criminals in a number of measurable physical traits. Murderers of white native-born American ancestry, he noted, had a narrower forehead and shoulders than non-murderers of the same stock. He offered no explanation for the murderous effect of these traits other than that they signified biological inferiority. Critics have faulted his work for the obvious deficiencies in sampling procedures and the failure to define "inferiority." The observed differences more likely reflect that the murderers in the sample, all-white, mainly descendants of settlers whose forebears emigrated from the British Isles and moved from Virginia to Kentucky, thence to Missouri, constituted a somewhat homogeneous breed. The comparison group was a more heterogeneous lot—firemen, policemen, visitors to the Chicago World Fair, and patrons of a New England bathing beach. Hooton should have controlled for the cultural factor by selecting the subjects for his control group from the same regional and ethnic stock as the prisoners.

The explanation of criminal tendencies as the expression of physical traits has as much logical validity as the attribution of picking pockets to finger dexterity. Studies by Sheldon and Eleanor Glueck showing that delinquent boys, compared with non-delinquent boys, more often possess a muscular athletic build indicate only that some individuals are better endowed than others with the strength, agility, and fleetness of foot needed for success in street crimes. The same traits in persons in the non-criminal vocations of professional athlete, soldier, police officer, or firefighter, lead to respect and honor. A leading researcher in this field, physician William Sheldon, found that certain temperamental and psychologic traits—low verbal intelligence, restlessness, feelings of not being taken care of, destructiveness, sadistic proclivities, feelings of inadequacy, and emotional instability—clustered significantly more frequently, along with muscularity, in a group of boys institutionalized for delinquency than among a control group of school boys. The significance of the association of the symptoms of psychological malaise with muscularity is problematic. Like the delinquency of the boys who display them, these symptoms are more plausibly understood as expressions of the social and cultural debilitation commonly found among persons of low socio-economic status.

The hypothesis that males possessing two rather than the usual one Y chromosome are endowed with an uncommon penchant for violent crime attracted serious attention in medical circles in the nineteen-sixties. Richard G. Fox's survey of the research literature put the notion to rest. "The reality," he concludes, "is that the XYY males in an institutional setting are less violent or aggressive when compared to matched chromosomal fellow inmates; and their criminal histories involve crime against property rather than persons." Fox goes on to speculate that the disproportionate number of prison inmates with double Y chromosomes results from the fact that the large physical proportions of many of them may present such a frightening aspect that judges and court psychiatrists are biased toward ordering or recommending institutionalization. (Fox, 59-73)

Not all biological explanations of violent crime focus on some form of organic inferiority. Martin Daly and Margo Wilson in their book, *Homicide,* set forth an "evolutionary psychological paradigm" tracing the origin of the homicidal impulse to the Darwinian process of natural selection. Murder, they claim, is the outcome of conflict in which the promotion of one person's fitness—fitness, in the broad sense of success in biological propagation—entails the degradation of another's fitness. That blood relatives seldom kill one another, is cited by the authors as proof of the instinct to assure propagation of the kin line. A more certifiable explanation springs from the practical consideration that not killing members of one's blood line makes sense: the closer the familial relationship among individuals, the greater their physical, social, and emotional interdependence, particularly in tribal societies organized on kinship lines.

Daly and Wilson's conception of homicide within the family as an expression of evolutionary mechanisms to promote fitness reduces the murderous impulse to some primordial force. Thus blind evolutionary imperatives induce infanticide when the child is of "inappropriate paternity," physically blemished, or unlikely to survive. A more direct explanation links the killing of stigmatized infants to harsh necessities arising out of the scarcity of basic necessities, particularly in social groups with marginal economies. Murray A. Straus's analysis of demographic factors in infant mortality from homicide in the United States makes the case for mundane considerations related to livelihood. He finds that non-white rates of infant homicide are about three times greater than white rates, socioeconomic status, not race, is the crucial factor. White and minority children of equivalent status suffer about the same child abuse rate. Straus observes a considerable spread, along cultural and economic lines, among the American states in homicide mortality rates of children under five years of age, from a high of 14.03 in Louisiana to a low of 1.51 in North Dakota. (Straus, 65-67) Similarly, birth control and abortion, as functional equivalents of infanticide, are most commonly motivated by economic considerations.

In accord with their evolutionary hypothesis, Daly and Wilson explain the male propensity for violence in terms of the struggle for superiority in the competition for propagation. Wife-murder and wife-abuse represent the striving for control over the reproductive capacities of women. Killings arising out of trivial altercations aim to deter rivals from threatening one's interests; they give tangible proof that any such attempts will be met with severe punishment. The predominance of males in robbery-murders is due to the greater need of men for additional resources with which to check rivals and attract women.

The facts of every-day life, however, do not square with the "evolutionary psychological paradigm." In fact they indicate the paramount importance of environmental factors. Most men proclaim their "fitness" for progenitorship in non-violent ways. Men from the sectors of society in which wife-murder or abuse is most frequent show the least concern for the welfare or survival of the offspring of their matings. A cross-cultural comparison suggests that the social requirements of the male role, rather than a natural process for determining whose blood-line is going to make the greater contribution to the next generation, provoke violent encounters between rivals. The explanation for the predominance of males in robbery-murder, that men need greater resources than women, collapses in the light of the the rapid changes in family structure and relations between the sexes. Women, particularly in the underclass, increasingly take breadwinner roles, often more effectively than their mates, and often as the head of single-parent households They are just as needy of material resources and still show no proclivity for armed robbery.

The Nobel prize winning work of animal behavior scientist Konrad Lorenz exemplifies the pitfalls of attributing complex social behavior to an inherent impulse. His book, *On Aggression,* propounds the theory that aggressive instincts developed in evolutionary adaptation underlie the human propensity to kill. Lorenz does not define *instinct.* He uses the term loosely to mean inborn drives set in motion by organic requirements or necessities of group life. The expression of these tendencies, however, is channelled by learning. Like other writers, who bring their expertise on animal behavior to the explanation of human behavior, Lorenz extracts his evidence for human instincts from the closed loop of tautology: the existence of instincts is inferred from uniformities in behavior; the uniformities prove the instinctual nature of the behavior.

Lorenz comes perilously close to affirming what for Darwinists is the Lamarckian heresy of the biological transmission of environmentally acquired traits. His argument, ironically, reads more like a case for cultural determinism than biological evolutionism. Cultural innovations favoring the inhibition or intensification of aggressive instincts may affect, even reverse, the direction of natural selection. In remote prehistory, the near equality in strength among humans and instinctive gestures of appeasement served to limit the quantity and harm of the expression of aggressive instincts. The development of conceptual thought and verbal speech made possible the devising of weapons, which encouraged aggression and increased the likelihood of a fatal outcome. The reduction of inhibitions on killing by cultural change unbalanced the biologically evolved adaptive mechanisms and spurred natural processes to create a new equilibrium to accommodate the violence. A strong regard for the traits connected with success in the martial arts, or on the material acquisitiveness which incites warfare and crime promotes "a high positive selection premium on the instinctive foundations conducive to such traits." (Lorenz, 237)

To show that changes in natural selection processes affecting patterns of aggressiveness can evolve in a few generations, Lorenz cites research by anthropologist Sidney Margolin who made "very exact psychoanalytical and psycho-sociological studies" of the Ute people, a native American prairie culture. (Margolin's findings, as reported by Lorenz, should be taken with the caution that the term "exact", let alone "very exact," applied to measurement in psychoanalysis or "psycho-sociological" studies is a contradiction in terms.) The results show that the Ute Indians suffer from powerful aggressions which they are unable to assuage in reservation life. Margolin believes that their killer instincts intensified through a process of natural selection during the comparatively few centuries when "they led a wild life consisting almost entirely of war and raids." (I presume that Margolin refers to the time in the history of the Ute between the introduction of the horse culture by the Spaniards in the late sixteenth or early seventeenth centuries, and their confinement to the reservation by the American government in the late nineteenth century.) The destruction of their old way of life has left the Ute more afflicted with neurosis than any other human group—a claim, I believe, that would be difficult, if not impossible, to demonstrate. The seed of the neurosis, according to Margolin, is undischarged aggression. Powerful taboos prevent them from attacking members of their own tribe, and the targeting of aggression in war against other native American tribes or the white man is no longer feasible. So they find an outlet in reckless motor vehicle driving, by which they have achieved an inordinate highway accident rate. If Margolin's analysis of the combativeness of the Ute, as interpreted by Lorenz, is correct, it would seem that as the most aggressive Ute males, by virtue of premature death in auto accidents, diminish their contribution to the gene pool of their society, natural selection will favor the propagation of persons of less aggressive instincts. Accordingly, we can look forward to a timely remediation of the problem.

Evidence of sudden change in patterns of aggressiveness of whole peoples, often occurring in less than one generation, shows that forces much quicker than evolution, essentially insightful intelligence, are at work. Prior to the establishment of the State of Israel, Jews were not known for physical aggressiveness. Through centuries of inquisitions and pogroms they accepted verbal and physical insults without reprisal for fear that to defend themselves would invite sterner persecution. Modern historians have noted, for example, the submissiveness of the Jews in allowing themselves to be rounded up and moved to concentration camps, not knowing what lay in store, and thinking that if they bowed to the yoke, this persecution too, would pass. Within the same generation, a new breed of Jews appeared among the survivors of the holocaust who reached Palestine, subsequently Israel. The world was electrified by their combativeness in a series of wars against vastly superior forces which challenged the existence of the new nation. The result of a speeded up natural selection? Hardly; more to the point, a change in attitude based on the conviction of the Jews that they must depend on themselves for their own security so that never again would they need to submit to oppression.

The recent history of Japan, as biologically inbred as any large nation, is another clear example of how rapid social change can influence attitudes toward physical aggressiveness. Prior to the establishment of the modern state in 1870, Japan was riven by feudal wars until the nation was united under the Meiji emperor. Adopting western technology to became a great military power, the Japanese directed their aggression toward other nations, defeating Russia in major naval battles, invading and annexing Korea, brutally subjugating large areas of China and southeast Asia, and then making the grievous error of attacking the United States. Upon defeat, Japan, first forcibly, then quite volitionally—even in the face of the entreaty of their recent conqueror, the United States, to develop a military force consistent with their international economic stature—adopted a pacifist role in world affairs. An evolutionary adaptation? Hardly; rather the lesson that the material goals once sought in military expansion are better obtained from disciplined commercial enterprise.

The Psychology of Murder

I include in this discussion understandings from psychiatry and neurology, fields which also contribute to the explanation of individual behavior. Contradictions are bound to develop in a field with as wide a variety of theories and methods as the behavioral sciences. The style of inquiry that attempts a deep penetration of the mind of the murderer, takes the investigator out of the range of science into the realm of speculation. Confining analysis to measurable external manifestations of the mind, as in laboratory studies of measurable responses to measurable stimuli, results in superficialities and truisms: for example, the solemnly proclaimed principle that people engage in crime because it is satisfying, or they refrain from crime because it is painful. (Wilson and Herrnstein, 44)

Psychological theories differ in the degree to which they give priority to the effect of innate or experiential factors in shaping behavior. The former put narrower limits on the potential for adaptation. Both, more or less, regard people's introspection about what they are doing as epiphenomena, the surface traces of forces outside of direct awareness. Recent developments in the psychology of crime tend toward the development of theoretical models that combine the two viewpoints, mainly by stressing the interactive effect of nature and nurture. (Pallone and Hennessy; Wilson et al)

Psychological theories that link behavior directly to some innate measurable factor make the stronger pretension to scientific virtue. An outstanding example is the relationship between intelligence and criminality. During the early part of the twentieth century it appeared that mental testing might add greatly to our understanding of the criminal mind. Intelligence, believed controlled by heredity, was thought to be the key to social adjustment. Retarded persons were considered especially prone to criminal behavior because of a deficiency of sound judgment, lack of self-control, or the inability to know right from wrong. The repeated finding that delinquents, compared with non-delinquents, and murderers compared with non-violent offenders, score significantly lower on intelligence tests has reinforced the conviction of believers in the genetic origins of crime. Skeptics interpret the results within a broader framework, observing that the vast majority of apprehended murderers come from lower social and cultural levels, in which the failure to acquire and pass on the skills measured by mental tests and required by the ordinary demands of life reflects a social rather than a psychological disability. They contend that intelligence test scores are so interwoven with other factors closely related to criminality—social class, ethnicity, the cleverness to evade apprehension, and the likelihood of diversion from the criminal justice system—that the relationship between intelligence and delinquency is somewhere between problematic and spurious. Anonymous self-reporting studies which inquire into the criminal conduct of high school and college students, the latter mostly of middle or upper class background and presumably of higher average intelligence than persons not in college, suggest that criminal deviance, though seldom of a violent kind, occurs quite frequently among the intelligent. Studies of corporate, political, and occupational crime perpetrated by persons of high social and educational levels establish that superior intelligence, although seldom associated with the *direct* infliction of violence, is no guarantor of obedience to law or respect for the lives of others.

Psychiatric theories connecting murder to mental disorders have evolved out of clinical studies of individual killers, hence have little relevance to epidemic levels of homicide in violence-ridden societies. Forensic psychiatry had its early development in orderly European countries with very low rates of homicide. The European psychiatrists who fled from Hitler's Europe to the United States in the period around World War II heavily stamped the American outlook on crime with the view, developed in a rather different cultural setting, that killers are mentally deranged. An example is David Abrahamsen whose early professional years were spent in his native Norway, a nation of several million people with an infinitesimal amount of homicide—two or three, seldom more than five killings a year, less than one one-hundredth the number in an American population of comparable size. Long after taking up professional practice in the United States, he held to the view that killers possess an abnormal mentality. He continued in his prolific writings to explain individual cases drawn from the thousands of homicides committed annually in the United States as the expression of neurotic or psychotic symptoms rather than socially learned deviant conduct. (Abrahamsen, 1973, 1-2)

Although psychiatry is a medical specialty, many of its concepts and theories are based upon thinly disguised psychological, not organic, facts. Psychoanalysis, a field of psychiatry locates the origin of motivated behavior in organically rooted instinctual drives, but specifies no organic site for the key concepts of the id, ego, superego, and unconscious. The psychoanalytic emphasis on the masked symbolic character of motives appeals to lawyers defending clients accused of unusually brutal crimes which carry the prospect of severe penalties. The psychoanalytic expert, unlike other kinds of psychiatrists, does not need to find some adversity of life— mistreatment in childhood, head injury, neurological disorder, glandular malfunction, or the like—to explain atrocious conduct. The resourceful psychiatrist can always identify stresses or strains in the life of the patient to concoct a diagnosis of unconscious motivation which, by psychoanalytic definition, frees the actor of responsibility. The forensic psychoanalyst digs into the labyrinths of the mind of the murderer to excavate his destructive impulses, wishes, and fantasies, and by linking these anti-social propensities to natural processes, purges them of their maliciousness. Psycho-analytic diagnoses conceive of violent crime as the outcrop of the inability of personality either to construct barriers to the anti-social expression of raw instinctual impulses or to groove channels for their socially acceptable expression. In the former instance undisciplined desires rampaging through fantasies are acted out in sadistic orgies of murder or violent sexual crimes; in the latter, repressed sexual desires find outlet in disguised form such as compulsive firesetting, shoplifting, and even killing.

In the name of clinical artistry, psychoanalysts bypass the rigors of scientific method to assert unprovable connections between disordered mental states, which they claim triggered the murders in question, and events that occurred in childhood or infancy. Psychiatrist Herbert Strean, writing with Lucy Freeman, in a book titled *Our Wish To Kill: The Murder in All Our Hearts* indulges this license. He and his collaborator conclude that serial killer Michael Kallinger, who included his son among his victims and tortured his own children as a form of discipline, was driven to murder by a lack of love, and cruelty in early life which made him a schizophrenic. (8-10) They challenge the commonly accepted belief that Sirhan Sirhan assassinated Senator Robert F. Kennedy because Kennedy was supporting Israel in its conflict with the Palestinians. Sirhan himself explained that he killed Kennedy because he felt politically frustrated. But Dr. Strean and Ms. Freeman profess to know better: "Sirhan Sirhan killed Robert Kennedy because in large part he felt like a jilted lover, as some of his imaginary conversations with Kennedy shows." The real motive, they say, was rage for a father who punished him when he disobeyed as a child. Sirhan's yearning for Kennedy was like that of a child's desire for the one in power, the man "at the top" like his father. At a more general level, Strean and Freeman account for the wish to kill by an extravagant rhetoric which begs rather than confronts the issue. To wit: Our culture is a "hate culture," or "[T]he wish to kill originates from fallen self-esteem." (Strean et al, 13)

Sensationalized media accounts of psychiatric testimony given in murder cases foster the popular belief that people who kill must be psychologically sick. The belief wavers before powerful statistical evidence to the contrary and the manifest practicality of the murderous act in resolving problems of adjustment. Few accused murderers meet rigorous standards of mental illness, and the proportion of the mentally ill who engage in homicidal attacks has not been shown to be greater than the proportion of killers among persons without symptoms of mental illness. The fact that a killer has a severe mental disorder does not prove that the illness in question caused the killing. Most of the very few killings by the mentally deranged spring from the same causes or desires that impel normal people to kill.

Undaunted by the ricketiness of their claims, psychiatrists and clinical psychologists testifying in court as expert witnesses invoke a murky terminology to claim that the killing in question was a result of a mental illness that so disabled reason, that the defendant is not legally responsible. Where independent evidence of mental incompetence is lacking, expert witnesses for the defense in an unabashed display of circular reasoning have been known to claim that the act of murder itself is proof of mental disorder.

Nevertheless psychiatry enjoys wide popularity in the explanation of criminal behavior. When a gruesome murder occurs, there is quick resort by the media and law enforcement to psychiatric expertise for a "profile" of the killer, if unknown, or, if known, an "autopsy" of his mind. The theoretical flexibility of psychoanalysis enables even lay persons familiar with its basic concepts to compose their own diagnoses for a particular crime. Some psychiatrists believe that diagnosis does not necessarily require a clinical examination. Analysts have ferreted out the behavioral dynamics of people long dead by applying their arcane terminology to subjects' diary entries and information obtained from interviews with associates. In response to criticisms of the unreliability of the results, practitioners characterize their work as art as well as science.

The ingenious psychiatrist can retrospectively find a disease in anyone who has committed a murder; he need only use the mysterious language of his craft to transform the passion that energized the killer into a severe mental disorder. The celebrated "Twinkie" defense mounted in the case of Dan White who killed san Francisco Mayor George Moscone and city supervisor Harvey Milk is a shameless example. Angered over the mayor's refusal to give him back the position of city supervisor from which he had resigned and Milk's role in fortifying the mayor in that decision, Dan White armed himself, went to the offices of his adversaries in City Hall, and killed them. The question of premeditation got short shrift, notwithstanding that White had avoided the metal detectors at the entrance of City Hall and had been heard to express angry opposition to the infiltration of city government by homosexuals, such as Milk. The circumstances of the killings clearly added up to first degree murder, but White was convicted only of manslaughter.

The credit for the jury's willingness to recognize White's case for diminished responsibility goes to a procession of psychiatrists. Dr. Donald T. Lunde maintained that White suffered from a long standing depression which he could not control because it was rooted in genetic factors which affected his biochemical balance. Dr. Martin Blinder supplied the jury with a rationale for the exacerbation of White's depressed state. When frustrated White would go on junk food eating binges, gorging himself on Twinkies, cupcakes, candy, and cokes which, Dr. Blinder claimed, alluding to studies of cerebral irritation produced by excessive consumption of refined sugar, results in violent tendencies, sufficient in White's case to push him over the border of sanity. Forensic neurologist Dr. Harold Klawans, commenting on the astonishment evoked by the conviction of manslaughter instead of the expected first degree murder, takes a skeptical view of the "Twinkie" defense: the prosecution's response was inadequate, and the defense has never been used since. He also notes the widespread opinion that there was contrivance behind the scenes by judicial and medical authorities to make the crime psychiatric, not political. (Klawans, 168-169)

Neurology, the medical specialty of diseases of the brain and the nervous system, has staked a claim to competence in the diagnosis of the homicidal impulse. The experimental and clinical evidence, however, scarcely justifies a belief in a connection between some pathology of the brain and murder. The theory that brain tumors or lesions may induce physical violence shows up in articles in medical journals and occasionally as a defense in murder trials. A review of studies on brain damage in violent offenders by Ron Langevin and associates finds no support for the role of brain pathology in violent crime. A major flaw in these studies is the lack of a comparison of the affected subjects with controls made up of non-violent individuals. In an attempt to remedy this deficiency the Langevin group compared eighteen killers and twenty-one men convicted of non-homicidal violent crimes, with sixteen men convicted of nonviolent non-sex offenses. Both groups underwent extensive neuropsychological tests and personality assessments. The results show only minor differences between the killers and the nonviolent offenders. Examinations for standard categories of mental illness, including depression, psychosis, paranoia, and personality disorder, yield no significant differences between the combined violent group and the nonviolent controls. (Langevin et al)

An instance of *sleep drunkenness,* a neurological disorder provoking an involuntary fit of violence, has been reported by forensic clinical neurologist, Dr. Harold L. Klawans (the debunker of the Twinkies defense) as the case of "The sleeping killer." The accused had been arrested for the murder of one girl and the attempted murder of another. A tax attorney, he had been working long hours to finish up an assignment to meet a deadline for the filing of taxes.

He decided to drive home so that he could be with his family on the occasion of his daughter's birthday. Overcome by fatigue he pulled off the road to get some sleep. The next thing he knew, a police officer awakened him and placed him under arrest for murder and assault. The victims, it appears, had run out of gas for their car and had knocked on his window to ask for help, whereupon he started the engine and ran over one, turned around and returned, hitting the other. He claimed to have no recollection of what had happened. Dr. Klawans ordered electroencephalographic tests. Two nights of testing revealed no sleep disorder. The third night the patient jumped out of bed visibly agitated, yanked off the electrodes, and wandered about throwing furniture around. The attendant finally got him back into bed. The report of the brain waves recorded by the EEG stated that the patient had not fully awakened, raising the presumption that he had attacked the victims while in this twilight mental state. The district attorney apprised of the results of the test dropped the charges, and the patient was advised to avoid excessive fatigue to prevent any recurrence. (Klawans, 130-137)

The statement of events which transformed the case from "open and shut" to unprosecuted strains credulity. The two bouts of sleep drunkenness occurred closely together in time, one just before the killing, and one very shortly thereafter. They were the only ones the patient claimed to have ever experienced. If such an episode had happened before in the presence of others, he would know about his vulnerability and would be on notice not to work to exhaustion as he did the night that he killed. If it had never happened before, its recurrence so soon after the first occurence, and after only two nights of medical testing, in a patient presumably no longer extremely fatigued was a remarkable coincidence and a stroke of good fortune, considering that it excused him from the charge of murder.

The strangeness of the case and the fact that "sleep drunkenness" is not listed in the *Diagnostic and Statistical Manual*, the clinicians's compendium of all behavior disorders, prompts the question of whether the disorder is clinically or statistically validated, and, if it is genuine, what is the rationale for its negation of criminal responsibility? Does sleep drunkenness have the same disabling effect as alcohol drunkenness? If the individual knows he is drunk, then by analogy to the law pertaining to alcohol drunkenness, he may be held accountable for the consequences of his conduct. On the other hand, the fact that sleep drunkenness is involitional may reduce or eliminate criminal responsibility. If, however, this kind of drunkenness is the same as total amnesia—and apparently the prosecuting attorney did not challenge that view in this case—acquittal is justifiable.

Undoubtedly there is a neurophysiological basis for the passions accompanying or triggering all expressions of violence. Endocrinology explains the powerful reactions of the hypothalmus, adrenalin secretions, thyroid, and deficiency of blood sugar to aversive stimulation. Neurology shows how pathologies of the nervous system excite response in untoward ways. But whether the heightened irritabilities from these organic states lead to violent crime depends not on the fact of the arousal—we all get aroused at times—but on how the person has learned to manage feelings of anger and aggressive tendencies.

Psychologist-criminologists steeped in the theory of behavioristic psychology seek to redeem the scientific integrity of psychology by explaining conduct in rigorously objective terms. Unlike the various schools of depth psychology which produce their data by speculation, behaviorism acquires its data through the direct observation of responses obtained from the controlled stimulation of experimental subjects in laboratory situations. Like the law, it excludes mind from its explanation of behavior, but for a different reason. The jurist regards the willing mind as the cause of action. The behaviorist assigns mind to the realm of subjective experience, uninvestigable by observation or the measuring devices of the natural scientist. Hence those reactions of mind known through introspection and inferred in others from the appearance of purpose in their behavior are not suitable data for behavioristic analysis.

Behaviorism explains the acquisition of behavior patterns in terms of *operant* learning. Laboratory studies with animals and humans have reliably shown that behavior patterns are established or abandoned depending on their consequences. Acts that lead to gratification are repeated; those that lead to pain are avoided. The process whereby a particular stimulus strengthens a response is termed reinforcement. The process for weakening or extinguishing a response is termed punishment. Assaultive behavior is often repetitive and rewarding, but seldom homicidal. How the theory might apply to homicide is puzzling since killing—with the rare exception of killings by serial murderers or hit-men—is seldom a repetitive act, the continuation of which depends on how rewarding or unrewarding the consequences may be.

Behaviorism underpins the systematic criminology of political scientist James Q. Wilson and psychologist Richard J. Herrnstein set forth in their book *Crime & Human Nature,* with the overblown sub-title, *The Definitive Study of the Causes of Crime.* Their pivotal theory of "crime as choice" has a volitional connotation suggestive of the doctrine of free will embraced by the law. It is stated at so broad a level of generality, as the authors diffidently point out, that it is not meant to supplant but to encompass other theories. However, their statement that "people when faced with a choice, choose the preferred course of action" (p.43) or that "behavior is determined by its consequences" seems little more than an attempt to give a scientific garnish to the rationalistic language of the criminal law or everyday discourse. It still boils down to the commonsense proposition that people do what they believe to be in their best interest. Or in an even greater reduction to absurdity, it proclaims the not so stunning truth that criminals have found crime to be a satisfying activity.

In order to impart a scientific aura to their pronouncements, Wilson and Herrnstein formulate an equation to the effect that the balance of positive and negative consequences of a particular act determines the avoidance or repetition of that act. Another equation states that the longer it takes for the positive reinforcement to occur, the less likely it is to engender the behavior that produces it.

The latter equation is given as follows:

$$\text{``}B = \frac{R}{R + Re + Di}$$

where: B = strength of a given class of behavior expressed as a fraction of total behavior.

R = net reinforcement conditional on B

Re = total reinforcements being obtained, exclusive of those conditional on B

i = a parameter—the "impulsiveness" parameter—whose value determines how steeply discounted the value of a delayed reinforcement is." (Wilson & Herrnstein, 531)

The expression of these relationships in the form of an algebraic equation cannot disguise the fact that the "factors" of the equation refer to highly subjective states, unamenable to the scientific requirement that things be defined in terms that enable other observers to recapture the same physical reality with a high degree of reliability. A reduction of the propositions of the equation to their essential meanings evokes the conviction that, rather than a predictive instrument of science, they comprise no more than a set of maxims which need no verification. How can you argue with a theory which says that people tend to avoid pain (unless there is some advantage in receiving pain, like undergoing surgery to remove a malignant growth) or to seek pleasure (unless there is some advantage in refusing it such as avoiding sexual contacts under circumstances where the risk of communicable disease is high); or that prudent people compared with imprudent people, will more often observe reasonable caution; and that the prospect of immediacy or delay in the expected gratification from an act will affect the likelihood of doing it? By the premises of such a theory it can be claimed that no matter what a person does, his acts are determined by judgments of the utility of the behavior based on past experience. In short, the theory is a non-falsifiable truism.

Another behavioristic principle states that individuals differ organically in the degree to which behavior can be implanted by conditioning. Psychologist Hans Eysenck observed that delinquent youths, compared to non-delinquent youths, are on average more extraverted and less conditionable. Also, consistent with the findings of William Sheldon and Sheldon and Eleanor Glueck, delinquent youths are more muscular, restless, and prone to physical rather than verbal expression compared to non-delinquent boys of comparable background. Their greater strength and impulsiveness underlie the propensity to take illegally what law abiding people acquire by exchange. There is no demonstration that these traits, by themselves, significantly affect homicide rates, either in the American populations studied by Sheldon and Eleanor Glueck and William H. Sheldon more than a generation ago or in the unhomicidal Britain of Hans Eysenck. The same personal traits are valued by recruiters of athletes for contact sports and by the military in the assignment of commissioned and non-commissioned officers to combat duty. The present day epidemic of murder among inner-city children and youth owes exceedingly more to the prevalence of hand-gun ownership than to the hyperactivity of heavily muscled youths.

The precision in the measurement of stimulus and response which behaviorists, conducting their research almost entirely in laboratory situations, find so appealing is offset by the truth that what is observed has little direct bearing on the distinctly human aspects of thinking, feeling, and acting. By applying the same denominator of determinism to humans as it applies to rats and pigeons in laboratory research, behaviorism reduces human learning to a mere reflexive process.

Clarence Ray Jeffrey, a proponent of the behavioristic model for criminology, proposes that many forms of criminal behavior are maintained by their adjustive consequences. He gives as an illustration the murder of an unfaithful wife by her husband. Are we to presume that the cuckolded husband has learned to kill his wife through the positive reinforcement obtained from killing previous cheating wives? Another illustration involves a little boy who steals from the cookie jar when his mother isn't looking; presumably the pleasure of eating the cookie leads to further thefts of cookies. (Jeffrey, 294-300) But what if mamma caught the child on the first try, before he obtained the positive reinforcement of consuming the cookie, and took it away? Does that insure the extinction of cookie eating or cookie stealing? The problem remains, concerning both the wife-killer and the cookie thief, of explaining the initial transgression. The emphasis in operant learning theory on the consequences rather than the suitability of behavior leaves out of account the insightful character of human learning: the ability without prior conditioning to relate needs and desires to appropriate objects or acts and proceed to gratify them. (Asch, 98)

No discussion of individual factors in the causation of violent crime would be complete without a consideration of the impressive body of research which finds that delinquents differ from non-delinquents in personality characteristics. Since good boys and bad boys may differ in socioeconomic status and cultural background, with all that this implies for attitudes toward conformity to law, some researchers have adopted the methodological device of *matched pairs* whereby each delinquent case is matched with a non-delinquent case of equivalent social background. With the contaminating effects of socioeconomic status presumably under control, differences between the two groups in the amount or kinds of miscreancy can be confidently ascribed to personality factors.

The ideal of equivalence between the two groups is difficult to obtain, however. The attempt by Sheldon and Eleanor Glueck in their classic study, *Unraveling Juvenile Delinquency*, to match a delinquent with a non-delinquent boy of equal socioeconomic status was not successful. The non-delinquents' families displayed more of the stability of middle class families. They had higher average earnings, higher levels of employment, better living conditions in the home, better educational achievement of parents, and less physical and mental illness compared with the families of the delinquent matches. Accordingly it should come as no surprise that the non-delinquents' personalities reflected a more supervised and caring upbringing. Compared with their delinquent counterparts, they exhibited tighter self-control and closer conformity to social standards.

Summary

Biological and psychological theories of murder relate to innate states or reflexive processes that are common denominators of all human behavior. They analyze the person in partial or complete isolation from the attitudes, values, and sentiments that give meaning and direction to life. They define what the individual professes to think about his killing behavior as froth from the churning of man's animal nature. In failing to respect the content of the human mind in ordering the direction and planning of conduct, they undervalue the social origin and meaning of the murderous wish.

Biological and psychological criminologists contend that the individual traits which they endow with causal power are predispositions whose effects depend on the experience and social situation of the actor. Lacking data on these traits in the general run of killers, they can only guess at, and tend to overvalue, their contribution relative to social factors. In the following chapter I shall make a more definitive statement on the relative importance of individual factors relative to social factors.

Despite their weaknesses, theories that attribute murder to some physical or mental abnormality hold a secure niche in scholarly and popular thought. Their dominant theme—that killing is the compulsive, spontaneous, or irrational product of some diagnosable disorder—makes intriguing reading and offers the reassurance that murder is not the sort of thing that "normal people" do. But the facts speak otherwise. By the "normality" of killing I mean that the perceptions, attitudes, beliefs, judgments, and emotional surges that prompt murder are explicable without resort to theories of abnormal psychology. Few murders are demonstrably a product of mental breakdown. Virtually everybody has problems, which interpreted clinically, can be woven into a diagnosis of mental disorder. Attributing to them the power to produce homicide rings false since so many of the complaints deemed sicknesses by mental hygienists are recognizable as states which all of us at some time experience in some degree .

Psychologist Israel W. Charny makes a recommendation in his work on genocide that could apply to any form of murder: "The social sciences need to have a language that makes it possible to think about how a human being who is not clinically mad or morally perverse can become a killer of many people." (Charny, 23-24) As I will note in Chapter 4, the grammar and vocabulary for such a language, whether the killing is of many or only one, can be found in sociological theories of motive. But first I lay a foundation for an examination of sociological theories of homicide by identifying the demographic characteristics associated with homicidal behavior.

3

Who Kills Whom

National and international statistics reassure that we need not submit to the fatalism fostered by biological theories of homicide that nature has endowed citizens of the United States more abundantly than those of other nations with an inborn streak of violence. The United States is composed of people whose forebears came from lands on every continent. A comparison of homicide rates between any ethnic group of the American population and the country of their national origin belies the inevitability of our murder epidemic. Nations that supply data on violent death to the World Health Organization produce homicide rates ranging from less than 1 per hundred thousand of population in the advanced industrial societies of western Europe and Japan to more than 30 per hundred thousand in conflict-ridden nations of the third world. Independent black African nations whose citizens share gene pools with American blacks have homicide rates varying from as low as 1 to as high as 14 per hundred thousand. The black American homicide rate, based on arrests for murder and non-negligent homicide, of 36 per hundred thousand, is several times that of any reporting black African nation. With the exception of certain nations of South and Central America, southeast Asia, and the Republic of South Africa, few countries exceed annual rates of 4 per hundred thousand. The United States with a stable annual average homicide rate of about 9.0 for the past twenty years compared with the 0.6 to 3.0 of other western style democracies, is a conspicuous aberration among nations.

International comparisons can lead to incautious generalization. There are so many differences between countries with very high and very low homicide rates. Nations may differ in demography, climate, culture, and political and social organization. The question of which, if any, of these factors accounts for the disparity depends on the intellectual or esthetic preferences of the observer. Social critics, unencumbered by requirements of rigorous evidence are free to put the blame on whaterver they believe causes the loss of moral bearing with the resultant rampant egoism. American criminologists, nurtured in a social order dominated by materialistic values, find ample evidence of a correlation between indices of economic deprivation and the bulk of American homicides. The effect of poverty in itself is refuted by the low rates of violent crime in Calcutta, India. This city of twelve million inhabitants, beset by all of the organic and psychologic ailments thought to cause violent crime, with 300,000 of its residents living on pavements, and nearly half of the population squeezed into squatter shanties had 100 homicides in 1990 compared to New York's 2,200. This sociological marvel is simplistically attributed to a network of relatively homogeneous subcultures. (*New York Times*, 1/6/91, Section 4, p. 18). A reading of Dominique LaPierre's absorbing word picture of Calcutta's slums, *City Of Joy*, sketches a mosaic of *heterogeneous* cultural groups packed together under conditions of incredible squalor. South Africa too, has its network of homogeneous subcultures, of which the Zulu and Xhosa tribes are major groupings, and for years, has had a record-breaking national homicide rate, independent of killings in civil riots, of over 40 per hundred thousand. Prosperous nations comprising cultural groups so diverse that they speak different languages but possess ingrained traditions of civility—Switzerland, Canada, and Belgium, for ex-ample—have low homicide rates. More culturally homogeneous na-tions with extensive poverty—Mexico, Colombia, Guatemala, and Thailand—have higher than average rates.

Actually there are greater differences in homicide rates among identifiable social groupings within nations than among nations. The massive South African rate derives preponderantly from conflict among blacks, who account for 80 percent of the population and provide the menial workforce of the nation. The violence erupts from strains peculiar to South Africa's riven social system: long standing inter-tribal feuds which, with the gradual breakdown of apartheid, have become civil conflicts, drunken quarrels in neighborhood Soweto pubs, and the stresses experienced by migrant workers from long periods of separation from families left behind in the tribal homelands. The white South African homicide rate, on the other hand, is low, in the same range as that of European countries.

The spread in American homicide rates ranges from about 2.0 in the North Central States to 70.0 in cities with a large black underclass. The stability of homicide rates for the United States as a whole over recent decades implies a constancy of the forces which prompt the killing. In the period from 1971 through 1989 the rate of criminal homicides known to the police ranged from a low of 7.9 to a high of 10.2, with an average rate of 9.0., and a mean deviation from the average of only 0.5. Although the number of killings rose in 1990 and 1991, the population also increased, keeping the rate under the 10.2 limit of the preceding two decades.

The homicide rates for specific regions, ages, sexes, and races of the nation also maintain a consistency over time. American murder rates have been historically highest in the southern states, followed by the western states and northeastern states, and lowest in the north central states. Rates for metropolitan areas are half again as high as for rural counties and twice as high as for cities not a part of a metropolitan area. Regional and rural-urban differences have tended to level since World War II owing to the exchange of population among regions and areas. The mass relocation of residents of the rural south, a region of high homicide rates, to urban areas has contributed to an increase in the homicide rates of cities. The influx of white middle class retirees to warm regions of the nation has restrained the growth of homicide rates in southern states.

Individual Traits: Age, Sex, and Race

The traits of race, sex, and age, routinely entered into official records of criminal arrest, far more than any known organic, psychological, national, or regional difference, differentiate killers from the rest of the population. American killers are disproportionately young, male, and black. In 1990, persons age 18-34 accounted for 58 percent of homicide arrests; males, about equal in number to females in the general population, made up 90 percent of arrests; and blacks, about 12 percent of the population, produced 55 percent of arrests.

Street gangs, mainly black and Hispanic teen-agers and young adults, contribute a substantial 16 percent of the homicide rate of large cities. A sampling of gang related homicides reported in metropolitan newspapers reveals a wide variety of forms of homicide, running the gamut from robbery-murders, through sexual assaults, the assassination of competitors and double-dealers in the drug trade, turf wars between rival gangs, recreational assaults, teaching a lesson to upstarts (like a youth from a different neighborhood who, provocatively or unwittingly, wore the local gang's colors), proving one's mettle to peers, and taking vengeance, to most lamentably, the killing of innocent victims from stray bullets in drive-by shootings of gang wars.

Gang activities are carried on in a mood of skylarking ("wilding" is the term popularized by the nationally publicized attack on the woman jogger in New York's Central Park), similar, but not identical, to that of school boys at sport or up to some harmless high-jinks. The games are highly competitive, but the "athletic" gear consisting of knives or automatic weapons renders the outcome absolutely conclusive for the losers. Some observers read a genocidal plot into the alarmingly high murder rate of young blacks: the conspirators assure the destruction of young black males by pushing the gun trade in inner cities. The facts more directly fit the doctrine laid down by the English clergyman Thomas Malthus almost two hundred years ago, that natural forces—famine, plague, and warfare—pare populations down to a balance with existing resources.

Rates of murder committed by females, like those of males, fluctuate in accordance with race and age, but less steeply. Marvin E. Wolfgang's classic Philadelphia study, *Patterns in Criminal Homicide*, yields a black female homicide rate of 9.3, less than one-quarter of the black male rate of 41.7, but almost three times the white male rate of 3.4 and more than twenty-three times the white female rate of less than 0.4. (Wolfgang, 1958, 33) Essentially the same proportional differences between the sexes are shown by Harvin L. Voss and John R. Hepburn in their analysis of Chicago homicides. The age distribution of females arrested for murder follows the trend for males, peaking at age 25 to 29, tapering down in the ages of 30 to 34, and declining more sharply thereafter.

Official compilations of crime statistics do not provide separate data on the crime of Hispanics in American society, understandably because the term Hispanic embraces such a diversity of racial and cultural groups—Chicano (Mexican), Porto Rican, and Cuban, in varying combinations of African, American Indian, and Caucasian racial stocks, as well as Spanish, and Portuguese—all of which have in common only that their constituents have Hispanic surnames. Most crimes committed by Hispanics are lumped officially under the category *White.*

Alex Pokorny's Houston, Texas study compares the frequency of homicide rates for Hispanic compared with other local cultural groups. Focusing on a Mexican-American population, the most numerous of Hispanic-American groups, Pokorny found a male rate of 24.6, one half of the black male rate of 54.5, but three times the white male rate of 7.9. The most striking finding is the total absence of murders by Hispanic females, suggesting that the traditional Hispanic cultural norm of female passivity and submission to men reduces the potential for female violence. Pokorny's study was published in 1965; quite likely Mexican-American women who came of age in the United States since then have been influenced by the new wave of feminism to be more assertive.

Explanations of women's low level of homicidal activity has ranged from the traditional view of the inborn passivity of the female, in contrast to an inborn aggressiveness of the male, to the contemporary emphasis on culturally acquired sex roles. Sociologist Otto Pollak combines the two perspectives in his 1950 publication, The *Criminality of Women,* contending that women are as criminal as men, but that the requirements of the female social role, rooted in nature as well as nurture, channel the mass of female crime into more covert and less visible forms such as shoplifting and embezzlement, or into the relatively infrequently prosecuted crime of prostitution. In her role as homemaker or nurse, woman presumably has opportunities for homicide of a less detectible form than available to men, such as poisoning members of the household for insurance. If women often get rid of unwanted associates by poisoning, they must be very successful at it since very few cases come to light.

The burgeoning women's movement has downplayed the influence of physiological differences between the sexes on behavior. Activists prefer the culturally toned expression *gender* to explain male or female differences in criminal behavior. Criminologist Freda Adler, in her pioneer feminist assessment of women's criminality, *Sisters in Crime,* anticipates that the criminal activity of females should rise to a level with that of males as the restraints of sexism wither away. Her prophecy finds support in the statistics of many kinds of occupational crimes situated in the workplace, but not in the statistics of homicide: the ratio of male to female homicides in the United States persists at a disparate ratio of 8.5 to1.

Feminists who tend to minimize the effect of sex differences on capabilities have not been able to explain away biological differences between the sexes which bear directly on violent tendencies. The female constitution is adapted to reproducing and nurturing new members of the species; the male constitution, to protecting and providing for females whose ability to look after themselves may be encumbered by pregnancy or child nurturance. The distinction is rooted in different hormonal makeups. Males secrete testosterone which arouses aggressiveness under threatening conditions; females secrete estrogens which are closely bound up with their reproductive function and lactation. In advanced industrial societies the physiological difference in sexual functions are less restrictive and have not stood in the way of women invading hitherto exclusively male occupations, even such bastions of maleness as the police, judiciary, firefighting, and combat roles in the military.

Nevertheless very basic differences in the homicidal behavior of the sexes persist. Women have as much opportunity and incentive as men to kill over insults or for material gain, but seldom do. Killings by females for material gain, to the extent that they are known, are mostly as accomplices to the men in their lives. A large proportion of the small number of women who kill on their own initiative have suffered brutal victimization at the hands of spouses or lovers and retaliate in retribution or desperation. An exception, a female serial killer convicted in Florida in 1992 of killing six men, demonstrated a calculated brutality in her motive pattern. She approached her victims with a plea for assistance in apparent highway breakdowns or a solicitation for sex, and when they complied, she shot and robbed them as they lay dead or dying. Another exception, Judias Beunoano, was convicted in Florida for a series of killings in which she was the beneficiary of large insurance policies on the victims' lives. She got rid of her first husband by poison. Her second victim was her common law husband who died of mysterious medical complications. Not even her son was safe from her devices; crippled by a toxic paralysis from a previous failed attempt by his mother to poison him, he drowned when she pushed him out of a canoe. A fiancé survived the detonation of an explosive placed in his car. (Anderson and McGehee)

The known personal characteristics of victims are similar to those of killers. The 1990 *Uniform Crime Reports* show that 78 percent are males; 70 per cent are age 15 through 39; 93 percent of black victims in cases involving one victim and one offender were killed by blacks, and 6 percent, by whites; 86 percent of white victims were slain by whites, 12 percent by blacks. An exception to the rule of offender-victim similarity is gender: in homicides involving a single victim and offender, 85 percent of males are slain by males, but only one in ten females is slain by a female. These differences have remained firm over the passage of years.

Cultural diferences in patterns of homicide influence the ratio of female to male victimization. A study by Simha Landau, Israel Drapkin, and Shlomo Arad shows that for the American cities of Houston, Chicago, and Philadelphia, females comprise from one-fifth to one-fourth of victims, and in the southern province of Sri Lanka, about one-sixth. In Israel, women account for two-fifths, and in England, three-fifths of victims. (Landau et al) Domestic quarrels are the commonest pattern of homicide in the countries with a higher proportion of female victims; robbery and male ego conflicts are more often the pattern in countries with proportionately fewer female victims.

For many Americans the most painful measure of racial inequality in America is the statistic that black males age 15 through 39, comprising 3 percent of the population of the United States, furnish 37 percent of the known murder victims. The homicidal harvest of blacks is not the inevitable product of some malignant racial gene, but rather the spoilage of a social system which fails to embrace a substantial proportion of the population into its moral order.

Social Status

While age sex, and race are highly correlated with homicide rates, the preponderance of individuals in the categories of highest risk don't kill. Provided they are of middle or upper class social status, they have what seems to be almost an immunity to committing homicide. Killing—by whites or racial minorities, females or males, old or young—is almost entirely a lower class behavior pattern. The class differences in homicide rates are measurably much greater than differences based on race or any measure of organic or psychological abnormality.

Occupation is the most practical and reliable indicator of social class. A comparison of black and white arrest rates, within the same occupational levels, substantially reduces the racial difference in rates of crime generally. (Green, 1970) Blacks at the lower social levels display higher homicide rates than comparably situated whites (Wolfgang, 1958, pp. 36-39), but decline to equality, or less, compared with whites at the middle and upper levels. (Green and Wakefield)

The primacy of social class over all other correlates of murder has been shown in every study which looks at the relationship. Marvin E. Wolfgang estimates that only about five to ten percent of the 621 killers in his study of homicide in Philadelphia exceed lower class status, as measured by occupation. (Wolfgang, 1958, 37) An analysis of the 612 homicides committed in Cleveland, Ohio during the period 1947 to 1953 (Bensing et al) found nearly perfect inverse correlations between homicide rates and the districts of the city differentiated by the socioeconomic variables of income, educational attainment, and occupation: the lower the measure of social status, the higher the homicide rate. Seven decidedly middle class districts had no homicides. The five districts which were adjudged the highest in social class yielded a total of five homicides which amounted to a rate of 0.6 per hundred thousand of population. It is not ascertained, however, whether these homicides were committed by residents, domestic servants, or outsiders. The remaining homicides, over 99 percent, occurred in the poorer districts of the city.

Research by Russell Wakefield and the writer (1979) indicates that fewer than one percent of all homicides in America are commited by the middle and upper classes which comprise just over one half of the population. In one inquiry a questionnaire was distributed to the eighty-three county prosecutors in the State of Michigan inquiring if over a three year period there had been any cases of homicide committed by persons in middle or upper level occupations—professional, managerial, skilled workers and proprietary. Only one out of the thirty-two replies, supplied a killer, a retired school teacher, who met the occupational criterion.*

Another inquiry by the same investigators examined the social class level of the killers in all news stories of homicide reported in the *New York Times* for the period 1955-1975. The killers were divided into two social tiers. The upper tier consists of professional, managerial, skilled, and proprietor occupations; the lower tier, of the semi-skilled, unskilled, and unemployed. Dependents not in the labor force were accorded the status of the employed member of the family. The procedure for obtaining the sample of cases assumes that the *New York Times* reports most instances of murder committed nationwide by people in the middle and upper levels of society. Confidence in the representativeness of the sample is bolstered by the fact that the killings are distributed among the states and the District of Columbia in numbers roughly proportional to the size of the various states' populations. Also, the population of killings found in the *New York Times Index* was virtually the same as found in the indexes of other major newspapers—The *New Orleans Picayune Times*, The *Washington Post*, The *Chicago Tribune*, and the *Los Angeles Times*.

The investigation turned up, nationwide, only 119 cases involving 121 offenders and 191 victims in which the killer was in an upper tier occupation. This number of offenders constitutes less than one half of one-thousandth (.0005) of the estimated 252,000 arrests for murder during the time period surveyed.

Some skepticism may reasonably attach to the drawing of a national sample of killings from a local newspaper, no matter how broad its circulation. To meet this objection a refined analysis of the homicide data of New York City reported in the *New York Times*

---

* The fact that we received responses from only 32 of the 83 district attorneys canvassed reflected the objection to the study by the head of the state's organization of district attorneys who pointed out that providing this information would be improper because some of the cases could still be pending disposition.

was undertaken as a check on the pattern of class distribution found in the national study. Presumably virtually all known local killings would be reported. The results support the national findings. Only 9 murders by middle or upper class people were reported over a twenty-one year period, an average of less than one-half per year. In 1965, the middle year of the time frame of the study, 702 cases of murder and non-negligent manslaughter were officially reported in the New York Standard Metropolitan Statistical Area. The *Uniform Crime Reports* for 1965 (p. 97) shows that 89.8 percent of the known cases of homicide are cleared by arrest. Applying that percentage to the 702 known cases of homicide for the same year, we estimate that there were altogether 630 arrests for homicide in New York City in 1965. The proportion of those arrests comprising middle or upper class persons is fewer than 1 out of 630, less than one-sixth of one percent.

The fact that the holders of occupations herein designated *middle or upper class* comprise at least one-half of the labor force points up the enormousness of the disparity between the upper and lower occupational tiers in rates of homicide. Briefly put, the lower occupational classes—the semi-skilled, unskilled, and unemployed, comprising between forty and fifty percent of the population—account for over 99 percent of homicides. Allowing for an undercount of middle and upper class murders by raising the observed number six-fold puts the proportion of middle and upper class murders at 1 percent.

The circumstances of the middle and upper class homicides delineated in the national results differ in all major respects from those of the lower class homicides except for the sex of the offender: males predominate at all social levels. In the upper tier:

—The killer is a white male over thirty, whereas in the lower tier he is a black male under thirty; in fact, none of the upper level murderers was identified as black.

—Very few have prior criminal records; a majority of the lower class offenders do.

—There are no ascertainable instances of victim-precipitated homicide, compared to the one-fifth or one-third found in the lower class cases.

—Intra-familial killings comprise 73 percent of the cases, three times the proportion found in lower class homicide.

—Murder capped by suicide, occurs in 27 percent of cases and in fewer than 1 percent of lower class homicides.

—The method of killing more often involves shooting and less often, stabbing, compared with lower class murders. The social class difference in the proportion of shootings is less pronounced when white upper level offenders are compared with only white lower level offenders. (Since the time period of this study, 1955-1975, the enormous inflow of firearms of all kinds into the inner cities has likely leveled the social class difference in the use of guns.)

—Alcohol is uncommon in the blood of offenders and victims; in lower class offenders it is present in more than one-half of cases.

—The killings, like those in the lower tier, occur mainly during the evening hours, 8 P.M to 2 A.M., but unlike lower-tier murders, exhibit no time pattern during daytime hours. Upper-class murders are significantly more likely to occur at the victim's home than away from home.

The enormous disparity between the upper and lower social classes in rates of homicide, provides a foundation for the evaluation of the claims of advocates of biologic, neurologic, psychologic, and other individual trait theories of violent crime. A recent publication of the National Research Council (1993) supportive of such claims takes the view that all causes of violent crime are created equal. The writers, a committee of twenty-one panelists representing the biological, medical, psychological, and social sciences express the view that "...violence arises from interactions among individuals' psychosocial development, their neurological and hormonal differences, and social processes. *Consequently, we have no basis for considering any of these 'levels of explanation' more fundamental than the others."* (Emphasis supplied) They go on to say, "Because existing studies rarely consider more than one of these levels simultaneously, very little is known about the relevant interactions." (Reiss et al, 102)

It is true that we lack data on the distribution of these individual traits in the general run of homicidal or violent offenders needed for a direct analysis of the interactions. We know enough, however to make some judgments about the interactions. Quite possibly, for individuals who live under social and cultural conditions of high risk for violent crime, the irritability arising from organic or psychological disturbances may fan the already powerful propensity for violence. On the other hand, these causes may have no independent effect; like the violent behavior they purport to explain, they are themselves products of life in a lower sociocultural environment. The latter interpretation is favored by the finding that under social and cultural conditions of low risk for homicide, as embodied in middle or upper class status, there is apparently no effect. This could mean either that organic and psychological causes have virtually no inherent effect or that their potential effects are cancelled out by the stronger self-control exercised by people in the uper tiers of society. Apparently under conditions of very high or very low risk to kill, represented, respectively, by underclass or upper tier membership, organic or psychological causes are neither necessary nor sufficient to produce homicidal assaults

Glaring inconsistencies in the relative weight accorded individual and social factors by the National Research Council attest to the perils of writing a book by committee. In contradiction to their conclusion that none of these levels of explanation is more fundamental than others, they say in another context, "To date, no known neurobiologic patterns are precise and specific enough to be considered reliable markers for violent behavior..." (Reiss et al, 12) And again, "...no patterns precise enough to be considered reliable biological markers have yet been identified." (p. 116). Even when such "markers' are accorded some positive consideration, the discussion is hedged by the repeated use of the word "may' in describing their probable effect. (p. 302) The same short shrift is accorded genetic factors in influencing potentials for violent behavior. On the other hand they find that social factors of all sorts—ethnicity, poverty, social and economic structure, and community organization—reliably correlate with violent crime. (Reiss et al, 129-147)

Gun Owners

The involvment of guns in America's very high homicide rate suggests another category of demographic analysis: the gun owner. Over sixty percent of the more than 20,000 people murdered annually in the United States die from gunshots. Handguns are the weapon of choice in 74 percent of gun killings. But that's not the total of gun-inflicted injury. Additionally there are annually tens of thousands of failed homicidal attempts by firearm among the million and a half violent assaults, not to mention the toll of accidental killings—children playing games with guns which their parents have left within easy reach, or suicide, which is simplified by the use of a gun.

Official crime statistics published by the United States Department of Justice regularly show that in cases in which the circumstances of the murder are known, only one-eighth of the offenders are the "criminals"—the rapists, robbers, or other forms of predator, featured in polemics opposing gun control—against whom law-abiding people might wish to keep guns for protection. The killers are mostly unresourceful people who, under emotional stress, their inhibitions dulled by alcohol or drugs, reach for their guns to resolve conclusively problems of interpersonal relations with people they know—relatives, spouses, and acquaintances. Fewer than one-sixth of the victims of homicide are strangers to their slayers!

Shifting the blame for the homicide epidemic from the widespread possession of guns to the characteristics of the people who own them or the frustrations of economic deprivation overlooks the powerful interaction betwen the two factors. The social system of Britain, for example, which shares a common language, literary tradition, and value of individual freedom with its American counterpart, presents more barriers to social mobility and begets a considerable social distance and mutual disdain between the social levels. Yet despite a disposition toward criminal violence displayed in internationally publicized soccer stampedes, the stormy poll tax demonstrations of 1990, recurrent race riots, and high rates of assault, the British produce homicides at a rate about one-tenth that of the United States. It takes no feat of interpretive prowess to account for a major portion of the difference. British law, supported by custom, stringently restricts possession of handguns; even the police do not carry guns while on routine duty. This is not to say that without the easy availability of guns, the American class difference in the rate of homicidal behavior would disappear, but it would be much less. The final chapter of this book will have more to say about the political and practical difficulties of attacking the gun problem.

Summary

The vital statistics of homicide chart the course for the next stage of this inquiry by showing that the probability of homicide depends much more on social factors than organic or mental defects. The pronounced variation in the distribution of homicide by nationality, age, sex, race, and most significantly, by social class, indicates that the murderous impulse develops out of the refraction of personal experience through the prism of social and cultural orientations. This theme receives tacit recognition by mental health professionals whose clinical diagnoses are frequently laced with sociological insights, camouflaged as psychological variables. We turn now to an examination of those insights expressed in their own terms.

4

The Social Context of Murder

The finding that social status influences fluctuation in rates of homicide more than any other individual or social variable narrows the focus of this inquiry to the question: What is there about lower class status that impels people to kill? Is the "mystery" factor absent in the middle and upper classes or does it find expression in other ways? The diversity of possible answers reflects the various perspectives that coexist within sociology. The sociology of crime is imbedded in the more general study of social control and and the relationship between society and the individual. These concerns inspire the key questions into the causes of serious crime: How does society achieves a balance between personal desires and the controls essential for orderly social relations? What is the source of pro-social and anti-social inclinations?

In advancing the claim that social forces activate the impulse to kill, sociology has had to deal with critics from psychology who affirm that society is purely an abstraction; the individual is the reality. To paraphrase the critics: societies don't kill, individuals kill. The issue boils down to the contention between the view favored in psychology that a complete knowledge of the processes which animate individuals is sufficient to explain the behavior of people in the aggregate, and the sociological view that interaction among individuals generates a reality exterior to the individual. This reality, broadly captured by the terms *social organization* and *culture*, sociologists insist, can be analyzed only in its own terms.

Sociology has not done as good a public relations job as psychology in engaging the popular imagination, and is misunderstood even by many well-educated people, lawyers and judges included. Although a staple of the college curriculum the sociological perspective, except in its mawkishly toned popular form, has yet to achieve wide currency in an ideological climate that favors individualistic interpretations of human conduct. It is often caricatured as an enterprise for do-gooders who put the blame for crime and deviance on the flaws of a "sick society" instead of the abnormalities of body or mind, or deficiencies of spirit, where, the critics believe, it belongs.

More sophisticatedly than in its sentimentalized representation, sociological criminology expounds upon the play of social forces in the generation and transmission of techniques of crime and sentiments favorable to criminality. The processes by which these factors penetrate individual awareness and shape response lie, to be sure, within the province of psychological theories of learning and motivation, but themselves have no bearing on the causation of criminal behavior. As sociologist Edwin H. Sutherland noted over a half-century ago, the mechanisms involved in learning criminal behavior are the same as those involved in learning non-criminal behavior. (Sutherland and Cressey, 82) Simply put, it's not the process of learning, but the content of learning that counts. Sociologists put small store in that workhorse of forensic psychology, mental derangement, to explain homicide, or other forms of crime. Distraughtness is a common occurrence of everyday life; to be homicidal it must be coupled with learned attitudes favorable to violence.

The scaffolding of modern American sociological thought on crime was erected by the generation of sociologists whose careers spanned the period between the two World Wars. Observing that crime clustered in urban neighborhoods with large concentrations of recently arrived immigrants or rural migrants, they attributed the pressures toward crime to the ineffectuality of the traditional values brought by the newcomers in responding to the demands of a strangely new environment. The strains were reflected in high measures of homes broken by desertion or divorce, inadequacy of parents, erratic or harsh discipline, poor housing, transiency, low income, menial occupation, and unemployment.

Post-World War II sociologists refined the views of their forebears addressing questions of how strains in the organization of society and the slippage of mechanisms of social control elicit crime. Whatever the differences among them in formulating the issues, they concur in the premise of a morally neutral "state of nature" in which there is no inherent commitment or opposition to conventional rules of conduct. A composite of their views, as follows, sets forth the main strands of contemporary sociological criminology.

—Criminality or conformity to law is learned. The moral order of civilization is a web of expectations which must be ingrained in each successive generation.

—The likelihood of deviant behavior depends on the strength or weakness of the bonds which curb self-indulgence and connect the individual to the conventional order and .

—Socially and culturally well integrated societies, those which rationalize inequalities in the distribution of privilege by some sanctified plan, maintain order better than culturally pluralistic societies since they are less vulnerable to the forces of discontent or change which undermine existing arrangements.

Homicide and the Social Order

The century-old reflections of the eminent French sociologist, Emile Durkheim, concerning the effect of organizational features of society on the degree of obedience to social rules have profoundly influenced American sociological thought. Durkheim traces the breakdown of traditional controls to the galloping economic expansion and urban growth unleashed by the industrial revolution. He used the term *anomie* to denote the moral vacuum left by the breakdown of the traditional arrangements for the allocation of material rewards. His insights apply today to the spectacle of enormous disparities in wealth and income which cannot be explained by variation in the value of the products or services rendered or by the rationale that the disparity is consistent with some transcendental scheme of things. The divine ordinance which justified the wealth and power of the ruling classes in pre-capitalist societies has been replaced by secularly conceived market forces. Commercial advertising and media accounts of the lives of the rich and famous stimulate material wants in the masses of people far beyond the means available for their satisfaction. The personal freedom accorded the individual in making moral choices, enhances the likelihood of advancing personal interests selfishly, regardless of the cost to others.

Durkheim's classic work, *Suicide*, constitutes a model of the application of sociological theory to behavior commonly attributed in psychology to personal disarray. Making use of the best demographic and statistical data available at the time (first edition: 1897), he finds no significant fluctuation in rates of suicide relative to individual states such as mental disorder, race, heredity, and cosmic factors of climate and seasonal temperature. The key factor in suicide, and homicide, is the way in which societies achieve cohesion among members and conformity to rules of conduct.

The *anomic* disconnection of persons from traditional moral moorings favors both suicide and homicide. Whether the state of exasperation that arouses the urge to kill is directed toward oneself or others depends on the "moral constitution" of the individual: "A man of low morality will kill another rather than himself." (Durkheim, 1951, 357) Contemporary research on the American scene demonstrating that suicide is relatively rare among the lower classes and homicide rarer yet among the upper classes suggests that the "moral constitution" referred to by Durkheim is an expression of social class differences in value orientation.

The American sociologist Robert K. Merton, in a publication dated 1938, developed further the implications of Durkheim's views for the understanding of deviance in the context of the American moral order. He states the paradox that individuals who profess to be committed to the moral order of society and think of themselves as good people misbehave because they wish to achieve the goals prized by conventional values. Merton explains this contradiction as an unintended by-product of the American value system which, depending on the ability of the individual to meet its requirements, generates both law-abiding and criminal behavior. So intense are the stresses from pressures to achieve the symbols of material success, that those who lack the qualities of character for successful competition—self-discipline, good education, industriousness, and skill in interpersonal relations—and those who possess these traits but accept no limits on their desires—wizards of financial manipulation, greedy or power-obsessed politicians, or corporate executives out to maximize their firms' market share—feel pressures to resort to illicit means.

Elaborations of Merton's *social strain* theme to explain the juvenile delinquency of the nineteen-fifties anticipate the formation thirty years later of drug-running youth gangs armed with automatic weapons whose nightly "bag" figures prominently in the hefty urban murder rate. One version, by Albert K. Cohen, in his book *Delinquent Boys*, contends that boys of lower class background lack the competencies to compete for success in accordance with conventional values. Reinforcing one another's grievances, they create a value system based on opposition to middle class values. The emergent delinquent subculture prizes non-utilitarian ends. Stealing is done for for kicks rather than for the value of what is stolen. The delinquent subculture's paramount values center around sentiments of deviousness, guts, and nerve, expressed in a short run hedonism and the pursuit of sensory gratification.

Richard A. Cloward and Lloyd E. Ohlin explain how the social composition of neighborhoods makes a difference in the forms of criminal opportunity available to youth. Their book, *Delinquency and Opportunity*, identifies three types of opportunity: the organized crime of white ethnic-American neighborhoods steeped in Mafia-style traditions of the merchandising of illicit goods and services, black and Hispanic fighting gangs which vie with one another over territory, and for those who can find neither legitimate or criminal work, there are loosely integrated groups of winos and drug-users. There is a prophetic touch in Cloward and Ohlin's assessment based on observations in the 1950's: The second group has displaced the first group as purveyors and enforcers in the homicide-ridden inner-city drug traffic; the third group has been absorbed into the consumer market for drugs.

Culture and Homicide

Cultural theories are basic to the sociological perspective on violent crime. Their affirmation of the psychological normality of crime opposes popular opinion and many enduring scientific myths about criminals. As a general concept of the social sciences, culture refers to the sum total of man-made things. As a specific term it refers to the unique combination of traits of a particular social order including its language, technology, customs, rules of moral and ethical conduct, laws, religion, and art.

Culture patterns, but does not strictly determine, the conduct of people as they take roles in major areas of group activity— reproduction, family, education, religion, economy, and polity—and specifies the criteria for sorting people into hierarchies of power and prestige.

In heterogeneous societies obviously not all people are fully assimilated to the culture pattern of the dominant group. Many are imbued with the values of an ethnic or class *subculture* whose rules of conduct are modifications of those of the dominant group's culture and may include elements of different cultural traditions; they dance to the same melody, but with a different arrangement and beat. *Part-culture* refers to the culture pattern of an age-sex grouping within a culture or sub-culture which develops out of historical change and differences in role training. The concept is useful in approaching age, sex, and generational differences in criminal behavior patterns, or to illuminate specific problems such as the puzzlement of parents with their errant offspring.

Cultural theories of crime focus on the content of ideas and their transmission. One line of thought, appealing in its simplicity, censures the glamorization and excessive use of criminal themes in popular culture for the reason that too much exposure to the depiction of enjoyment or profit from acts of lust, greed, or violence may instill and whet an appetite for crime. A more sophisticated insight blames lawbreaking on the conflict of conduct norms between the dominant culture and one or more subcultures within the same society: the criminal, strictly speaking, is not a non-conformist; he is following a different set of rules. The classic statement of this view by criminologist Thorsten Sellin, in his treatise, *Culture Conflict and Crime*, cites a Sicilian immigrant father in New Jersey, nonplused at his arrest for slaying the sixteen year old seducer of his daughter, a morally correct act by his lights.

Edwin H. Sutherland's theory of *differential association*, a mainstay of sociological criminology, explains how culturally induced tendencies favorable to criminal behavior are transmitted. In an earlier period, when many authorities proclaimed the innateness of criminality, Sutherland's pronouncement that criminal behavior is *learned*, published in 1938, was a needed corrective. The learning, writes Sutherland, occurs in small groups and consists of techniques of committing crime and definitions of legal codes as favorable or unfavorable. The crux of the theory is the proposition that a person becomes delinquent when the weight of definitions favorable to obedience to law is exceeded by the weight of definitions favorable to violation of the law. Critics have noted that there is no scale by which to objectify the weight of such definitions. Proponents can counter that the definitions are essentially attitudes and these can be objectively investigated, as in survey research.

While purporting to set forth a theory of criminal behavior, Sutherland more nearly describes the process by which a person acquires positive or negative attitudes toward engaging in crime. Holding a favorable or unfavorable outlook toward a legal requirement influences, but does not determine the course of action an individual will take. The theory of differential association specifies neither the conditions under which criminal attitudes activate criminal behavior nor the conditions under which anti-criminal attitudes fail to uphold obedience to the law. A person may be favorably disposed to the killing of a certain individual or class of people, if the gain is sufficient, but exercise restraint for reasons which are independent of attitudes toward the law, such as fear of the consequences if caught, or lack of opportunity, incentive, or nerve. Conversely a person may have acquired "an excess of definitions" favorable to the law, and may be an honorable upright person, but under the goad of unusual temptations or pressures, augmented by some rhetoric of justification, commit murder.

Perhaps the chief value of Sutherland's statement is the prompt to search culture for criminal themes. All societies have a rich tradition of violence, but all societies are not equally violent. Indeed the approval of violence in a culture's literature, mythology, history, or religion is no reliable guide to what people will do. Few national cultures have literary heritages exceeding that of Japan in ferocity and goriness, so terrifyingly yet intriguingly and dashingly depicted in films and novels about the outlaw warrior tradition of the feudal period; nor do many national cultures produce as few murders.

A collaborative effort by sociologist Marvin E. Wolfgang and clinical psychologist Franco Ferracuti (1967) forges a more direct connection between culture and homicide. They attribute the disproportionate rate of criminal assault in the United States among male youths of lower class background to a *subculture of violence,* a set of values and sentiments which endows violence with an aura of valor and fortitude and justifies it in the name of personal honor. This powerful sentiment accounts for the willingness of young "bloods" to stake their lives in combat over such momentous challenges as "What you staring at, man?", contention over sitters' rights on a barstool, or territorial claims to a street location for drug selling.

The ideal of violence attains its most direct expression in those levels of society which possess the least legitimate power. Claude Brown in his autobiography, *Manchild in the Promised Land*, tells of the significance of physical aggression in the culture of the Harlem ghetto of the nineteen-fifties. Boys were reared to be more afraid of not fighting than fighting. Claude's father, himself a knife-carrier, would brook no reluctance of his son to fight in situations which required it. Honor consisted in the inviolateness of one's money, woman, and manhood. People killed over a gambling dispute or a small debt. To leave unredressed a slight to one's sister compromised the shirker's honor. Twenty years later Brown (1984) paid a visit to the old neighborhood and reported that these conditions had hardly changed.

Whether lessening the exposure to media sources of criminal stimulation will reduce the risk of doing criminal acts depends on who is targeted for such treatment. We all acquire the information needed to engage in crime without any special indoctrination. The knowledge to do criminally forbidden acts is just as widely disseminated a cultural product as recipes for cookies. The gamut of transgressions—infamy, sin, crime—involves behavior patterns which are learned in much the same way as any other part of the social legacy. The individual does not need any specialized knowledge or association in groups organized for crime, in order to be able to engage in crime. All it takes is ordinary insight. Murders are thoughtfully planned and executed by people with no prior experience in crime. Virtually all culturally acquired behavior can be done in such a manner or circumstances as to be illegal. The lawful acquisition, conveyance, or use of firearms, medicine, narcotics, or other peoples' property; indulgence in sensual pleasure or emotional release in hazardous pastimes or contact sports—all have their illegal counterparts. Indeed in learning good conduct and good character through moral indoctrination, one cannot help but learn about their opposites. Codes of laws and morals are least

ambiguous in their identification of forbidden conduct. Folklore—
ballads, poems, sagas, myths, fairy tales—indeed, all literary forms
and media deal extensively with the exploits, capers, or abominable
deeds of criminals. Business corporations and banks, even political
and religious organizations, offer on-the-job training in techniques
and practices easily transferable to crime. The mass media of information and entertainment—true crime books, press, films, and
television—provide detailed instruction in all manner of homicidal
techniques.

Yet no matter how widely and deeply criminal knowledge extends in a particular sociocultural order, most people seldom or
rarely engage in serious criminal behavior. This observation does
not, however, disprove the influence of the media. As Paul G.
Cressey noted more than fifty years ago, the stimulation from films
with criminal themes interacts with pre-existing personality
tendencies to activate delinquent behavior. Youths raised in
unstable families without adequate moral education are excep-
tionally vulnerable to the appeal of "role models" depicted in
violence-ridden films aimed at black audiences. After a two-hour
emotional binge with the films *Superfly* or *The Legend of Nigger
Charley,* inner-city youth audiences have spilled on to the streets,
the adrenaline still surging, to smash windows and loot stores. No
more than the anticipation of violence was needed to set off
disorders in a number of American motion picture houses across the
nation on the opening night of *Boyz 'N the Hood*, a film deploring
the problem of violence and drugs in inner-city ghettoes. Before the
showing began in one theatre, there was a shooting death.
Youngsters whose personalities are intellectually and emotionally
impoverished by neglect are highly suggestible to the aura of
glamor cast on violence by films and television and find in the
characters of such films examples to follow in terrorizing and killing
other inner-city children.

The Failure of Social Control

The sticky fact remains that many people situated at the points of
greatest exposure and vulnerability to criminal influences do not
engage in violent crime. *Control theory* attributes the predictive
limitations of cultural and social strain theories to misconceptions

that prompt asking the wrong questions. The central issue, as put by Travis Hirschi, a leading advocate, is not why people commit crime, but why they don't. Hirschi proposes that there is no innate restraint that precludes the victimization of fellow beings. The forging of the emotional bonds essential to the cultivation of forbearance is acquired in a sequence of developmental stages. The process begins in earliest infancy when parental nurturance reinforces the transmission of culturally expected patterns of thought and action to offspring. The child's fear of losing parental love strengthens commitment to rules of conduct. Rewards for conformity to conventional norms reduce the likelihood of straying into deviancy. A breakdown in the bonding process, due to parental neglect or harsh treatment, particularly if it occurs in the early stages of life, produces a morally and emotionally stunted person, devoid of the attachment or commitment to others needed for caring relationships. (Hirschi, pp.16-34)

In a more recent statement, Hirschi, joined by Michael R. Gottfredson, distances control theory further from conventional criminological thought. The only reliable correlate of crime or other forms of disapproved deviance, they find, is *low self-control.* But the traits which they identify as signs of lack of self-control, shown as follows on the left, more than casually resemble those of the traditional criminology, shown on the right, which they find wanting. (Gottfredson and Hirschi, 90-91)

impulsive	short-run hedonism
insensitive	sociopathy
risk-taking and short-sighted	time sense rooted in the present
non-verbal	a deficiency of intelligence

A deficiency of control theories, generally, is their lapse into circularity: the very fact of committing crimes is proof of the the lack of self-control which causes the crimes; not committing crimes is proof of self-control. An example is the version of control theory which expounds that a good *self-concept* insulates boys who live in high delinquency neighborhoods from delinquency. (Reckless et al) . The proof is that boys picked by teachers as good boys and who think of themselves as good boys stay out of trouble.

Although it is difficult to separate the qualities of nurturance, discipline, or training associated with self-control or the lack of it, self-control, in itself, does not necessarily repress serious crime, including murder. If the notion of control is broadened to include the disciplined command of emotions, thoughts, and reflexes required for calculatedness—an indeterminate number of lawbreakers, some of the most notorious murderers among them, have shown themselves to be quite capable of self-control. What is lacking is not control, but commitment to minimal standards of civic virtue.

The Radical Critique

The scientific commitment to objectivity does not eliminate the ideological underpinnings of criminological theory. Putting the blame for crime on defective cultural transmission in the family, rather than on the organization of society, places control theory on the conservative side of the political spectrum. Theories of social stress and violent culture project a liberal view in their implications for needed social reform. Marxian criminologists take a radical stance, placing the blame for crime squarely on the evils of capitalism. In an idealistic statement published in the first decade of the twentieth century, the Dutch criminologist, Willem Bonger, wrote that the egoism of capitalism, in contrast with the altruism of socialism is the energizer of crime. (Bonger, 12). Exploitation by the ruling classes produces the deprivation that pushes the poor into property crime and young women into prostitution. The hopelessness and despair of chronic poverty drive people to seek forgetfulness in drunkenness or narcotics. The profit motive is the driving force behind the racketeering and gang murders of organized crime. The desperation of the impoverished or the overbearing egoism of the rich can provoke alienated individuals to remove human obstacles to personal desires by killing them. For those who accept the doctrine of class struggle, the only solution is drastic social change to produce a non-exploitative social order which will give rise to a populace imbued with altruism.

Marxism did not command a wide following among American sociologists in the post-World War II period. In the 1960s stirrings of discontent with the war in Vietnam and impatience with the progress of civil rights reform touched off a new radical movement in criminology, styled *critical criminology*. Devotees took the iconoclastic position, that there is no objective basis for the definition of acts as crimes; crime is in the eyes of the beholder. They combined traditional Marxism with the study of how the observer's perception of things affects his understanding of them. The synthesis alleges a virtual conspiracy of the upper class, abetted by an ideologically misguided middle class, to suppress the lower class. To these radical criminologists, no patterns of behavior are innately offensive; they are labelled criminal because they threaten the interests of the dominant classes who control the enactment of laws. Thus behavior which grows out of adaptation to the uncertainties of life in the lower classes and threatens the dominance of the upper classes has a greater chance of being dealt with by the criminal sanction. The peccadilloes of the powerful— fraud, tax evasion, malpractice, monopolistic practices, and the like—are more often dealt with in civil procedures, thereby escaping the criminal sanction. (Richard Quinney, 99-105)

The stridency of the radical position has moderated during the conservative political shift of the 1980's in Europe and America. The challenge of the radical criminologists to the fixity of existing standards of any kind—moral, intellectual, cultural, and legal—is nothing new, nor is it confined to radicals. More than a half-century ago Thorsten Sellin noted the impermanence of law and morals in time and space observing "...that everything the criminal law in any state prohibits today it will not prohibit at a given future time." (Sellin, 1938) Jural philosopher Morris R. Cohen regards the assignment of acts to the category of *mala in se* (intrinsically evil), as a matter of local preference "...with no clear criterion by which to judge what acts should...be included and what acts should be excluded from the category of crime." (Cohen, 29)

The gauntlet of moral relativism has been flung by movements in all branches of the humanities and social sciences. The proponents of the new relativism, not unlike those of earlier periods, argue that standards emerge historically and in a sociological setting. Hence *objectivity* is a delusion, a cover for the imposition of ideological domination. None of the contrarian thinkers, however, has yet made an adequate case for the relativism of killing without justification, or even the crimes of assault, rape, robbery, or theft.

The existence of a common ethical orientation underlying cross-cultural uniformities in the criminal law finds powerful support in anthropological and sociological research. A conclusion drawn more than fifty years ago by anthropologist Ralph Linton declares the indispensability and universality of laws securing property and person. As Linton put it, "Virtually all societies...protect property rights and restrict acts of aggression among members." (Ralph Linton, 534-44) In a monumental study of ethical and legal variations among historical societies, Pitirim Sorokin found a number of acts—including murder, assaults, and robbery—that were universally defined as criminal and punishable. (Sorokin, 523)

The stacking and selection of evidence to conform to ideological preconception is the least engaging intellectual habit of American Marxist scholars. The classic Marxist and Neo-Marxist indictments of American capitalism are conclusions drawn from a comparison of capitalist American society with some hypothetical idealized socialist counterpart, certainly not any existing socialist state. Inequality resulting from the struggle for power is not unique to capitalism. It is characteristic of all social life. As the revelations from the *glasnost* policy of the now defunct Soviet Union, the collapse of communism throughout eastern Europe and the accounts of political dissidents make clear, underdogs in the power struggle in communist states have suffered harsh suppression by harrassment, banishment, and incarceration in mental institutions. (Solzhenitsyn; Sharansky) The much higher levels of civility observed in some European democratic socialist nations are more validly attributed to the common moral base of cultural homogeneity than to their political economy, as witness the increase of civil disorders in reaction to the massive immigration of alien racial or cultural groups to Britain, France, Germany, and Holland and the ensuing problems of accommodation in the past twenty years.

A Sociological Psychology of Murder

Since sociological pronouncements on crime consist mostly of relationships between social and cultural variables and criminal behavior, the question arises: How do social influences become transformed into the intent to kill? What is the ideational link between those influences and the act of killing? We still need a factor, the equivalent of the law's *intent*, to complete the chain of causation. In one of the rare instances that behavioral science has addressed the matter, the answer has followed the circular route of defining *intent* in terms of other behavioral variables rather than as a force in its own right. Social psychologists Martin Fishbein and Icek Ajzen regard *intention* as a form of belief, namely the individual's conception of the likelihood that he will perform some behavior. They propose that the intention to perform any behavior is determined by the person's attitude toward the behavior and by his idea of whether the people whose opinion he values think he should do it. (Fishbein and Ajzen, 288) Thus the likelihood of committing murder for any individual would depend on a number of considerations: his assessment of the prospect of getting away with it, his own attitude toward homicide, and how he thinks others would perceive it.

An area of sociological inquiry with the formidable title *symbolic interaction* has developed a distinctive set of concepts to address the missing link between attitude and behavior. A central theme of symbolic interaction is the attempt to forge a sociological approach to the question of motive, a concept regarded by psychologists as exclusive to their intellectual turf. The result is a conception of *motive* that is out of step with either the psychological or ordinary usage of the term. On the positive side this inapt conception of motive serendipitously comes closer than anything else in the behavioral sciences to a researchable conception of *intention*. *Symbolic interaction* denotes an area of sociological inquiry which takes the vocabulary and rhetoric embodied in language as the outward expression of the speaker's inner mental life (which is one of the ways by which the law ascertains an offender's intents and purposes). Unlike animals whose interaction relates to sexual approach, territorial claims, or other survival functions, and is accomplished mainly by signs expressed through instinctual mechanisms—odor excretions, body movements, and vocalizations—humans interact foremostly by means of language symbols. The fact that a criminal offender's statement is contradicted by physical evidence or testimony, may signify that he is mentally confused or doesn't mean what he says. Or the suspicion could emerge that he is trying to deceive his listeners.

Symbolic interaction regards the offender's utterances as elements of a culturally patterned "vocabulary of motives," in effect, culturally prepackaged reasons for conduct in standard situations. Unlike the subject in psychoanalytic theory who acts and then rationalizes, the subject in symbolic interaction rationalizes before he acts. The vocabulary of motives enables people to engage in criminal conduct, yet avow commitment to conventional values. The transgressor admits the crime while contending that there was no wrongdoing or that the infraction was necessary to correct a worse wrong. A seminal article by Gresham M. Sykes and David Matza identifies the grounds for self-absolution as "techniques of neutralization." They include the appeal to a higher loyalty such as friendship or some abstract moral principle; condemning the condemner for being a worse malefactor (crooked cops and judges, for example) than the accused; the denial of the injury (no harm was done); denial of responsibility (society or mental illness is to blame); the denial of the victim (no one was hurt); and the denial of the crime (there are no valid grounds for the criminalization of the act). (Sykes and Matza)

Political terrorists or gangsters excuse themselves by an appeal to familiar sentiments which many people endorse, but hardly consider justification for murder. The celebrity Mafia hit-man, "Joey," justified his "hits" by the waywardness of his victims in violating rules for the orderly management of business dedicated to supplying people with the goods and services prohibited by puritanical laws. As Joey puts it: "There are many reasons why an individual is killed. He may be a stool pigeon, he may be too greedy, the man he is working for might suspect he is talking too much...or is too ambitious; he might be blown away because he has not lived up to an agreement he made, the job might be planned by an underling trying to take over from a boss, the target could be a mob member who has become a junkie and is therefore unreliable, it might be a gang war and it could even be payment for an attempted double cross. There is always good reason and it involves doing something you shouldn't be doing as a member of organized crime." (Joey, 60-61) In recounting the details of his work routines, Joey betrays no sign of a troubled conscience. After a kill he returns home to a meal prepared by his wife, has a few beers, and watches television before retiring to a sound sleep.

The justification of the drug trade, with its homicidal overhead, is nowhere more spirited than among those who suffer the most from it, but also have the potentiality to gain from it. Wiley A. Hall, a columnist for the *Baltimore Sun* (November 13, 1990) tells of a speech he made to a class of a high school with a predominantly black enrollment. He told his audience that he thought drug dealers were bad people. A female student in the audience disagreed. Dismissing the speaker's condemnation of the homicidal violence of the drug trade, not to mention the pernicious effects of drugs, she declared that drug merchants "...were only trying to make money like everybody else...[they] helped their communities by giving people jobs..[A]uthority figures who attacked the drug trade were a bunch of hypocrites." To the columnist's astonishment, her classmates, who, he had no reason to doubt, were decent youngsters and not involved in the drug trade, agreed with her.

If criminal behavior is the rational projection of images connecting wishes with plans of action, how can we explain "compulsive" crimes which seem to have no rational basis and which are interpreted in psychoanalytic theory as the neurotic expression of unconscious wishes? Donald R. Cressey reconciles the seeming contradiction by providing the quintessential socio-logical explanation of how criminality gets into the head of the criminal. Going beyond the use of blame-disavowing language to justify infractions, he hypothesizes that language constructs themselves are the motivators of crime. His critique of the psychiatric interpretation of repetitive theft as *kleptomania*, a compulsion to steal over which the the afflicted person presumably has no control, could apply as aptly to serial murders. To paraphrase Cressey, an accused murderer may identify himself as having any of a variety of psychiatric ailments said to impel the sufferer to kill repetitively. To quote him, "A full commitment to such an identifica-tion includes the use of motives which release energy to perform a so-called compulsive act. The fact that the acts are recurrent does not mean that they are prompted from within but that certain linguistic symbols have become usual for the person in question." (Cressey, 1969, 1126)

Cressey's statement, with some modification, could also be applied to the individual killer in a crime of passion. A sudden murderous assault triggered by an insult or gesture is not as spontaneous as it may seem. The planning and calculation are in sequence, but in a highly compressed form. The attack may erupt out of a history of the nursing of grievance accompanied by an internal rehearsal of what the individual will do when a tormentor burdens his endurance with the final straw. In the dialogue with himself the potential killer constructs an image of the enactment of the attack linked to notions prevalent in his cultural community of adequate provocation and the severity of the punishment due his tormentor. By imaginatively weighing the incentives for committing a crime against the probability and pains of getting caught, the would-be offender can decide whether to proceed or stop.

The effort to distinguish between people who think about killing, but don't, and those who do falls prey to the error of imposing a psychological interpretation on social and cultural facts, An example is Edwin I Megargee's distinction between the *undercontrolled* and *overcontrolled* personality based on tests administered to convict populations. The *undercontrolled* exhibit a greater tendency to engage in violence, but do not commit the most destructive assaults. They are able to displace aggression in ways that enable the ventilation of hostility in assaultive, but non-lethal ways. The overcontrolled type appears to be a passive person, often with no prior history of aggression. He "is often a fairly mild-mannered, long suffering individual who buries his resentment under rigid but brittle controls. Under certain circumstances he may lash out and release all his aggression in one often disastrous act. Afterward he reverts to his usual overcontrolled defenses. Thus, he may be more of a menace than the verbally aggressive, 'chip-on-the-shoulder' type who releases his aggression in small doses." (Megargee and Mendelsohn, 437. Quoted in Megargee, 128)

Stuart Palmer's psychological study of fifty-one white murderers confined in the New Hampshire State Penitentiary supports the view that the overcontrol of hostility is a significant factor in deadly assaults. Palmer compared his subjects with a control group of siblings of the killers with respect to scores on scales of acceptable and unacceptable release of aggression. The murderers, he found, "...tended to be overconformists a great deal of the time, avoiding even socially acceptable releases and yet used relatively extreme and unacceptable releases the rest of the time." (Palmer, p.156)

A more broadly based analysis suggests that the distinction between the *undercontrolled* and *overcontrolled* depends more on situational and sociological factors than on personality differences. In the first place, the distinctions made by Megargee and Palmer are based on studies of incarcerated populations, hence test score differences may reflect attitudes related to conditions of imprisonment rather than personality structure. A second reason stems from evidence bearing on the racial factor in violent crime. The travails of growing up in the black underclass, particularly the tolerance for the physical expression of hostility permitted by violent subcultures, would seem to conduce to an *undercontrolled,* hence more frequent and less lethal, expression of violence. To the contrary, evidence reported by Howard Haven shows that blacks not only engage in violent crime more frequently than whites; their violence is also decidedly more lethal. Following procedures developed by Megargee and associates, Haven found that blacks score significantly higher than whites on measures of over-controlled hostility. (Megargee, 1971, 143). The markedly higher frequency and lethality of black compared to white violence suggests that the distinction is less a product of personality differences than of environmental adaptation and that what is expressed in the test results are culturally induced differences in patterns of violent crime. The nature of these patterns will be developed in the next chapter.

Summary

Sociology does a remarkably better job of interpreting the vital statistics of violent crime than the biological or psychological sciences. Still the social and cultural factors which feature in sociological analysis comprise no more than the setting for violent crime. As destabilizing as some of the settings may be, they do not compel people to kill. Rather they represent the conditions of life which place individuals at highest risk to kill. The anonymity of the individual in mass society encourages alienation. The impairment of the socializing function of family and school results in the development of self-absorbed individuals lacking in sentiments of honesty and compassion. Key concepts, such as the *subculture of violence* and *differential association*, reinforce the emphasis on the social acquisition, as opposed to the innateness, of violent crime. The lack of internal restraint posited by control theory may be less a deficiency of self-control than of assimilation to attitudes favorable to crime. The radical critique of mainline criminology may provide useful insights into the processes whereby minor crimes, mainly of the public order variety, come to be defined as criminal, but these insights do not extend to the more serious crimes, and certainly not to homicide.

Symbolic interaction, more cogently that any psychologial theory, provides a linkage between social forces and individual behavior. Although designed as a theory of *motive*, the language constructs which represent mental blueprints for action more aptly correspond to what the law and everyday usage define as *intention.* Symbolic interaction does not supply a powering force which activates the "vocabulary of motives" and galvanizes the individual into action. While it is true, as advocates of symbolic interactionism maintain, that programs of thought and action directed toward the achievement of group values are propelled by the individual's need to comply with social expectations, the values prescribed in the linguistic constructs are not embraced for their own sake. The fact that the most esteemed practices, objects, or sentiments relate to the satisfaction of biological or derivative social drives is what makes them values. History tells how values which cease to be serviceable in these regards, tend toward obsolescence.

Reconsidered as a theory of *intention*, symbolic interactionism opens a window into the world of meanings in terms of which the murderer acts; it supplies a mirror, albeit of flawed reflectance, for viewing the offender's image of his completed act. Compared to psychological theories, this sociological construct is much more finely attuned to the varied interests which the act of killing serves. We turn now to the identification and discussion of those interests.

5

The Kinds Of Homicide

Homicide varies greatly in the circumstances of its occurrence—in behavior patterns, in the traits, and intents and motives of the perpetrators. Obviously generalizations derived from the observation of many slayings can not apply to every case. To make sense of all known things of a kind we sort them into categories according to similarities and differences. Homicide is a category of a more general class of things known as crimes. It bears a behavioral resemblance to the various forms of assault and mayhem, and may be grouped with them under the heading of *violent crime*. The singular characteristic that separates homicide and unsuccessful homicidal attempts from other forms of violent crime is the intent to kill. Existing schemes for the classification of crimes do not deal with significant behavioral differences among homicides, tending to lump them all together.

There are many criteria by which we can classify homicide. Each or any particular combination reflects a distinctive perspective on the nature or causes of crime.

The criminal law, concerned with the suppression of crime, and only incidentally with the goal of ascertaining the causes and control of crime, categorizes offenses on two dimensions. The first is the interest protected by law which corresponds obversely to the interest of the offender in violating the law. *Crimes against property* separate the individual from the fruits of his labor; *crimes against the person* threaten the viability of the individual; and *crimes against public order* offend against public morals or disturb the peace. The second dimension is the gravity of the crime, which the law divides into two categories, *misdemeanor* and *felony*, the latter calling for harsher penalties than the former. The law also takes cognizance, for purposes of sentencing and treatment, of degrees of gravity of the offender's prior criminal record.

Classification in the sciences is dictated by the principle that different effects result from different conditions. Every branch of natural science has its own distinctive concepts for differentiating among the phenomena embraced in its purview. Chemistry has the periodic table which distinguishes among all basic forms of matter. Biology has the phylogenetic series which distributes all creatures in the animal kingdom into successively smaller categories denoted phylum, family, genus, and species.

The rules governing the design of classification are the same for all branches of science. They require precise standards of differentiation in order to avoid ambiguities in assigning things to one category or the other and the breadth to accommodate all instances of the phenomena under investigation. The satisfaction of these two requirements automatically satisfies a third: that the categories be mutually exclusive. These requirements are as yet unmet in criminology.

Since many branches of science makes pronouncements on the causes of crime, we find a variety of classifications of crime. Some fields of knowledge have more than one system of criminal classification depending on the number of schools of criminological thought thought within the discipline.

The lack of any system of classification for climatic and biological perspectives on violent crime reflects the obscurity of the connection between the "causes" and the effect. Genetic theories of crime, for example, are based on studies which lump together miscreancy as varied as intoxication, theft, indecent exposure, abortion, prostitution, rape and robbery, as well as homicide. One can only imagine the basis for a climatic or genetic classification: whether crime varies in type or intensity by thunderstorms, temperature, or lunar cycles; or by the particular genes that incline one toward property or personal crimes.

Psychiatry and clinical psychology, as official purveyors of judgments on mental states to the criminal justice system, have evolved classifications geared to legal criteria of criminal responsibility as well as scientific terms of diagnosis. Their classificatory systems differentiate between normal and abnormal killers, and among the latter in terms of standard personality disorders which represent varying degrees of release from criminal liability. The *sociopath*, in whom inadequately formed inner controls permit anti-social impulses, inhibited in the "normal person," to dominate choice, is the least excusable type; presumably, he is attuned to reality and knows the difference between right and wrong. The criminality of the *neurotic* is the outward manifestation of disturbed inner personality defenses, expressed compulsively in theft, firesetting, or kinky sexuality, but rarely in murder. Affliction with a neurosis seldom weakens the individual's connection to reality to a degree that negates criminal responsibility. The *psychotic* killer suffers from acute disorders of perception or conception revealed in illusions, delusions, or hallucinations. Since psychotics may kill for the same reasons that normal people kill, psychosis, in itself, does not necessarily excuse the killer from the consequences of his act. The killing must be a result of the psychosis. The claim that a killing resulted from a psychotic state is rarely as incontrovertible as the example, so appealing to commentators on the insanity plea, of the hypothetical killer who in slitting his wife's throat believes he is slicing a tomato. This deluded salad maker would, of course, be found not guilty by reason of insanity. The *normal* killer is presumably "none of the above," but I have complete confidence that an imaginative clinician could assimilate any killer to "one of the above." Although the "normal" killer accounts for the vast majority of homicides, psychology and psychiatry offer no formal classification of their homicides. Rather they deal with them on an *ad hoc* basis, improvising some disturbance which may momentarily disable self-control but not qualify to exculpate the offender.The mushiness of the definitions of diagnostic categories and the lack of consensus on theirs application have done more to fog than clarify understanding. (See Chapters 11 and 12).

Sociological systems of classification focus on the social and cultural nature of crime. Most take their inspiration from Edwin H. Sutherland's organizing principle of *behavior systems* in crime. Each system is essentially a "group way of life" comprising techniques of criminal behavior, codes and traditions. It is common rather than unique behavior. Thus each behavior system is a cluster of for-bidden behaviors which presumably have common causal antecedents. (Sutherland and Cressey, 274-277) Other investigators have modified or extended the criteria of classification to suit their theoretical preferences. Some of the commonest criteria are the degree to which a criminal activity represents a career pattern, the degree of social tolerance accorded the act, and techniques of lawbreaking. (Clinard, Clinard and Quinney, Cavan, Gibbons, Roebuck)

A misconception in sociological classifications is the core assumption that various criminal career patterns, including for example, armed robbery, professional theft—shoplifting, burglary, or auto theft—organized crime, and fraud constitute distinctive behavioral entities. Evidence of the "career" patterns of repetitive property offenders shows that the same offender may engage in some or most of these forms of crime. All of these forms, however, plus certain forms of homicide, comprise a general pattern of *predatory* crime, sharing a common objective: getting something for nothing. The same conclusion applies to the differentiation among such categories as "conventional criminal behavior...occasional property criminal behavior [and] professional criminal behavior." (Clinard and Quinney, 10-21) They are all varieties of predatory crime.

Sociological classifications dilute the gravity of homicide by combining it with other assaultive crimes, as minor as the assault and battery of a tavern brawl, into *violent personal crime*. One classificatory system Clinard) pigeonholes murder along with such disparate crimes as statutory rape, forgery, arson, vandalism, and some theft into the behaviorally meaningless category *occasional crime*. Except for the relatively rare serial murders and gangland slayings, homicides hardly qualify as a "behavor system" since they are seldom committed more than once in the life of the killer.

Violent personal crime is sufficiently varied to deserve a more refined classification than it gets in sociological classifications. Most instances are means of enforcing demands in relations with persons associated in various degrees of intimacy—lovers, spouses, parent-child, friends, and neighbors. Property offenders, whatever their preferred technique—violence, stealth, or duplicity—whatever their station in life, common thief, robber, or crookedinvestment adviser, are intent on material gain. Crimes of sexual violence are sought as ends in themselves for their sensual or psychic returns. Certain crimes for certain people may be morally principled acts. Killing can occur in all of the above contexts.

A Classification of Homicide By Interests

However they may differ, all systems of criminal classification, psychological and sociological, are alike in that they have evolved from an ideology which devalues the self-determination of the human actor. The cause of crime, as conceived in this book, is not some complex of material manifestations associated with the act, but rather the intents and purposes of the offender. The classificatory system herein proposed reflects that killing can be instrumental to the attainment of any human interest. The personal and social variables associated with homicide are only the background against which volition operates. In the foreground are the patterns of thought and action implicated in deadly assaults. These divide into five categories of interests embodied in the intents and purposes of people who kill—interests which the law, from its side, seeks to regulate in the interest of social stability. The similarities in behavior patterns within each category result from common social, cultural, and situational restraints within which the killers operate

(1) *Predatory* killings are for material gain, to collect life insurance benefits or inheritance, or to facilitate robbery or sexual gratification. This type, more than any other, fits into the economic model of the free market which proposes that criminal behavior is governed by the same rational calculation of profit and loss that applies to other forms of enterprise. Like the non-lethal forms of predatory crime, predatory murders are perversions of lawful economic behavior.

(2) *Defensive* killings are reactions to perceived threats to bodily safety, property, status, or self-esteem. Their manifest purpose is to dominate others physically or to repel attempts at domination by others. That the offender may be the aggressor does not contradict the self-protective character of defensive assaults: a first strike is a sound tactic for people who feel threatened, .

(3) *Hedonic* killings are for pleasure: excitement, thrills, or sensual pleasure are the payoff. A recurrent factual theme in case studies of serial killers, for example, is the thrill of the hunt.

(4) The hired killer joins relatively inoffensive criminal special-ists such as the fence, prostitute, smuggler, and loanshark in the *purveyance of forbidden goods and services*. They consider their work an unappreciated public service. Like the pest exterminator, the hired killer rids the world of undesirable elements.

(5) *Moral* killings are the criminal counterpart of the orderly show of opposition to the prevailing moral order. Common examples are government-directed genocide, mercy killing, assassination, political terrorism, and revenge killing. Accused killers often take on a righteous air of self-sacrifice in the service of a higher morality.

The application of the proposed classification deserves some com-ment. The categories of interests span the whole spectrum of human striving. The interest advanced by any particular killing is inferrable from the circumstances of the crime and statements of offenders and witnesses. There is little doubt, for example, of the interest of a suspect in a killing who greatly increases the amount of insurance on the life of his spouse before seeing her aboard an airplane to go visit an ailing relative, and after an explosion which destroys the plane in mid-air, traceable to a bomb in the luggage compartment, goes to join his erstwhile secret paramour. Nor are we puzzled by a shooting in the course of a heated argument involving the exchange of threats.

The assignment of motives for killings of a particular kind may be unnecessarily muddied by facts with only an indirect connection with the circumstances of the killing. An example of such a miscalculation is the perception of a staggering increase in "drug-related" murders. The opinion is widely expressed by authoritative sources, mainly law enforcement officials, reported in the media that the drug trade accounts for as much as 40 percent of known murders. If correct, which is not the case, this figure signifies a major change in patterns of homicide with profound theoretical and policy implications. Since murder rates remain fairly constant from year to year—in fact they diminished slightly in the nineteen-eighties compared to the nineteen-seventies—this belief lamely presumes that a new cause for the generation of homicide, namely the booming drug trade, has replaced other causes.

A *New York Times* article titled "Crack Hits Chicago, Along with a Wave of Killing" (September, 24, 1991) exemplifies the exaggeration of the connection between drugs and homicide. It reports that by the end of August, 1991, Chicago had racked up a toll of 623 murders, exceeding the 593 by that date in 1974, the year with a higher total of homicides than any since. The number of killings for the month of August, 1991 was 120 compared to the previous record of 117 for the month of November, 1974. Allowing for a modest increase in that segment of the population most likely to kill and be killed in the drug trade, namely inner city youths, the "wave" of killing is hardly a ripple on the preexistent wave.

The increase nationwide in murders attributed in official reports to narcotics rose from 2.9 percent in 1985 to 7.4 percent in 1989, and then dropped to 6.5 in 1990, hardly the heralded increase to 40 percent. The modest increase may reflect no more than a policy decision in response to public or official pressures at local levels to shift cases from the category, "arguments over property or money," which indeed is the essence of drug altercations, to "narcotics."

The meaning of "drug related," as it applies to murder, is seldom specified, although the implication that drug dealers are disposing of rivals or dishonest associates by killing them holds out the prospect that if we could get rid of the drug problem, by suppression or legalization, we could substantially reduce homicide rates. This view oversimplifies the problem since the drug trade, like homicide, is as much an effect as all of the other ails churning out of the rampant moral disorganization of the American inner-city. Killing is not distinctive of the drug trade, but a common method of conflict resolution in the levels of society which supply most of the sales operatives in the drug market. The same function applies to Mafia killings which originated in the culture pattern of the Sicilian vendetta. The loyalties to the Mafia family secured by the benefits flowing from membership, and the traditional Sicilian sense of separateness between extended families outweigh any considerations of mercy toward the targeted victim. Whether we ascribe a killing to the drug trade or to organized crime, the killing is a service supportive of the marketing of illegal goods.

The amount and proportional distribution of the types of homicide in any particular social grouping depend on organizational features which embody, paradoxically, the highest ideals of the social order. There is little predatory killing within simple societies organized on the basis of kinship with an ethic of cooperative sharing, but there may be much blood-feuding between extended families, clans, or tribes in competition for limited natural resources.

The larger the groupings, the more nearly the conflict resembles a state of war.

Paul Bohannon's anthology of studies on African homicide contains very few instances of murder with an economic motivation. (1967, 249) Bohannon explains that the state of economic development in the African nations at the time of the studies, shortly after independence, did not offer many opportunities for economic crimes. The predominant interests in killing were fear of witches and revenge upon them, herein categorized, respectively, as *defensive* and *moral.*

The value system of the United States with its cardinal themes of individualism, consumerism, and a free market economy, surcharged by ambivalence toward external controls, is a potent prescription for predatory crime of all sorts—robbery, burglary, fraud, extortion, embezzlement, confidence games, and all the varieties of common theft, as well as murder. Unlike the value system in more socially stratified societies, the American value system sets no clear limits to aspirations, an omission which weakens the restraints that bind individuals into a sense of community. Alienation in the upper levels of society appears in the more covert forms of property and white collar crime, but only rarely, in assaultive crime. In the lower levels alienation festers out of low self-esteem stemming from the lack of employment opportunity and the inability of agencies of socialization—family, school, or religion—to inculcate the competencies required to earn a livelihood and the qualities of character required for harmonious inter-personal relations. It is therefore not surprising that the lower classes in the United States hold a near monopoly on killing, and that almost 65 percent of all murders in which the circumstances are known turn out to be of the *defensive* variety, most arising out of altercations between people who know one another.

Predatory killings involved in robbery, gang warfare, or sex offenses, almost entirely lower class activities, account for almost 35 percent of known murders and non-negligent homicides. Premeditated calculated murders for insurance or inheritance, or to get rid of an unwanted spouse, lover, or business associate receive the widest attention in the media, fiction, and true crime literature, but are rare among known killings.

Headline grabbing mass murders, which provide the stuff of sensational true crime biographies published while the event is still fresh in the public memory, are even more rare. Levin and Fox (p. 47) report that FBI data for the years 1976-1980 show that out of the total of 96,232 cases of homicide, those 156 cases involving the death of four or more victims, exclusive of arson deaths, comprised one-sixth of 1 percent. Mass murderers, of the multiple or serial variety, are atypical in that they are virtually all white and of lower middle class origins.

Summary

The most enduring systems of classification, whether in science, law, or the humanities, are based on a clearly defined subject matter. The parts of speech specified in the rules of grammar, the molecular composition of matter, or the cellular structure and morphology of organisms attain the ideal of precision because they apply to insensate things. The attempt to adapt the same procedures of classification to human affairs erroneously takes for granted an oversimplified materialistic model of human conduct. Whether killing occurs in the context of a domestic argument, drug dealing, robbery, political conspiracy, arson, or rape has less to do with the material circumstances accompanying the act than with the wishes and aims of the offender.

The next four chapters (6-10) elaborate upon the devices and desires of people who overcome the inhibition against killing other people. Chapter 6 deals with predatory and mercenary forms characterized by calculation, connivance, or conspiracy—the kind most commonly associated with people of substance. Chapter 7 describes the uses of murder as an adjunct to robbery. Chapters 8, 9, and 10, respectively, detail the non-mercenary aims of murder: the defense of person and esteem, the indulgence of perverse pleasures, and the advancement of cherished principles.

6

Killing For Profit

The blatant greed displayed in predatory murders makes them the least puzzling of homicides. More than any other form of murder they display clear signs of the cognitive linkage between the wish and the act. Those which are the outcome of a robbery are treated separately in the next chapter. This chapter deals with the more sophisticated calculated killings for material gain in which the offender attempts to conceal his involvment.

The money and power sought in pedatory behavior represent powerful values. Killing, as the means for their attainment, is eminently efficient. Virtually all people have close relationships which at times deteriorate or no longer satisfy. When the termination of the relationship can lead to financial or romantic gains, the incentive to kill increases. We can do no more than speculate on how many people toy with the idea of terminating soured relationships by killing. Known cases may be only the tip of the iceberg. The calculatedness of the methods and the efforts to evade detection in the known cases imply that there may be many more instances in which the killer is not apprehended or the death is reported as accidental or from natural causes. This possibility is not as remote as it may seem since the singular characteristic of this class of killers, based on the observation of those who get caught, is an overweening confidence in their ability to fool the police.

Killing for profit by rich élites is an unfailing source of tabloid amusement. The victim is most commonly a family member, usually a spouse. The notorious cases of the physicians, Dr. Bernard Finch and Dr. Carl Coppolino, each of whom was convicted of killing his wife in order to collect the insurance on her life and to replace her with a new love, exhibit a cool rationality, and in the case of Dr. Coppolino, a remarkable ingenuity in the alleged method of killing. Coppolino, an anesthesiologist, was alleged to have given his wife a lethal dose of succinlycholine, thought to be an "undetectible" anesthetic. Dr. Milton Helpern, a New York medical examiner called into the case, testified that he had developed a test which disclosed lethal amounts of the poison in the dead woman's body. Years later new revelations disputed that Helpern, since deceased, had proved the presence of the succinlycholine. Inconsistencies marred the testimony of another expert, also deceased, who vouched for the presence of greater than normal desposits of succhinic acid in the brain of Mrs. Coppolino. Still another expert submitted that no definitive test for the detection of the poison had yet been developed. Doubts implanted by the new evidence may have helped Coppolino obtain a release on parole after twelve years of confinement, but were not sufficient to gain him a full pardon. (Coppolino, 265-290) As a condition of parole he was restricted from the practice of medicine.

No doubts surfaced in Dr. Finch's case. He dispatched his receptionist-paramour to Las Vegas to hire someone to kill Mrs. Finch. She located a man who accepted the assignment, took a sizable cash advance, and later reported he had done the job. The conspirators were astonished to find Mrs. Finch alive and well on their return. The contractor turned out to be a con-man rather than a hit-man, apologizing that he had killed a woman he mistakenly thought to be Mrs. Finch. Thrown back on their own resources, the plotters assembled a kit of killing instruments—rope, knife, and other useful tools—and did the job themselves, so unskilfully that they were apprehended and convicted.

The scenario of profit-motivated killings more often conforms to the fictional detective story narrating an ingeniously planned upper class murder than to the impulsive, alcohol-sodden outburst of lower-class violence. But even when premeditated and carried out by holders of professional or graduate degrees, known predatory killings often betray an artlessness in planning or execution. The sensationalized wife-murder case of Dr. Sam Sheppard in 1954 furnished the prototype of the *intruder defense* for a a number of notorious cases. Dr. Sam, as affectionately known to his sympathizers, claimed that a bushy-headed burglar broke into the house, knocked him senseless, and killed his wife. Inconsistencies in his recital of events, plus evidence that he maintained a mistress and stood to gain financially from his wife's demise, moved the jury to a verdict of guilty. Twelve years later the verdict was vacated on the ground that the sensationalism attending the inquest and the trial infringed on Dr. Sheppard's right to a fair trial.

One of the most publicized "intruder" killings, inspiring a best-selling book and a television movie, was the case of Captain Jeffrey MacDonald, a Green Beret medical officer. His tale that hippies high on narcotics broke into his house, shouting "acid is groovy," killed his wife and children, and injured him gained him an acquittal in a court martial. On retrial by a civilian court eight years later, he was convicted. He too allegedly had a mistress offstage.

Lew Graham, an assistant dean at the Louisiana State University Medical School, also having an adulterous affair, could have taken the leaf of his disputed account of his wife's murder by an intruder directly from MacDonald's story. An ingenious analysis of the blood spatter on his garments resulting from the battering of his wife's head by a sledgehammer was sufficient to convince the jury that he, rather than an intruder, did the slaying. (Lewis)

Restaurant manager Steven Steinberg blamed the murder of his wealthy wife Elana on two burly white intruders who broke into their bedroom, killed her, and injured him, but not severely. Skepticism toward his story prompted a change in tactics. He shifted from a denial of the killing to a plea of insanity. His recollection of "intruders" was reinterpreted in friendly psychiatric testimony as a hallucination in a dissociative sleepwalking state during which he committed the killing. The jury acquitted him. (Frondorf)

In a plan evocative of a screen play, Dr. Robert Reza, pulmonary specialist, and respected church member, established an alibi for an intended crime by leaving his Long Island home to attend a professional conference in Washington. During his absence an "intruder" broke into the house, shot, and strangled his wife. Arriving home the distraught husband broke into tears while speaking to an investigator. His anguished mourning didn't fool the police. Their investigation revealed that he had been carrying on an affair with the church organist. Within a few days he confessed that he made a round trip home from Washington to kill his wife. According to a news account, Dr. Reza explained that "...he had been under pressure and killed her because he could not cope with success." (*New York Times*, December 29, 1990, 25)

Rob Marshall, a successful real estate agent in Toms River, New Jersey, adapted the intruder theme to the automobile. He had been carrying on a torrid love affair with a married woman of the social set in which he and his heavily insured wife mingled. He was accused of paying a hit-man to lie in wait at a designated spot on the road between Atlantic City and Toms River and to kill her in a contrived robbery. He denied the charge testifying that he and his wife had gone to Atlantic City for an evening's diversion. and on the way home he drove off the road to check an automotive problem. Suddenly he was struck on the head, hard enough to render him senseless but not inflict serious injury, and while he lay unconscious, his wife, seated in the car, was fatally shot. The police and eventually the jury didn't buy the story. He was sentenced to die. (McGinniss, 1989)

Diane Downs' defense in the trial for the murder of one of her three small children represents an unusual variation on the intruder theme. She claimed that a "shaggy-haired stranger" flagged her down on a country road, demanded the keys to her car, forced her into the back, shot her and her three children, killing one and critically injuring the others, but inflicting only minor injuries on her. An investigation by a skeptical prosecutor and police department found gaping holes in her story and a motive. Unlike her male counterparts she killed not to get rid of an unwanted spouse, but to get a spouse. She hoped by getting rid of her children to win back a former lover whom, she believed, had rejected her because he didn't want to involve himself with a woman who had the responsibility of looking after three children.

For some curious reason physicians feature prominently in true crime murders. Not necessarily because physicians are disproportionately represented among the "better" class of persons accused of murder, but because the paradox of killing by members of a profession pledged to save life heightens interest. Also it is satisfying to the reader to know that members of an élite, comprising one of the most respected and highly rewarded professions, succumb to the passions that beset the lesser folk.

William Randolph Stevens chronicles one of the more convolutedly calculated murder attempts by a physician in the annals of true crime. Dr. Patrick Henry, a dermatologist, claiming to be angered by his ex-wife's refusal to let him visit their son, by his own admission set out to kill her. Four years after the divorce, and after he had remarried, he put into motion a diabolic scheme which neatly fits the mold of the script in the Columbo television detective series. The police strongly suspected Dr. Henry, but needed the evidence to make a case against him.

His plan, detailed in memos to himself recovered by the police, reads like instructions to a secret agent for the "termination" of a troublesome dissident. It entailed travelling from Baltimore, Maryland where he resided, to Dallas, Texas to attend a professional conference. There he would take an evening plane for the short flight to Tucson, Arizona where his ex-wife and son resided. He would make the trip under an assumed name, carrying false identity papers, and wearing a disguise of several layers of clothing which puffed up his appearance so conspicuously that ticket agents, flight attendants, and fellow passengers could hardly fail to remember his presence. He would then go to his ex-wife's residence where she lived with her parents and child and using a key which he retained from the time of their marriage, get into a nursery school operated by her next door to her residence. He would enter the house through a window in the early morning hours, find her, and kill her. Each step of the plan except the last was carried out. The final step was abandoned, he claimed, because he had changed his mind about killing her before he arrived in Tucson; all he wanted was to see his son. The prosecution, however, charged that he deferred the killing after arriving in Tucson only because indications of movement in the house and other unpropitious signs scared him off.

Dr. Henry rested his contention that he had renounced the intention to kill his wife on the claim that he had left his murder tools in an attaché case checked at the airport. Here's how the prosecution invalidated his defense. The intended victim told detectives that she had seen her ex-husband across the street from her house and recognized him under his bizarre disguise. Later in the morning he phoned his ex-wife introducing himself as a parent who desired information about the nursery school and asked her to meet him at the facility. She knew his voice and fearfully thought he was trying to get information to use against her in a possible hearing over custody of their child.

Dr. Henry had left a noticeable trail of events to give the impression that his presence in Tucson occasioned no threat to his wife. Prior to his departure for Tucson, he sought to check an attaché case, *identifiable by a broken handle*, at the Dallas airport. Security personnel, alarmed by his grotesque appearance, detained him and insisted that he submit the contents of the attaché case to the scanning of an airport security X-ray machine. The technician operating the machine observed suspicious materials which on direct inspection by agents of the Federal Bureau of Alcohol, Tobacco and Firearms turned out to be a gun, knife, blackjack, and burglar tools. Since Henry had not attempted to carry the case with him on the flight to Tucson, no serious charge could lie against him. The federal agents released him, but held the case, and agreed to send it and its contents to him on the next flight to Tucson.

When the attaché case *apparently* did not turn up in Tucson on the scheduled flight, Dr. Henry loudly upbraided the clerk at the the lost luggage office of the airline. The prosecution believed he made the fuss in order to establish that he did not have the case in his possession while in Tucson. Thus if Henry's ex-wife should meet a sudden death and suspicion should fall on him, he would have solid evidence that he did not have the lethal equipment with him while he was in Tucson. Or if she were not killed, but for some reason the police should question him, he could claim that he had left the case behind because he had given up the scheme.

The intended victim, however, reported having seen the attaché case *with a broken handle* when she spied her ex-husband across the street that nearly fateful morning. The prosecution believed, and later convinced the jury, that the case did indeed show up on the luggage carousel in the Tucson airport, and that Henry took it and replaced it with a different attaché case. He then filed a loss claim, describing the replacement case in misleading terms so that the Tucson luggage handling personnel would not be able to identify it among other pieces of unretrieved luggage. Later when Henry returned to take his flight back to Dallas, he found the substitute attaché case with other unclaimed luggage awaiting pickup. He notified the attendant that he had retrieved it, and received a slip acknowledging the retrieval, willingly supplied by the attendant, who did not notice that the case was not as described in the loss claim.

The prosecution's portrayal of Dr. Henry as a malevolent Mr. Hyde prevailed over the defense's characterization of him as a kindly Dr. Jekyll. He was convicted of attempted murder.

The fact that the typical true crime account of predatory murder features a killer of some substance in the community, a white business or professional person, may give the impression that people of the lower social tier don't do the more calculated forms of killing. The settings may differ, but the intents and purposes can be quite the same. An occasional pattern, the actual number of cases, likely, far exceeding the known cases, involves the "kindhearted" lady who takes in elderly boarders and helps them with their personal affairs. After a while she poisons them, one by one, and, when they unsurprisingly "pass away," she collects insurance naming her as beneficiary. In an alternative version, instead of getting insurance money, she covertly disposes of the bodies and continues to manage the deposit of their social security, pension, or disability checks.

The frequency and unimaginativeness of predatory killing in the lower classes deprives the event of the shock appeal of killings by the rich or famous. True crime writers and the editors who review their book proposals are apt to take a dubious view of the sales appeal of books about lower class killings for profit. The performance of lower class killings, however, is often not appreciably cruder than those of many true crime accounts, and has the same adjustive value for the offender as for more affluent counterparts. A young black woman and her male friend, both addicted to crack cocaine, moved in, uninvited, with the woman's grandmother and established a parasitic relationship with the elder woman, known to her friends as a kindly generous person. The granddaughter had no unusual problems of growing up until at age eighteen she became a mother and shortly thereafter took to drugs. Once addicted her life revolved around maintaining the supply. The young woman opened her grandmother's mail and found a retirement check which she attempted unsuccessfully to alter and cash. The grandmother threatened to have her and her boyfriend arrested. They smothered her with a pillow, at the same time cutting her wrists to make the death appear a suicide. (*New York Times*, 10/13/91, p.1)

The implications for material gain and the fragility of the moral restraints on killing gives pause to wonder why the deadly solution is not used more often. Quite possibly it happens more frequently than comes to light. The concealment characteristic of the more calculating predatory murders, except for those committed in the course of a robbery, suggest that the known instances comprise an unrepresentative sample of an unknown total. There lurks the powerful suspicion that the undetected homicides are more skillfully executed, with the deaths attributed to natural causes, accident, or suicide.

Killing for Hire

Because killing can be a messy chore, people with murderous wishes may hire somebody less fastidious to do the dirty work. Leaders in organized crime reduce the risk of incrimination in serious crime by reliance on a professional killer to get rid of rivals in other mobs or traitors within the organization.

Hired killers vary in skill and disposition to violence. The assassins described by Peter Wyden in his book, *Hired Killers*, were recruited by citizens of good reputation from the small-time criminal fringe of the lower classes. Wyden's generalized portrait of the hireling suggests no particular combination of traits that would account for their acts of violence. They were ordinary people, neither irrational nor unintelligent, whose failings were no worse than those of non-criminals of their social set. All of the employers, except those in organized crime, were highly respected members of the community. Prim, matronly, well groomed Elizabeth ("Mother") Duncan was a model of respectability except for those who knew her intimately, notably the pair she hired to kill her daughter-in-law. The neat methodical accountant Joseph Selby suffered no scruples in contracting for the elimination of his unloved wife. The murder of Judge and Mrs. Curtis E. Chillingworth in 1955 was plotted by Joseph Peel, a suave municipal court judge who feared that Judge Chillingworth was about to expose his entanglement in local criminal rackets. These recruiters, paragons of community virtue who conducted their personal affairs prudently, displayed an astonishing lack of discretion in seeking out and retaining people of unknown reliability to do a hazardous job. They compounded the risk of exposure by giving in to the demand of the contracting killer for an accomplice, "an assistant murderer, an unnecessary eye-witness to give the chief executioner a feeling of security."

Fred Milo, co-owner with his brother, Dean, of a barber and beauty supply business headquartered in Akron, Ohio displayed the height of incaution in the procurement of the services of a hit man to get rid of Dean. The account, as related by private investigator William C. Dear and writer Carlton C. Stowers in their book, *"Please Don't Kill Me,"* counterpoints the risks of killing by proxy with the frustrations of homicide detectives, having little more than the evidence of a dead body to guide them.

Stripped of its tragedy, the tale reads like a farce. Dean, the victim, had taken control of the firm when his father, an immigrant from Albania, retired. He had successfully expanded the business from a small operation to a chain of ninety-seven outlets, while relegating brother Fred and a sister to minor roles in the organization. Fred became so incensed that he confided to an impecunious lawyer friend his wish to get rid of Dean and asked him to cast about for someone to do the killing. The lawyer approached a woman reputed to have ties with the local underworld, mostly small time operators in burglary, robbery, and narcotics. She in turn solicited two hoodlum acquaintances who feigned interest in doing the job; they were interested in the money, but were not inclined to risk a murder charge.

Impatient with the lack of results, brother Fred set out on his own to recruit a killer. The chain of incrimination grew as one contractor subcontracted out the assignment to another, each taking a cut of the prospective pay-off. Despite the large circle of involvment, the police assisted by a full-time private investigator, were unable to extract any significant clues from the physical evidence of the killing, business documents, or interviews with family members, employees, and other associates. Not until a substantial reward was posted did a number of informers from among those solicited for the venture come forth with information that gave the police helpful leads. When the case was broken and the judicial process had run its course, eleven defendants, including Fred, more than had ever been tried in a single case in Ohio, were convicted—the principals, of first degree murder, and the lesser players, of obstruction of justice. The actual trigger man—described by investigator William Dear as a social misfit from a broken home, leading an aimless life supported by petty theft and drug dealing—received, ironically, only six hundred out of the eighty thousand dollars expended by Fred Dean to kill his brother.

In contrast to the inept amateur, the professional hit man, such as described by "Joey" (with Dave Fisher, 1974), works alone, quickly and cleanly, unless the contract requires doing a particularly gory job for its exemplary effect. "The thing about hit men that is so unusual," observes Joey, "is that they are so usual." People whose personalities or appearances stand out in a crowd are unsuited for the job. The motives of employers of professional killers most commonly represent solutions to business problems, particularly in organized crime. The death sentence is imposed for violating the "ethics" of organized crime which may involve being a stool pigeon, unreliability, overambitiousness, or greed. The killer gets his satisfaction from a mixture of gratifications: the high pay, the ego inflation from the power of life and death over others, and the awesome status and respect commanded by the job of hit-man not only in gangster circles but from straight admirerers, particularly women who get "turned on" by the idea of sex with a killer. (*Joey*, 1974: 60-61)

Testimony by ex-hit man Philip Leonetti in recent trials of Mafia leadership figures, gives an insider view of the "administrative" uses of murder by the underworld. Leonetti, who entered a government witness protection program after achieving the rank of number two next to his uncle, Mafia family head Nicodemo Scarfo, dims the glamorous aura bestowed upon the hit-man by Joey. He tells how the killing may serve personal as well as business interests of the Mafia dons: the redress of lack of respect, paranoid fears, or personal dislikes.

Leonetti admitted to killing two gangsters at Scarfo's orders and conspiring in other killings. He defected because Scarfo was gripped by an obsessive mistrust of some of his closest associates. When he ordered the deaths of loyal followers, even his wife, his gang turned against him. Leonetti reportedly told his lawyer that it bothers him that he killed people and he's sorry for their families, but true to the tradition of the Mafia hit man, he believed "...he was doing the right thing by punishing those who violated the laws of a society they voluntarily joined and whose rules they were familiar with." In a comment that aims to moderate the savagery of his client with a touch of perhaps psychoanalytically inspired pathos, the lawyer adds, "He [Leonetti] was punishing men like himself." (Del Giudice et al)

Summary

Calculated killings figure most prominently in the detective mystery novel. Once exposed there is seldom any mystery as to the motives—financial gain from insurance, inheritance, or business takeover. The handling of these themes by fiction writers often comes closer to the truth of human nature than that of mental health experts whose testimony in court is distinguished more by obscurantism than intellectual rigor. The public's obsessive interest in murders motivated by greed is shown in the disproportion between the insignificance of their numbers and the media attention accorded them. Perhaps the primary reason for the interest is that if any among the "gentle" readers were to contemplate killing, this would be the preferred form.

A less inhibited element of the population doesn't need some crisis of relationship to kill for material gain. They account for the 10 percent of killings that occur in the course of a robbery. We turn now to an examination of the situational contexts in which they kill.

7

Robbery Murder

To grasp a robber's motive for killing his victim requires no unusual insight. The robber has material wants which he is unable or unwilling to gratify licitly. His intentions are clear: to get the victim's valuables and make a clean getaway. To accomplish this the armed robber destroys the existing order of civil understanding and by the use of force creates a new order in which his commands become "law," enforceable by the sanction of death. By the logic of the new order, the robber may kill when he perceives the victim as a "lawbreaker," an appearance created by resistance to the robber's authority. Or the robber may decide that the very existence of the victim constitutes a threat that justifies execution: dead men or women can make no identifications to the police.

Social behavioral scientists and their followers among true crime writers disdain the notion that the motive for killing robbery victims coincides with the practical objectives of the act. For them the real motives spring out of emotions clogged by past events in the life of the killer and suddenly released in a a spasm of catharsis. John Bartlow Martin's non-fictional novel of a middle American tragedy, *Why Did They Kill?*, illustrates that perspective as it unravels the forces in the lives of three white adolescent males which drove them to a fatal assault on a lone woman, ostensibly to steal her purse. Martin goes far beyond the compass of the bare facts, which in themselves add up to no more than a bungled mugging, to explain the killing as the combined product of unconscious needs and social ailments arising from rapid social change. The event, rendered all the more tragic because there was no intent to kill, had that impromptu quality displayed in robbery murder committed by two or more persons: that were it not for a chance spark ignited by the interaction of the personalities of the offenders, it never would have happened.

The boys passed the early part of the fateful evening driving around Ypsilanti, Michigan with girl friends. They stopped at a tavern in a nearby town where beer was sold to persons of doubtful legal age. By the time they dropped the girls off, about 11:30 pm, they had consumed a case of beer. One of the girls recalled that her date appeared unsteady from the effects of the drinking. The boys then headed for the adjacent city of Ann Arbor hoping to find excitement. Finding themselves in the neighborhood of the University of Michigan Hospital, they decided to rob a nurse. Pauline Campbell had just finished her shift and emerged onto the street when the boys spied her. Bill took a rubber-coated mallet, sneaked up and hit her repeatedly on the head. Assisted by Dave he dragged her body to the car. Noting the extent of her injuries—her head was badly crushed—they dropped her to the street, got into the car driven by Max, and fled from the scene.

The intention to rob a nurse did not arise on the spur of the moment, although there was no indication that it included any plan to kill one. Several days earlier, Bill and Max—this time, without Dave and joined by Dan—had driven by the University Hospital to steal hub caps; Dan wanted to steal a chromium exhaust pipe extension. Seeing nurses moving about on the street, Bill proposed robbing one of her pocketbook by hitting her over the head and dragging her into the car. The added element of abduction suggests that in both episodes, he had more in mind than robbery, but little was made of it in psychiatric or legal examination. He walked up behind his quarry and struck her on the head with a small wrench. She withstood the blow, screamed, and ran.

The police arrested Bill, Max, and Dave for murder on the basis of a tip from a friend in whom the boys confided that they had committed the earlier unsuccessful attack. Bill and Max were convicted of first degree murder; Dave, of second degree murder.

The social and developmental histories of the youths revealed nothing out of the ordinary, certainly nothing suggestive of homicidal tendencies. Bill and Max came from lower middle class backgrounds. Bill's father was an inspector in a factory; his mother, a schoolteacher. Max's parents worked and hired a succession of housekeepers to look after Max until they got home. By all indications, both boys had caring parents. If an unstable family background augurs trouble in later life, then Dave clearly was at higher risk than his companions. Yet Dave was a minor player in the killing. He was one of ten children. The father, a tenant farmer, had been disabled in an accident before his birth. After his death the mother bore the burden of raising the children. She was later committed to a mental hospital and upon release remarried. Dave lived with an older brother during his mother's illness and by age seventeen was on his own. The boys were caught up in the youth culture of the early nineteen-fifties which valued driving souped-up cars noisily about town, getting drunk on beer, cruising to pick up women, and drumming up excitement. Although none had a felony record, all had brushes with the police involving minor crimes.

Martin explains the murder as an outcome of the conjunction of a psychopathic individual, namely Bill, with a delinquent society, a view which reduces the role of Dave or Max to that of supporting player. In Martin's scenario, Dave's participation was the bid of a socially inept teen-ager to be accepted in friendship by the others. Martin thinks that Dave's presence may have unwittingly prompted the vicious beating by hardening Bill's determination not to botch the attack, as in the previous try, lest he become the target of Dave's gibes. Max provided the example of a hardened delinquent. He displayed the traits of a sociopath—shrewd, cunning, egoistic, unable to forge any deep emotional relationships. His career in deviance started as a troubled child and traversed the stages of rebellious boy, truant, runaway, and thief.

Bill was the principal actor. The others did not join physically with him in the attack on the victim; their legal guilt derived from complicity in the mugging that led to the killing. The boys sought to diminish the seriousness of the crime by denying that they were intent on robbing the nurse. Martin grants Bill's disavowal of a need for the small amount of money she might be carrying. (It turned out to be $1.50) The denial of the intent to rob on the basis of the meagerness of the loot lacks credibility since the boys didn't know how much was in the nurse's purse until they stole it. The crime clearly met the legal and moral definition of robbery. The boys' claim that they had some money of their own, does not suffice to nullify the predatory intent exhibited by their conduct.

Bill took the nurse's purse, examined its contents, kept the money he found, and threw the rest in a nearby river. They stopped at a gas station and bought ninety-four cents worth of fuel, then proceded to a hamburger drive-in where they spent the dollar and a half.

Martin raises the presumption-laden question: Why did Bill need to hit his victim? As a practical matter the apparent reason was to make it easier to grab her purse. The power of the blows, in light of the previous failed attempt, was intended to disable any resistance. Martin, however, denies the obvious, instead seeing the assault as the expression of some deep inner compulsion. He reasons that if robbery only was the motive, Bill could have grabbed her purse and run. Max and Dave, it may be added, certainly didn't need to hit her; they were only after excitement. Bill on, the other hand, says Martin, did have a need to hit the victim, a need arising out of internal conflicts, which had nothing to do with the robbery. He drank excessively "to quell the stirrings of the higher brain centers where the conscience dwells." He was paranoid in relationships even with those who loved him. Although not a very good fighter, he looked for scraps, perhaps because he thought he needed to live up to his rather impressive appearance. He threatened escape from an aimless life by plans to join the Army or the Navy, but found it easy to be dissuaded by the entreaties of his parents. In the year before he killed he was undergoing some typical adolescent crises—rejection by his first girl friend for cheating on her and rebellion against his overprotective mother. In short, by Martin's assessment, Bill hit the victim because he was in a desperate struggle to break away from dependence on his mother, resolve inner conflicts, get rid of aggressions by physical assault on society, and fulfill the demands of his egocentric nature.

Martin interrupts this line of conjecture with the critical observation that Bill is not much different from the mass of teen age youth who encounter the strains of adolescence without killing. So why didn't Bill resist killing? Unable to advance a sensible reason, he falls back on the insensible: a mixture of psychoanalytic theory, psychopathy, and breakdown in the moral order of society.

In the psychoanalytic portion Martin takes the reader through a labyrinth of unconscious needs in which the selection of a nurse to be the victim takes on a deep significance. The fact that he beat her far more savagely than necessary to rob her suggests that she was a symbol of some hated object. Martin found out that when Bill was ten he discovered that a nurse was to blame for the near death of his mother in giving birth to his sister. Any resulting antipathy for nurses may have been reinforced in Bill's unconsciousness by Max's having been raised by housekeepers, whom he detested, because his mother worked as a nurse. Martin connects the nurse symbolisms of the two boys by means, in Bill's words, of a "chemical reaction" between them. Indeed, speculates Martin, "it is also possible that the victim could only have been a nurse. And it is also possible that the murder could be viewed as symbolic matricide." (Martin, 129) It is not clear, however from Martin's account whether the symbolic matricide is of Bill's mother, against whom he was in rebellion, or of Max's mother, toward whom Bill acted as a surrogate killer. Martin strengthens his case for the play of unconscious forces by the observation that Bill's recent rejection for admission to the University of Michigan may have helped channel his aggression by moving him, unconsciously, to direct his companions to the University campus that evening.

Martin's judgment that Bill was a psychopath with a need to kill suffers from a flaw common to that diagnosis: the inference of psychopathy from the fact of killing; in other words, deriving the cause from the effect. The label of psychopath could easily attach to a larger number of youths than those who get into serious trouble with the law. A lag in moral development is not abnormal at this time of life for boys from stable as well as unsettled family backgrounds. Adolescence breeds rebellion and hostility toward a social order which levies expectations that the untried youth fears he may not be able to meet. Having the physical needs and wishes of adulthood, but lacking the experience of maturity and being shackled by the restraints of childhood foments evasiveness and hostility. The negativeness in the usual case eventually gives way to positiveness as the individual achieves success in the handling of adult roles and finds his niche in the existing order.

Almost as an afterthought Martin lays the blame for Bill's misconduct on the fact that "our free society is sick." The portentous language of Martin's indictment charges that cultural contradictions produced by the rapidity of social change since the beginning of the century have loosened the bonds of traditional social controls. Young people, Martin believes, are overindulged and overprotected by parents and authorities while witness to glaring inconsistencies between precept and practice. (Martin, 130)

This perennial complaint of the older generation applies to all young people who grow up in periods of rapid social change with its inevitable accompaniment of value conflict. Since most of them don't commit serious transgressions, there is no way of knowing how much, if any, force to assign moral confusion in generating delinquency.

All of Martin's speculation on the motive for the crime presumes that Bill intended to kill. The very title of the book, *Why Did They Kill?*, takes for granted that all three of the boys intended to kill. The facts seem otherwise. Dave and Max did not join Bill in the assault; clearly they had no discernible homicidal intent or motive; their legal and moral guilt lay in being accomplices to a mugging in the course of which a killing occurred. The fact that the mallet Bill used to hit the nurse was rubber-coated weakens the assumption that he intended to do more than stun his prey. The plan, in the fatal robbery and in the earlier failed attempt, to drag the victim into the car argues for the intention to abduct a live victim. To maintain that Bill wished to kill the victim requires agreement with Martin's tenuously drawn, but untestable, assumption of unconscious motivation. More consistent with the totality of facts is the inference that the fatal outcome was an unintended by-product of the bungled adolescent caper of three beer-sodden young men intent on a robbery and, plausibly, a gang-rape.

The saga of Gary Gilmore, recited by Norman Mailer in his celebrated true crime documentary, *The Executioner's Song*, tells of a rather different robbery murder, in which the killing was built into the planning. Mailer provides an abundance of information from which adherents of almost any school of thought could piece together what they need to fit a preferred theory of robbery-murder. His account invests the life of an unregenerate killer with an aura of bittersweet tragedy. He fancied Gilmore as a mystic who looked back on his years of imprisonment as a foul karma from which death was a "species of romantic solution." (Mailer's Introduction, in Abbott, xi) To put Mailer's thought into plainer language: Gilmore was suicidal.

The killings to all outward appearances were uncomplicated. Gilmore, a convict on parole for armed robbery, robbed a service station attendant, forced him to lie on his stomach with his arms underneath his body, and shot him in the back of the head twice.

The next night he held up a motel manager and, following the same procedure, fatally shot him. Both jobs were botched. Gilmore was seen carrying the dead service station attendant's money changer, trying to dispose of the murder weapon, and leaving the motel after killing the manager. His bloodied trouser cuffs were observed by a female companion later in the evening. In getting rid of the murder weapon after the second killing, he accidentally gave himself a painful wound in the hand when a twig from a shrub caught the trigger and fired the gun. He called his cousin for help. She guessed his involvment in the killings and informed the police.

Gilmore was convicted of first degree murder and sentenced to die. He elected death by firing squad. His refusal to allow his attorneys to pursue every legal recourse to stave off his execution made him a celebrity. His willingness to die upset partisans of the anti-death penalty movement, which had gathered momentum in the wake of a ten year period with no executions nationwide.

The Gilmore case ignited a media explosion. Extensive interviews in American and foreign publications, the lurid revelations of tabloid weeklies, and a television mini-series added to heavy coverage in the daily press. Mailer's book of more than one-thousand pages—based on conversations with virtually everyone who had been a significant player in Gilmore's life before and after the killings, letters, official documents, and court records—creates an expansive context, much greater than needed, to explain those two momentary acts of pulling the trigger of a gun held to the skulls of the piteous victims.

The narrative relates the early onset of a pattern of incorrigibility met by parental inconsistency: a lenient mother and a strict father. The father's attitude had less effect on young Gary because business kept him away from home much of the time. The male members of the family had a penchant for getting into trouble that did not jibe with the family's middle class complexion. Gary's father had been convicted of passing a bad check and had spent eighteen months in prison. The father was not a habitual deviant. He possessed some literary talent. Upon release from prison he made a living by rewriting the building code digests of cities into more understandable language. A younger brother who wrote poetry was said to have passed a bad check; apparently nothing came of it. He was mortally stabbed in an altercation. Another brother avoided trouble and attended college. Gary was the worst. At the age of thirteen he was committed to reform school for stealing a car. When he reached the age of criminal responsibility he received a sentence in the Oregon State Penitentiary for robbery. Upon release he came to Provo, Utah at the invitation of a cousin who helped him find work and get settled.

Gary did not give up his errant ways. He shoplifted items for personal use and for sale. He easily formed relationships with women. Nicole, who lavished her passions casually and promiscuously, became the love of his life in a stormy relationship inflamed by her infidelity. His letters to her from jail are a strange mixture of the language of romantic love and unrestrained eroticism. She reciprocated his ardor and entered into a suicide pact with him, smuggling pills of a potentially lethal dosage, secreted in a condom in her vagina, into jail. The plan failed; both received emergency treatment before the ingested pills had their full effect.

Gary's defense attorneys were unable to find a psychiatrist to declare him insane. A psychological assessment put him in the range of above average to superior intelligence with a vocabulary IQ of 140, an abstraction IQ of 120, and a full-scale IQ of 129. Gary was an inveterate reader, a habit he had picked up during his years in the penitentiary. A neurologic report noted his admission of a tendency toward compulsive behavior but did not accord it much significance. A question and answer session conducted by the medical staff found Gary competent and responsible. Their diagnosis defined his problem vacuously as "personality disorder of the anti-social type." Interviews by medical staff and journalists to ferret out his thoughts and feelings in doing the killings were unproductive. Nor could they extract a plausible motive from the mass of details dug up by investigation. Looking at one side of the obvious, they thought correctly that Gilmore didn't need to kill to effect the robberies; the victims cooperated in turning over the receipts and did nothing to provoke him. They overlooked the other side of the obvious, the most cogently practical reason for the killings: he wanted to eliminate any chance of identification by the victim.

Gilmore's language in describing himself to interviewers aimed to create the impression that he was mean and tough. His affectation of macho courage does not square with the cowardliness of the killings. His answers to questioners were not the exculpatory bleatings of a person trying to stir up sympathy. He seemed to be taking some perverse gratification in posing as a gutsy bad guy—a thug to be sure, but true to the values of thuggery—a role common to "heavy" criminal types confined in maximum security prisons.

The flipness of his remarks about the killings and his self-presentation as a rotten apple—so puzzling to the journalists, mental health workers, and law enforcement personnel, intent on fathoming his motives—are not so mysterious when understood as a product of his imprisonment in the Oregon State Penitentiary during the highly impressionable formative years of his life. The real audience for Gilmore's tough guy rhetoric were the cons and ex-cons who shared with him the sentiments of the subculture of predatory violence. He admitted to interviewers that he intended to kill the victims when he went to rob them. He shamelessly affirmed his identity as a robber, a thief, a con. His responses conveyed an impression of barely regretted meanness, deserving of the death penalty. He took a casual view of the killings—no particular reason for them: "I'm impulsive. I don't think," he explained to one interviewer. He pumped an extra bullet into his first victim "to make sure he wasn't in any pain." The second victim didn't receive that mercy; the gun jammed after the first shot; so Gilmore left him to die as best he could. Gilmore repeatedly pressed the point to interviewers and judges that he wished to die soon, and with dignity, like a man. He had to wait longer than he expected since the state was reluctant to apply the death penalty until a Supreme Court decision on the Utah capital punishment statute could be delivered.

Yet, as portrayed by Mailer, who seems to find violent men fascinating, Gary Gilmore wasn't all bad. The malevolent side of Gilmore's self-presentation was offset by his avowed affection for family members, his mother in particular. Many who dealt with him in a variety of relationships found him an attractive, likeable person. He enjoyed the give and take with doctors, lawyers, writers, and television producers, and disarmed them with the apparent honesty of his responses. In reply to the frequently asked question of why he killed the two young hard-working family men, both of whom had been Mormon missionaries, Gilmore responded with some version of *I am simply no good.* Attempts to invest his utterances with any more than this disclaimer of worth came to naught. After repeated interviews, Gilmore may have felt some need to vary his response. One time he came up with a reply that would certainly win the endorsement of a practitioner of depth psychology: "because I did not want to kill Nicole." What killing the victims of his robberies might have to do with killing his girl friend is unclear. The thought makes sense only in the context that killing is a symbolic act which cannot be understood in its own terms. Gilmore also expressed the wish that he hadn't killed the two young men, but whether this was meant as remorse for the killings or regret over the consequences to himself is unclear.

The infliction of cruelty by a robber before ending the life of the victim signifies a malevolence that overwhelms reason. Social-behavioral scientists who think in terms of cause and effect rather than moral depravity attribute the origins of extreme callousness to an impairment of the killer's empathic faculty. Gary Kinder's book *Victim* provides a rich vein of data by which to reconstruct the social context of a multiple murder aggravated by cruelty for its own sake. The premeditation and viciousness of the event exceeded anything in the memory of the community. Dr. Louis G. Moensch, a psychiatrist retained to test the sanity of one of the killers said "...it's probably the most gruesome crime that's ever occured in this state...the sadistic quality here, the unmitigated and unneccessary cruelty, the ingenuity and variety of indignities to the people...this is the worst."

The binge of torture and murder took place on a spring day of 1974, in Ogden, Utah. Two men waving handguns held up a music record store near closing time. The salesclerks in attendance were Stan Walker, age 20 and Michelle Ansley, age 19. No sooner was the hold-up in progress, when a customer, Cortney Naisbitt, age 16, entered the store. The robbers threatened to kill him, kicked and punched him in the stomach and groin, pushed him down the basement steps, and tied him up. Cortney was soon joined by Stan and Michelle who were also bound. When Cortney did not come home for dinner as expected, his worried mother, Carol, went looking for him and eventually came to the record shop where she too was taken captive. The victim list was swelled by the advent of Stan Walker's father who came looking for his son. The robbers meanwhile were shouting curses and threats and adding to the terror by firing shots.

Stan, in an action that would clearly strengthen the prosecution's case for premeditation, urged the robbers to give second thoughts to what they were about. He pleaded with them, to no avail, to take whatever they wanted and go, and promised that none of the victims would identify them.

One of the robbers prepared a mixture of vodka and what he termed a "German drug"—in fact, a drain pipe cleaning fluid—which he claimed would sedate them. Saying, "We're going to have a cocktail party," he forced Cortney, his mother, Stan, and Mr. Walker to drink it. The scorching liquid burned stomach lining and esophagus and induced spitting, retching, and coughing. To keep them from spitting out the caustic liquid, one of the robbers tried to cover their mouths with masking tape, but it wouldn't stick.

Meanwhile the robbers relieved their victims of wallets, watches and jewelry. One of them, frightened by the horrors they had unleashed, refused to go any further and excused himself. The other then proceeded to execute the victims. First, Carol Naisbitt: shot in the back of the head; next, Stan Walker and his father got the same dispatch. The killer later returned to Stan's father, examined him for a pulse, tied a cord around his throat and pulled it tight, then wedged a ball-point pen in his ear and stomped on it forcing the point into Walker's throat. Michelle pleaded for her life. The killer forced her to remove her clothes, raped her, then fatally shot her.

Three of the victims died. Cortney survived in a permanently disabled brain-impaired condition, unable to recall the events of the crime. Mr. Walker, despite the bullet in his head and the ball-point pen rammed in his ear, both of which missed any vital organ, and the attempted strangulation which did not prevent some air from getting into his lungs, recovered, He testified at the trial of the accused who were convicted and sentenced to die.

The robbers turned out to be airmen, both black. stationed at a nearby Air Force base. Of the two, Dale Pierre dominated in the planning and was the one who committed the killings, torture, and rape. He was born and spent his formative years in the West Indies. Teachers and neighbors in the West Indies recalled that he was an intelligent but devious child, who in adolescence was involved in thefts and had problems with authority. He migrated with his parents to the United States when he was seventeen years old. A succession of unsatisfying menial jobs stimulated a desire for more lively activity. He learned to drive and enjoyed the excitement of speed, but the thrill soon wore off. The glamor of piloting an airplane attracted him to enlist in the United States Air Force. When he discovered that admission to pilot training required more education than he had, he soured on his job in helicopter maintenance and applied for a separation from the service. The Air Force was not averse to Pierre's departure. He was regarded by his fellow airman as a troublemaker and had been arrested for a number of auto thefts off-base. His separation from the service was held up pending the disposition of the cases in the civilian court since the military authorities were disinclined to grant him an honorable discharge. Meanwhile, his acquaintance with a black airman, William Andrews, ripened into a conspiracy to rob the music store. A third airman who participated in the holdup, but withdrew and did not participate in the torture and killing which followed, was convicted of robbery only. The author focuses on the character of Dale Pierre since he was the ringleader, torturer, and killer.

The robbers' decision to rob a music store reflected their appreciation of expensive high fidelity sound equipment. Evidence of events before and during the robbery indicates that the motive for the killings was the elimination of anyone who might identify them. Pierre could not have been unaware that in the white Mormon precincts of Ogden, Utah, it would not be difficult to narrow the search for two black suspects, one of whom spoke in a West Indian intonation. A fellow airman testified that the decision to kill the victims entered into their planning. "I heard them talking about it. They said they weren't going to leave any witnesses [to the crime]." At the scene of the crime, Pierre in remonstrance to Andrews fear of the consequences of killing if caught, exclaimed, "What about me being booked?" to which Andrews replied, "You been booked before...but I ain't got a record, man."

The understandable desire to eliminate victims who might later testify against robbers or rapists doesn't account for the heartless pain inflicted by Pierre. Calling the torturer a sociopath is less an illuminant than an abandonment of understanding. Another equally nebulous explanation, stemming from Pierre's references to popping pills and smoking marijuana, asserts that the influence of drugs had undermined any empathic sensibility and self-control. Dr. Moensch, the psychiatrist who pronounced Pierre sane, was not called upon to conduct the kind of full scale examination which would be necessary to lay a foundation for a diagnosis of Pierre's brutality.

He did, however, make some pertinent observations. He got the impression that Pierre was withholding relevant information. Pierre covered his reluctance to talk claiming that he didn't remember much about the day of the murders, that he didn't know where the stolen speakers in his possession came from, and that later, while putting some of the loot in a garage he rented, he blacked out. For Dr. Moensch the sharpest impression was that Pierre "...has a tremendous sense of inferiority, and at the same time he goes through the process of denying it. Then it becomes a sense of power. His feelings of wanting power, I think, represent the feelings of inferiority. It's an attempt at compensation."

Remarks by Pierre to Gary Kinder and others after the trial coincide with Dr. Moensch's judgment. Pierre's posturing conveyed an unrealistic view of himself and his conception of how others perceived him. He bragged about his knowledge on virtually every subject, affected a superior air, told of various plans to make a fortune, and laid out his strategy for getting a retrial and an acquittal. His pretenses bared rather than concealed his feelings of inferiority. Commenting on racial matters to an acquaintance visiting him in his cell, Pierre declared, "I often feel that I am white, but I don't feel bad being black." He believed that his upbringing in the West Indies, where blacks are in the majority, gave him a strong character and spared him the sense of inferiority found in many American blacks. He criticized other black airmen for their boisterousness, bad manners, and bad habits, their smoking and blaspheming. He found fault with their passivity, rationalized by them in terms of not being able to rise in the white world, their flashiness in dress, and vulgar taste in music.

The language by which Pierre set himself apart from American blacks is a textbook example of the psychological defense mechanism of *reaction formation*, the denial of disapproved tendencies in oneself and their projection onto others. Moensch remarked that Pierre tends to blame his problems on everything but himself. Dr. Moensch's judgment that Pierre may have been driven by a need to compensate for a feeling of inferiority does not convincingly explain the killings or the unnecessary pain inflicted on the victims. Pierre's ramblings convey an intense animosity toward white people. The excessive denial of anti-white feelings in his claim to feeling white, suggests that the lad "doth protest too much." But unlike the psychodynamical interpretation of reaction formation as an unconscious process, the broader context favors the judgment that the denial is a deliberate untruth. Pierre evinces an ill-concealed resentment toward whites for treating the superior person he considered himself to be like the blacks who deserved to be demeaned. Here was a chance for revenge, a chance devoid of risk because there would be no survivor to identify him.

There is pause to wonder why Pierre's attorneys did not order a full scale examination of his mental state, even if only for evidence of some degree of impairment, not enough to claim insanity, but perhaps enough to make the difference between the death penalty and a life sentence. There is reason to think, however, that the sheer ferocity of the treatment of the victims inhibited any move to initiate a plea for reduced responsibility on any ground. Pierre's first attorney felt the pressure of an aroused community and withdrew from the case recommending that her replacement be from another area of the state. The value of comprehensive mental tests did, however, occur to her. Like any resourceful defense attorney seeking to cushion the case against a client, she suggested that the maladroitness of his auto thefts pointed to an impairment of judgment which, if amplified by tests, could somehow mitigate the offense.

The major obstacle to understanding ruthless savagery is the presumption that only a person depraved beyond common comprehension could do such vile things. Shocking as extreme cruelty may seem, historical, legal, and clinical evidence suggests not only the banality of the infliction of unnecessary pain and suffering, but that committing or viewing such atrocities can bring a perverse pleasure. Pierre and Andrews had gotten the idea of pouring the caustic drink into the victims' mouths from a film, *Blackbelt*, they had seen a few days before the holdup. The relish and deliberateness with which they performed the torturous acts, the "fun and games" posture of the actors, and their enjoyment at the pain and terror of the victims pose disturbing questions concerning human nature. They require us to confront the prominence in historical and contemporary human affairs of torture, not only as a means of coercion or punishment employed by institutions of government and religion, but as a means of titillation and public amusement. We no longer have public amputations, tongue or eye removals, followed by beheadings and drawings and quarterings. Instead the movies provide realistic enactments of torture and executions; horror novels describe unspeakable abominations inflicted by human monsters. All of this suggests that although the infliction of pain for its own sake may be exceptional, the beholding of torture appeals to a human appetite, which, in the moral atmosphere of our times, may be activated by impersonal as well as personal hatred, and abetted by the deinhibiting effects of drugs, alcohol, or a perception of the victim which transforms the sufferer's agony into just deserts.

The maxim of law that the facts speak for themselves enjoys no credence in the scientific community, particularly among forensic psychiatrists testifying for the defense in apparently open and shut cases of robbery-murder. In the name of some mystique-enshrouded wisdom they dig out a different set of "facts" from a more profound reality than inferrable from what the killer says or allegedly did. This obliqueness can take a variety of forms. Truman Capote gives a psychoanalytical example in his tale of the murder of the Clutter family—husband, wife, and two children. His celebrated documentary "novel," *In Cold Blood*, tells of the invasion of of the Clutters' prosperous Kansas farmstead at night by two small-time hoodlums, Perry Smith and Dick Hickock, bent on robbery. Disappointed at not finding a safe full of money rumored to be in the house, Perry, by his own admission, slashed Mr. Clutter's throat in order to prevent him from identifying them. The wound did not prevent Clutter from straining against the ropes by which the robbers had bound him, and it appeared to Perry that he might succeed in breaking loose. Perry screamed at Dick to "finish him" but Dick panicked and Perry, himself in an agitated state, administered the *coup de grace* by shooting. The robbers completed the caper by killing Clutter's wife and two children.

The manifestly predatory motive for the act by moral defectives—devoid of the capacity for empathy, except for themselves, as expressed in their self-pitying maunderings after they were caught—was subordinated by an examining psychiatrist to the excusatory interpretation, approvingly quoted by Capote, that when Smith killed Clutter, he was "under a mental eclipse...it was not entirely a flesh-and-blood man he 'suddenly discovered himself destroying, but a key figure in some past traumatic configuration: his father? the orphanage nuns who had derided and beaten him? the hated Army sergeant? the parole officer who had ordered him to

stay out of Kansas'? One of them, or all of them." (Capote, p. 302).
The court did not buy this alternative "truth"; the two killers were
eventually hanged.

A rather different but equally indirect interpretation of killing in the
course of armed robbery subordinates the aim of getting money to
the assertion of power. One psychoanalytical version invests the
killing with erotic significance, hypothesizing that the gun symbolizes the penis of the robber. A less oblique analysis regards the
killing as the assertion of awesome power by which the robber
wishes to cement a reputation as a fearsome character. Sociologist
Jack Katz's work, *The Seductions of Crime*, develops and applies
this theme to the murders treated in *Executioner's Song*, *In Cold
Blood*, and *Victim*. From his reading of Truman Capote's text, Katz
rejects the notion that Perry Smith slit Mr. Clutter's throat to
forestall identification, or that he was he in a state of mental eclipse,
or even that robbery his true agenda; after all Smith and his partner
could have worn masks, and a take of $40 or $50 hardly makes
killing sensible. (To rescue the sensibility of the miscreants, the
reader should be reminded that Dick and Perry expected to find a
safe full of money on the premises.)

Professor Katz offers two reasons for rejecting the notion that
the elimination of witnesses could have been the motive for the
killing. One is that the police devote a great deal of their investigative resources to homicides. However valid this observation
might be, there is no reason to suppose that it was a damper on the
calculations of the two men or that they even took it into account.
The other reason is that robbers have ways other than killing
victims for concealing their identity: they could wear masks. Why
they didn't was made clear by the declaration of Dick en route to
the crime that they were going to wipe out the Clutters.

The motive Katz assigns to Perry for killing Mr. Clutter
developed out of a contention between the two unreformed
delinquents over who is the hardest and meanest. On the way to the
Clutter's house and once they broke in, Dick assumed the posture
of being more committed than his partner to the nefarious scheme
on which they had embarked. He chided Perry for his hesitancy and
took a more brutal attitude toward the Clutters. So why did Perry,
and not Dick, kill Mr. Clutter? To explain the sudden switch in
aggressiveness Katz creates a mystical metaphor of fateful

determination. The murderous impulsion moves to fruition through a process of gestation involving events in the life of the individual which set the stage and reach their climax in the killing as an exercise of "cosmological control." The primitive god, who is a destroyer as well as a creator holds sway over the universe, getting human attention by hurling thunderbolts, as in Greek mythology, or the sudden burning of a bush, as in the Old testament. "[I]f one is effectively to mobilize the form of primordial evil, he needs a situation structured for cosmological transcendence." (Katz, 304)

The robbery, then, is merely the setting for what Katz terms the exercise of "primordial" control, and by what more awesome means than killing a human being. What drove Perry to his assertion of "primordial power"? Perry responded to Dick's disparagement of his hardness by exposing Dick as a fraud and asserting his moral superiority at the game they were playing. When Dick hesitated to finish the assault on Mr. Clutter, "...Perry stepped in triumphantly, demonstrating, in what he would take to be a timelessly revealing moment, which of the two really had the primordial power." (Katz, 307) In plainer language, it would seem that Perry killed Mr. Clutter to best his accomplice in a game of one-upmanship.

The scenario of the Clutter murder, taken without psychodynamical or metaphysical embellishments, indicates a more mundane motive: the panic of two men overwhelmed by the failure of events to go as planned, each calling to the other to finish the failed robbery and remove the only living witnesses, *as they had planned from the outset.*

Professor Katz applies the same "primordial power" metaphor to the case of Gary Gilmore. Gilmore's two murders were waiting for an appropriate context to happen; the robbery merely set the scene. Katz finds the interpretation that Gary Gilmore killed to eliminate witnesses inconsistent with five attendant facts. Four have to do with actions which to Katz seem highly imprudent for a robber seeking to elude detection. First, when Gilmore committed the initial murder, he left Nicole's sister, unmindful of what Gary was up to and hallucinating on drugs, sitting in his truck waiting for him to return. Second, he sought help from strangers after he ran out of gas and "allowed" them to see him recover a gun, bullets and a coin changer taken in the robbery and secreted behind some bushes. Third, the day after the robbery he made an "unprecedented" offer of $50 to a cousin, which he must have known would arouse some suspicion in her mind. Fourth, the second murder was committed near his uncle's home after he had left his truck in a repair shop with an acquaintance who was able to link Gilmore to the crime. In noting these circumstances, Katz implies that Gilmore either was motivated by an unconscious need to get caught or was indifferent to the possibility of getting caught. Or to revert to his metaphor of the primordial god who transcends the mundane by being the enigmatic giver of evil as well as good, "His shooting was not only revenge or a symbolic suicide, it was a positive act of reclaiming his status as an awesome deviant." (Katz, 306)

A more pragmatic explanation of the trail of evidence left by Gilmore, aside from carelessness due to being in a chronic mental haze induced by drinking and drug-taking, is, that like most small-time hoodlums, he did not plan his capers with due regard for risk. He had a deluded confidence in his ability to get away with flagrant rip-offs. Hadn't he repeatedly entered stores and under the unobservant, or frightened, eyes of clerks, walked out without paying for whatever he chose to take, things as varied as a six-pack of beer and skis? The klutzy ineptness that marked Gilroy's judgment in the management of his life carried over into his career as a small time robber; extended to murder, it was his downfall.

The fifth "fact" advanced by Katz, that wearing a mask would have been a more prudent way of avoiding detection is a judgment, not a fact, and does not negate Gilmore's belief that killing the victim is an efficient way of accomplishing that end. The assumption that a sensible robber would wear a mask to avoid having to kill the victim imputes to robbers a degree of forethought that many do not exercise and a humaneness which in the general run of cases doubtfully influences their designs. Very few hold-up men are of the ilk of Willie Sutton, who proudly claimed that in his career as a bank robber, he managed his robberies so successfully that he never physically hurt anyone.

Katz imposes the "primordial power" solution on Dale Pierre's case, observing that, "'Eliminating witnesses' in robberies of this sort is another way of referring to the killer's objective of stamping the scene with an uncontroverted meaning." Katz vouches for his analysis by noting that Pierre succeeded in killing only three of his five victims. Like Gilmore and Hickock and Smith, he was more intent on "...defining the situation as one [he] dominated without opposition than in actually eliminating all the witnesses." Kinder's account in *Victim*, however, makes it perfectly clear that it was not from lack of diligence on Pierre's part that the survivors weren't killed. Cortney nearly died and was left with permanent brain damage from the bullet in his head. Mr. Walker who Katz described as getting up and walking out, the ball-point pen "waggling" in his ear, to report to the police what had happened, had been forced to drink the caustic fluid. A gunshot to his head, miraculously, did not kill or disable him. An attempted strangulation failed only because the rope had not been tightened sufficiently to completely close off the flow of air into the lungs. The fact that none of these methods of execution worked on Walker and that the ballpoint pen stomped into his ear missed a vital part attests to the victim's exceptional good luck and not to Pierre's indifference to his task.

In rejecting the view that the act of killing in the course of robbery is instrumental to the job, Katz declares that, for the offender, the exercise of physical force which may culminate in the death of the victim is the resolution to be a "hard man...a commitment to the transcendence of a hard will."(Katz,187). As Katz conceives it, the robber kills to proclaim his meanness and thereby vindicate his integrity as a source and enforcer of a situational order that transcends mundane morality.

A literary imagination can transform virtually any murderer into an unwitting agent of transcendental forces. The widely publicized case of the fatal stabbing of a young tourist from Utah on a subway platform in New York when he tried to defend his mother against muggers has all the ingredients for an interpretation of that kind. According to the police, the four men arrested and bound over for trial "...belonged to a gang that required prospective members to mug someone to gain admission [to the brotherhood]." (New York Times, 10/13/91, p. 40) Imagine the metaphor an imaginative writer could create with that story line. How strikingly reminiscent of the rites of passage in nomadic warlike preliterate societies by which a youth qualifies for the status of a warrior. The Masai youth was required to kill a lion with a spear; the plains Indian brave was required to "take coup", most often translated as scalping the victim. Their aboriginal New Guinea or Jivaro Indian counterpart obtained a human head, separated from the rest of the body. Only in the rhetoric of writers more habituated to the licenses of fiction than the constraints of fact could an explanation that removes a murderous assault from its situational context and endows it with mystical significance be given serious utterance in explaining urban street crime. The application of such a metaphor to the killing on the subway platform would have to ignore the incidental fact, given in the videotaped admission of the culprits, that they robbed the victim and his family in order to get the money to go dancing at a nearby public ballroom where, as a matter of fact, they were enjoying themselves when apprehended.

The presumption that a drive for power motivates robbers to kill their victims is belied by a mass of statistical and anecdotal evidence. The statistics show that the use of force in robbery is a means to an end rather than an end in itself. The injury rate in robbery reported in the pertinent studies varies widely, from 5 to 45 percent. The death rate is much less. Of the 21,500 cases of murder and non-negligent manslaughter known to have been committed in the United States in 1989, the circumstances of the killing are given for 18,954 cases. Of these 1,725 occurred in the course of a robbery. This number amounts to a bit less than three tenths of one percent (0.3%) of the 580,055 known robberies, including the number which resulted in a murder. If the expression of "primordial power" is an overriding objective in robbery, and murder its ultimate expression, we should obtain a toll of robbery killings far in excess of 0.3 percent.

The robber is primarily intent on getting money. Systematic evidence of career patterns in crime and criminal biographies confirms the instrumental rather than the consummatory nature of the use of force in robbery. For the habitual property offender, robbery is one of several shortcuts to making a living. Personal accounts by seasoned criminals mention the practice of shifting around among criminal groups and filling in at illegal activities involving non-violent as well as violent ways of making money. (E.H. Sutherland, 1937; 1972; Joey, 1974) A table dubbed "Rearrest Crime Switch Matrix" in a United States Government report shows that over 90 percent of the arrests for any of the property crimes of robbery, burglary, larceny, and car theft, are followed by subsequent arrests for one of these crimes. For persons whose last arrest was for robbery, the chances are that the subsequent arrest will be for a property crime are 82 percent, and the chances that it will be for a property crime other than robbery are 47 percent. (*President's Commission*, p. 63)

Field studies show no evidence of a homicidal impulse in the mass of predatory crime. André Normandeau concludes from his study of robbery in Philadelphia that offenders participate in a subculture of property crime which rarely involves violence. (cited in Conklin, 102-103) John E. Conklin's study of robbery in Boston found that the 396 cases in 1964 and the 847 cases in 1968, yielded, respectively, 1 and 2 murders. Professor Conklin views the robber as a larcenous individual with a penchant for violence that spills over into non-larcenous activity. His observation is supported by the "Rearrest Crime Switch Matrix," which reveals that of all types of property offenders, the robber has a slightly higher probability of rearrest for murder and non-negligent manslaughter than other types. He often has an arrest record of assaultive crimes in which the attempt to steal was not involved. Also the robbers exceed larceny and and auto theft offenders, but not burglars, in the probability of rearrest for aggravated assault.

The view that the motive for predatory violence is the assertion of power rather than material acquisition does not jibe with the autobiographies of ex-career robbers, notably Willie Sutton's *Where the Money Was* and Ray Johnson's *Too Dangerous to Be At Large*. Both emphasize the pecuniary gain from robbery. The purpose of the threat of force is to get control so that the use of force will not be necessary. One of the most feared contingencies in professional robbery, more than a would be hero, is a hysterical victim out of control. Johnson debunks the image of the cool, self confident bandit, and by implication the robber who seeks his *karma* in a blaze of homicidal glory. Instead he describes himself in the course of a "job" being in an acutely jumpy state that magnifies the risk of injury to an uncooperative victim: "My mouth would get so dry I couldn't spit for hours. All the robbers I know will tell you the same thing. There's great pride in acting cool, but underneath the robber is tense, keyed up, super alert, and nervous as hell." (Johnson, 160)

Summary

Attempts to invest the act of killing in armed robbery with a significance far beyond the robber's immediate need to control the situation do not square with the realities. The statistical marvel is that so small a proportion of armed robberies, fewer than 0.3 percent of a total well in excess of a half-million, involve killing. If the transcendent motive in the robber's use of deadly weapons were the assertion of power or proof of badness, we should expect far more killings from robbery than we get.

The setting and action of robbery-murder in case studies attests to the pragmatic uses of killing by people who are psychologically normal, but unassimilated to social rules of decency. Gary Gilmore, Dick Hickock and Perry Smith, and Dale Pierre and William Andrews were small-time hoods; Gilmore, Pierre, and Andrews were drug-besotted to boot. Their crimes are typical of the robberies on the streets, in gas stations, convenience stores, and fast food restaurants committed in the tens of thousands annually by kindred souls who exhibit as little imagination and compassion as their more celebrated colleagues. The killers among these rank and filers, however, lack a Capote or a Mailer to make them heroic figures of an American tragedy. To grace the killing by any robber as an epic reach into the existential void for self-affirmation takes a bit of stretching.

8

Defensive Homicide

Most murderous assaults are not aimed at material gain. As pointless as they may seem, and therefore dismissed as "senseless," they serve vital interests. Killing an antagonist in a quarrel can conclusively establish domination of a situation. The violent act has adjustive value because it purges emotions inflamed by stressful relationships and restores psychological balance.

Defensive homicides are reactions not only to physical threats, but to insult, rejection, or challenge to personal worth. Against a background of drug using and boozing, demanding and denying, feelings are bruised, blows exchanged, and weapons brandished. Which of the antagonists turns out to be the survivor or the victim is chancy, often depending on who has the killing weapon or the luck of the draw.

The unremarkableness of the killing scenario and the social unimportance of the participants accord this type of killing a perfunctory coverage in the news media, the routine of a negotiated plea in the criminal justice system, and scant interest from the true crime literati. The fact that most killings are impetuous acts of people lacking in self-control has prompted the observation that homicide is the most easily explained crime. Often the death is the fortuitous outcome of a confrontation out of control. Were it not for unplanned events—the intervention of a bystander during an assault, the deadliness of a weapon, the effectiveness of emergency medical treatment to make the difference between death or injury, a false move by a robbery victim, or the return of a householder in the midst of a burglary—the episode would be just another assault on the police blotter (Gottfredson et al, 31)

The progression from stimulus to act in most killings done in the throes of passion is a bit more complex. There remains the enigma of how, in the majority of homicides, a trivial word or gesture can set off so disproportionate a response. The case of the murder of Richard Adan by Jack Henry Abbott instructs how soaking up the sentiments and values of a violent social environment skews perception and judgment to an extreme. Abbott, a prison inmate, became a literary celebrity when he was taken under the wing of Norman Mailer who admired the style and anti-establishmentarian fire of his essays on the searing effects of prison life. Abbott's praise of violence, so eloquently expressed in his book, *In the Belly of the Beast*, was no mere literary affectation. He had spent over half of his life in prison for a variety of offenses, including the slaying of a fellow inmate and a bank robbery during a brief period of escape from prison. His defiance of authority and violent outbursts kept him in solitary confinement during much of this time. Abbott denies the common belief that Mailer's praise of his writing won him a parole. He claims he got it because it was due him.

Abbott had so acute a sensitivity to perceived affronts that a serious miscalculation after he was released on parole prompted him to slay a young man who intended him no harm, but according to Abbott, looked as if he did. Abbott and co-author, philosophy graduate Naomi Zack, whom he married, wrote a book about the slaying titled *My Return* in which they literally choreographed the movements of the two men from the moment their paths crossed until Adan lay dying a few minutes later. By Abbott's account, after an evening of drinking and dancing, he and two women companions went to a restaurant in a neighborhood frequented by drunks and unruly characters. Abbott perceived that a young waiter, actually the night manager, Richard Adan, was staring intently at him. At his trial Abbott said he thought that the look was one of hostile envy because he was accompanied by two attractive women. [Abbott would later realize that Adan's attention was to Abbott's half Chinese, half Irish, features; Adan's wife was also Eurasian. (Cox)] When they were seated, Abbott recounted, Adan threw menus on the table and for no good reason laid his hand heavily on his shoulder and spoke to him in a hostile manner. Abbott demanded to know why Adan was picking on him. The two got into a shouting match and went outside. Adan made gestures shooing Abbott away and ordered him not to return to the restaurant. In the face of Abbot's remonstrances, Adan brandished a knife, reportedly his practice in dealing with boisterous patrons who refused his order to leave. Whereupon Abbott pulled out his knife and stabbed Adan in the heart.

Another version (Cox, 185), has it that there was no toilet facility for customers in the restaurant and Adan thought that Abbott needed to urinate. Male customers who expressed that need were shown a spot around the corner next to a dumpster. Abbott took the invitation to step outside as a challenge to fight. He claimed that as Adan left the counter, it looked as if he had picked up an object which Abbott took to be a weapon. When they got outside Adan directed Abbott to the dumpster and followed to show him the spot. Abbott thinking that attack was imminent, turned and stabbed Adan. An eye-witness disputed Abbott's version, testifying that the stabbing was without provocation.

The difference in accounts do not alter the realization that the tragedy was the outcome of misunderstandings by both men, particularly Abbott. Adan's mistake lay in handling the hypersensitive Abbott the same as other difficult patrons, if indeed Abbot was difficult. Abbott's interpretation of Adan's words and gestures was mediated by attitudes developed out of of his life experience in a prison environment where there is constant fear of mayhem and murder. Mailer's literary assessment of Abbott, written prior to the killing of Richard Adan, ironically notes that Abbott's writings reveal a loathing of death; but, as the killing of Richard Adan suggests, not as it might apply to anyone Abbott might wish to kill. For, as Mailer also observes, Abbott "was not interested in the particular...but only in the relevance of the particular to the abstract." (Abbott, xi)

Making Sense of "Senseless" Murders

The defensive function of much violent crime, even in encounters initiated by the offender, is recognized by psychiatrists in diagnoses which regard the victim as a symbol of some repressed traumatic event in the life of the killer. The act of killing, psychiatrist Fredric Wertham (1949) has noted, may free the killer of an unbearable emotional conflict. The calm resignation and quiet diffidence displayed by killers taken into police custody is typical of the "cathartic" killing and a common aftermath of a violent blood bath (Fredric Wertham, 1937: 974-978). In a similar vein, psychiatrist David Abrahamsen, hypothesizes that the violent offender "uses his aggressiveness as an unconscious defense mechanism in order to conceal his basically passive personality. Thus when faced with a threatening situation, he feels forced to prove that he is aggressive and does so either by protest, bullying, rebelliousness, or by an outright criminal act." (Abrahamsen, 1962: 41) Suzanne Richard and Carl Tillman construe the "senseless" act of violence as a means of protecting the wholeness of personality against disintegration by discharging unassuagable anger through an act of violence. (Richard and Tillman, 149; quoted by Manfred Guttmacher, 63)

Even in cases involving randomly selected victims unknown to the killer, for example mass murders so apparently unreasonable as to be labelled "psychotic," a common diagnostic theme is self-protection from conspiratorial machinations. Mass killer Howard Unruh, who one morning in 1946 claimed thirteen victims on a murderous shooting spree on a Camden, New Jersey street, was portrayed by newspaper reporters as a mild-mannered person who, unfathomably, ran amok. Police investigation disclosed that over a period of years he had built up an intense hatred of Jews who were the primary target of his wrath. (Bandura, 180-181) While in the army in World War II he acquired a weapons collection which he brought home. In the period preceding the murderous spree he underwent a period of withdrawal devoting himself to reading the Bible, target shooting, and nursing grudges against his neighbors who, he believed, were defaming him. The decision to kill was not an explosion, but a cool resolve. He calmly walked down the street and into stores shooting neighborhood merchants and customers who were unlucky enough to be in his path.

The incidental quality of so many murders, the seeming incongruity with the circumstances in which they occur that earns them the tag "senseless," poses no problem to the depth psychologist who locates the taut spring of unleashed violence in the unconscious mind. What the actor thinks concerning his actions is merely the shadow projection of a reality which eludes conscious awareness. Forensic psychiatrist Andrew Ruotolo develops this theme claiming that internal conflicts, unwittingly aroused by the victim, activate violent propensities by threatening the pretenses which maintain the killer's neurotic defenses. "They [the victims as instigators] are impediments to the return of the killers to their characteristic neurotic solutions. Therefore, they had to be eliminated." (Ruotolo, p. 201)

The case studies presented by Ruotolo in the serpentine language of psychoanalysis are better understood as the frenetic attempts of socially maladroit, badly educated persons to stabilize troubled lives. One instance involves a robber who shot at but missed a bank employee who pursued him as he attempted to get away from a hold-up attempt. Ruotolo assimilates the robbery, along with a number of burglaries committed by the robber, to his diagnostic scheme as essentially "healthy" attempts of the patient, "a detached, resigned personality type", to bring himself into a "more comfortable integration" with other people. The neurotic defense identified by the physician was the patient's conception of himself as a Robin Hood who stole from the rich to give to the poor. Ruotolo's assessment of the Robin Hood delusion, however, gives it more the aspect of a schizophrenic psychosis than a neurosis. The import of the shooting, so evidently a panicked but nonetheless focused attempt to avoid capture and hardly consistent with the altruism of the Robin Hood image, is minimized in the analysis, perhaps because the shooter missed.

Ruotolo diagnoses a Puerto Rican immigrant who killed his common law wife as an expansive person whose neurotic defense consisted in fancying himself a great provider for his womenfolk—mother, sisters, and the woman he took as his common law wife. After his wife admitted to infidelity, he beat her, then displayed a willingness to forgive her and avowed a need for her. They made love; her giggling indifference to his magnanimity in forgiveness and confession of love angered him. He threatened to kill her; she laughed, declaring, "You wouldn't dare." But he did, thereby removing her as an impediment to his neurotic conception of himself as a magnanimous person. A sociological interpretation would adhere more closely to the social meaning of the event and focus on the culturally ingrained conceit of the male role in Hispanic society. In ridiculing the assertion of manhood embodied in her husband's threat, the victim uncorked a subcultural genie of rage and thereby entered the considerable statistical category of Puerto-Rican women murdered in domestic quarrels.

A woman of Italian extraction, the fifth of eleven children, shot an abusive husband to death. As if his meanness was not sufficient to explain the act, Ruotolo hypothesizes that the wife, a self-effacing person, had a "neurotic pride syndrome" based on her ability to maintain a loving relationship with her spouse, no matter how great his abuse of her. Repeated mistreatment exhausted her patience. She called the police to arrest her husband. Finding quiet restored when they arrived, the police took no action. When her healthfully assertive act was frustrated by the indifference of the police, she was forced from the perch of her neurotic defense and killed the person who, as the analyst puts it, "had seemingly prevented her from making her original neurotic solution work." After her apprehension she returned to the state of neurotic dependency in relations with the people who would minister to her medical and emotional need in the hospital ward where she was placed for examination. Whether her submissiveness was less a "neurotic pride syndrome" and more, the proper behavior of a woman taking the traditional wifely role is a reasonable conjecture. Either way it may have cloaked the sense of despair, mother to the thought common to battered wives that the only alternative to putting up with their misery is the eradication of their tormentor.

The circumstances of these cases and the obvious motives of the assailants—attempting to avoid capture, punishing an unfaithful wife, and protecting against a brutal attack—exemplify the run-of-the-mill murders relegated to the inside pages of the newspaper. By the "neurotic solution" theory of homicide, all impulsive violent assaults can be fitted into a mold of mental impairment, severe enough to warrant a plea of insanity; and, indeed, some forensic psychiatrists take that position.

Ruotolo is not alone among psychiatrists in construing socially transmitted lower class behavior patterns as neurotic or psychotic symptoms. David Abrahamsen, for example identifies "...difficulty in communicating, rebellion against parents, little or no male identification, a rich fantasy life, a feeling of unworthiness, the wish for revenge, fears, frustration and depression" as the "casebook" characteristics of killers. (Abrahamsen, 1973, 2) If it is reasonable to suppose that such tensions occur at some time in the lives of everyone, and very frequently in the lives of many people, the pivotal issue is not why some people kill, but why most people don't kill.

Where Ruotolo, along with Abrahamsen and other mental health therapists, abnormalizes the show of violence, sociologists consider the outburst as a culturally appropriate response to the perception of threat. The fact that emotions can be inflamed to a point that people will kill does not prove the abnormality of the offender, only that he or she falls beneath some accepted standard of self-control or follows a subcultural norm that requires the violent expression of anger.

Sociology is more respectful of the scientific virtue of parsimony in making sense of violent assaults. Unlike psychiatric accounts grounded in an elaborately constructed netherworld of non-rational thought and feeling, sociological interpretations hold that the killings are the rational, if immoderate, response of persons connected to reality by understandings forged out of experience in an environment in which threats to life, limb, and self-esteem are unexceptional. The frequently expressed bafflement at the motive for killings deemed "senseless" reflects a lack of appreciation of the world of meanings in which the act is embedded.

The typical "senseless" murder is not without reason. Unlike the sensational front page or fictional murder motivated by greed or power, the bulk of homicides are triggered by fear, anger, or resentment. They occur with the highest frequency in social settings which endorse violence as a means of demonstrating that the actor can enforce his demands and protects his interests. Defensiveness is reflected in killings to uphold reputation, to demand respect, to protect or promote self-image, and to neutralize persons perceived as threats. Typical cases of "senseless" violence involve lower class persons who can neither cope with threatening situations non-violently nor escape from them. Under conditions of reduced inhibition or increased excitation brought on by liquor or drugs, the magnification of old grievances, and the resulting distortions of perception, the homicidal attack becomes a solution, short run to be sure, but one that is conclusive.

Role Patterns in Defensive Homicide

The feelings of inadequacy which engender domestic violence fester in those unable to meet standards of competence in the performance of primary roles which structure the relationships of everyday life. Each role embodies the socially expected conduct of the player in a relationship and has its complement in the roles of the other players. Getting gratification in interpersonal relations entails giving gratification. The more crucial the relationship for the realization of individual needs and the stability of society, the more upsetting the failure of the relationship to deliver. That is why breakdowns of reciprocity in role relationships are much more crucial to the generation of a homicidal rage than any personality disorder; and why, paradoxically, murder so often involves offenders and victims locked into highly interdependent relationships as spouses, lovers, friends, parent and child, and work associates.

Social settings in which the give-and-take of interpersonal relations is directed by clearly defined requirements within the practical capabilities of individuals have low rates of assaultive crime. Where the requirements are unclear or the person has difficulty in meeting them, there is a greater likelihood of aggressive conduct fueled by the defeat of expectations. The denial of reciprocity in role relationships incites most spousal homicides. Given the traditional emphasis on the connection between male dominance and the role of breadwinner, the man who fails to meet his mate's standard of adequate support may encounter opposition to demands for sexual or other marital rights. Rebuff swells resentment; strains in maintaining a balance between giving and getting heighten sensitivity to slights. In this highly vulnerable state, an argument over some trivial matter, an affront, fancied or real, is all it takes to spark a homicidal explosion. In the usual case the man kills the woman in venting his passion. Less often the woman kills the man in defending herself.

Lee Rainwater's portrayal of family relations among lower class black people insightfully depicts the effects of the instability of the lower class family structure in the production of high homicide rates. His survey of residents of housing projects in St. Louis details the erosion of the bonds of intimate relationships between men and women. Husbands and wives think of themselves as having distinctively different roles in the family. Both pursue separate recreational and outside interests. Even when the husband is a stable provider, which is often not the case, the woman's conception of men is such that she doubts that he will continue to be a stable provider. Where husband and wife both work, the separate incomes are regarded as individual rather than common property. Family arguments between siblings of the opposite sex in the parental family provide training in unmasking anatagonists' pretensions to competence. The ability to demean the already vulnerable sense of masculine worth of brothers is carried over into relations with lovers. Thus for the male, growing up does not entail the acquisition of competence and mastery of the environment, but rather an increasing awareness of his deficiencies. Family solidarity is eroded as parents and their children, husbands and wives, and siblings become embroiled in quarrels so violent that the police are called in to settle them. (Rainwater, 1966)

The incubation of violent tendencies under conditions of male role impairment is not exclusive to the American underclass; it occurs in societies with remarkably low rates of homicide. In a review of English studies of the "battered wife syndrome," P.D. Scott finds that assault by husbands against wives reaches its highest concentration in the lower class. The violence is a product of the failure of reciprocity in marital relationships combined with socialization in a cultural setting which fails to restrain the expression of physical aggression. F.H. McClintock's study of violent crime in London notes that most crimes of violence are not committed by criminals for criminal purposes. The offenders are predominantly Irish or colored immigrants whose violent assaults erupt out of quarrels over sexual infidelity, marital discord, neighborly feuds, or petty arguments in pubs. (McClintock, 1963: 57) Edwin D. Driver's study of homicide in India yields a similar pattern. Of 144 killings only 9 were committed in the course of a robbery or other crime. The remainder resulted from quarrels arising out of sexual betrayal and disputes with kinsmen or neighbors over land or implements. (Driver, 1961).

The uncertainty over the dependable gratification of creature and social needs within the underclass begets brooding anxieties over getting along in a hostile world. Anthropologist Walter B. Miller (1958) has developed this theme in terms of "focal concerns" which give direction to the lives of underclass youths. The concerns of *trouble, fate,* and *autonomy* relate to the sense of impotence which conduces to a mood of desperation. The concerns of *smartness* and *excitement* channel desperation into acts of danger and violence.

Individuals who feel threatened gravitate toward the companionship of others who perceive the same dangers. Out of the exchange of common concerns, groups form for mutual protection. Juvenile fighting gangs, motorcycle bands, activist racist organizations, and terrorist political societies exemplify arrangements for subculturally validated illegal aggression. Membership is an antidote to the sense of impotence and feelings of inadequacy. The desire for the approval of comrades pushes members to participate in group activities with a much greater potential for violence that they would engage in by themselves.

In violence-ridden communities the options available to cope with threat are narrowed by subcultural conceptions of "the right thing to do." The individual could retreat from ominous encounters, but in lower class circles this could mean stigmatization as a coward. The folkways of the lower class require meeting the threat of force with force. A vocabulary and gestures of intimidation become a standard element in the culture of the underclass. People react by carrying guns, knives, razors, or clubs. Anecdotal lore concerning offensive and defensive tactics of fighting and killing heighten a readiness and competence for violence.

Deficiency in Verbal Skills

The ignorance and inarticulateness so pervasive in the underclass handicap the ability to control others by appeal to reason or by redefining situations in ways that are less menacing. The failure of dialogue in diplomacy can lead to war; in interpersonal relations, it can lead to deadly assault. The person who is unable to get what he wants from others by persuasion is more apt to impose his will by force and punish those who withhold compliance.

An impressive body of research speaks to the importance of verbal ineptness in the predisposition to violence. Marvin W. Kahn (1959) compared fifteen murderers with twenty-four burglars admitted to a psychiatric hospital with respect to personality factors and social history. He found that the murderers are generally more conforming and had records of greater occupational and marital stability and fewer arrests than the burglars; but they also scored lower in tests of abstract reasoning and exhibited fewer resources for coping with emotions. The murderers, Kahn concluded, are less able to contain the expression of sadistic hostility and have fewer resources for the expression of feelings.

The controlling factor in verbal skill is intelligence. Experimental studies indicate that frustration born of verbal ineptitude tightens the trigger of violence. A study of prison inmates by Gordon P. Waldo (1970, 66) shows that murderers score significantly lower on intelligence tests than non-murderers. Ernest A. Wenk and Robert L. Emrich (1972) administered tests to more than four thousand wards of the California Youth Authority and found that those who committed violent crimes while under supervision, compared with those who did not, score lower on tests of intelligence and aptitude; even greater differences were obtained on non-verbal tests of intelligence. M. Joselson (1971) in a study of forty-five black and the same number of white inmates of the Florida State Penitentiary observes that those incarcerated for violent crimes score significantly lower on tests of language skill compared with those incarcerated for property offenses. In each of these studies, blacks, comprising a disproportionately large number of the violent offenders, obtained lower average test scores than whites. The extent to which the racial difference in test performance is inherent or environmental is problematic. Whatever the ultimate truth of the matter, much of the variance in test scores results from socio-economic and educational differences associated with race.

Learning Violent Defenses

Despite the highly significant association of social class with the show of violence, the fact remains that most members of the underclass do not engage in serious violence, certainly not to the extent of killing, and members of the middle and upper classes do on occasion kill. Although the classes differ considerably in the amount of killing they do, the latency for killing is rather evenly distributed among them. Accordingly, the activation of the violent propensity must be sought in some complex of factors related to class, but not class itself. Various schools of social behavioral theory agree that the failure to control aggression originates in the denial of affection and abuse in early life, but differ on the dynamics of the process. Psychoanalytically inspired psychologists and psychiatrists in a line of reasoning that ignores social factors (See Chapter 2), link violent behavior to deformities of personality imbedded in the unconscious mind. Social psychologists, more keenly attuned theoretically to environmental and situational stimulation, affirm that the perception of persons and acts as threatening and the means for coping with threats are instilled early in life through a process of learning. As psychologist George F. Solomon has pointed out, children raised in families where aggression rarely exceeds the level of verbal slights and where insults are not a sufficient instigation to physical attack seldom engage in violence. Children frequently beaten by parents or parent-substitutes can either become subdued frightened individuals or they can identify with the aggressor, becoming aggressive angry individuals. It is possible that both tendencies may be incorporated and elicited under different circumstances, as in the person who is alternatively a cowardly bully and an obsequious toady depending upon his view of the power of the person with whom he is interacting. The passive person, by the appearance of vulnerability, may unwittingly invite aggression from a domineering person, and if pushed too hard, may turn the tables against the tormentor and become the offender in a killing assault. This is a typical scenario of the female killer no longer able to endure spousal brutality.

Seymour Feshbach explains how we acquire the motive to injure others by learning the social rule of retribution from parents or other caretakers. When the child is punished for aggression he learns to associate the infliction of pain on others with the experience of pain in himself; the more intense the pain inflicted, the greater the punishment received. From the example of the discipliner, the child learns that the infliction of intentional or unfairly inflicted pain should be met with retaliation in kind.

The theme of inability to cope with insecurity in socially acceptable ways runs through a survey by James M. Weiss and associates of thirteen clinical studies of persons without past records of anti-social acts who suddenly and with little provocation killed or attempted to kill. The killers' mothers tended to domineer, overprotect, and require strict conformity to rules of conduct. The fathers were negative figures—hostile, rejecting or overstrict in one-half of the cases, or indifferent in the other half. Unable to make a satisfactory identification with either parent, the children developed feelings of insecurity, doubts about their own adequacy, and deepening dependency needs. As adults they tended to be drifters. Failure, so magnifying resentment that a slight became an intolerable affront, triggered the discharge of tension into fantasies of murderous assault. Such provocations, present in twelve of the thirteen cases, included rejection of the individual's sexual advances by his paramour, withholding of a paycheck by the employer, a wife's criticism of her husband's drinking behavior, and an ejection from a public library. Insult added to the injury of an already wounded self-esteem. "At that moment the murderer seemingly experienced the ultimate rejection, a feeling of 'I am no good, but it's your fault.' " (Weiss et al, 674)

Fights With No Rules

The escalation of fear and anger in the violent confrontation creates a situation out of the control of either combatant. The only termination, save for surrender or third party mediation, is for one or the other to prevail. Marvin E. Wolfgang applies the term *victim-precipitated* to cases in which the victim initiated the show of force by threats, the display of a weapon, or an assault. About one-fourth of the 588 homicides he studied met this condition. In most of them the offender and the victim were associated by sexual liaison, in or out of wedlock, kinship, friendship, or acquaintance. They were strangers in only 12.2 percent of the cases. Even when not the first to act aggressively, the victim is an eliciting factor by emitting the stimulus for aggression—stinging words, challenge, rejection of a dependent lover, discharge of an employee, spousal brutality or nagging. (Wolfgang, 1958)

The degree of harm portended in the initial show of aggression may influence the intensity of the response. Whether an attacker kills, wounds, or merely repels an assault often depends upon a quick assessment of the danger which confronts him. Police often justify the killing of a suspect by his apparent move to reach for a weapon. The law allows a person to do whatever is *reasonable* for self-protection in the face of perceived danger. The actor's judgment of what is reasonable embodies situationally and cultur-ally-toned attitudes, hence may differ from the judgment of a judge or jury. In indicting and convicting for victim-precipitated homicide, the court is not necessarily disagreeing with the killer's assessment of the danger to himself, but with the amount of force used to repel the attack.

Whether an assault is fatal or non-fatal depends upon a conjunction of chance and the deadliness of the offender's intentions. David J. Pittman and William Handy compared the results of their study of aggravated assault in St. Louis with the results of Wolfgang's study of homicide in Philadelphia and concluded that the two forms of crime are essentially the same, differing only in outcome, due presumably to chance factors. Their data however reveal important analytical differences. The aggravated assault cases do not match the homicide cases in two important respects. The first is the choice of weapon. The St. Louis assaults involved shooting in only 16 percent of cases compared with a much larger proportion in homicide research: 33 percent in Wolfgang's Philadelphia study, 49.5 percent in Voss and Hepburn's Chicago study, and 63.5 percent in Pokorny's Houston study. The second difference is the degree of violence-proneness of the offender as revealed by his criminal history: two-thirds of the killers in the Philadelphia study, but only a few of the assaulters in the St. Louis study had prior records of violent crime.

The Complexity of Defensive Homicide:
A Case Study

Fleshing out the statistical portrait of defensive homicides has not engaged the interest of true crime writers, primarily because these murders are committed mostly by lower class persons and lack the sensational appeal of upper class killings. Digging into the particulars of run-of-the-mill cases could reveal more than the usual drunken quarrel rising to a homicidal crescendo. The story of Bernadette Powell, convicted of second degree murder in the shooting of her ex-husband, would not have been memorialized had the case not become a *cause célèbre* of feminist activism on behalf of battered wives. Writer Ann Jones insightful account portrays the insecurities which course through the lives of socioeconomically marginal black people.

Other than Bernadette's admission that she shot her husband, the circumstances of the killing were not definitively ascertained. The details of the incident, as originally revealed to the police, fit the mold of domestic crime endemic to the ghettoes of American cities. Herman Smith, Bernadette's ex-husband, had checked himself,

Bernadette, and their six year old son into a motel one evening. At 5:45 the next morning a shooting was reported. When the police arrived, Bernadette said that the shooting was an accident, that the man had kidnapped her and her son, and when he dozed off she tried to get the gun, lodged in his pants pocket, away from him, but it "went off," the bullet striking him in the chest.

What seemed like a routine manslaughter took on a more sinister cast when the district attorney obtained evidence that the murder weapon belonged to Bernadette, that she had purchased the gun and bullets from a friend, and had been heard to say that she intended to kill Herman. Bernadette was indicted for second degree murder. She rejected an offer of the district attorney, strongly recommended by her attorney, to accept a plea to manslaughter. She insisted that she was the victim and that the killing was an accident. She apparently expected that her denial of a murderous intent could prevail against evidence that she had initiated the meeting that led to their being at the motel, had participated recently in an assault against Herman, had uttered threats to kill him, and was the owner of the killing weapon,

The all-white jury found her guilty of second degree murder. A legal support movement, organized around the issue of the battered wife syndrome and the charge that the prosecuting attorney was, himself, a wife abuser and hence not a disinterested people's advocate, provided the resources for a series of appeals, all of which failed. An attempt to reopen the case based on evidence indicating that the murder weapon belonged to Herman, as Bernadette claimed, also failed.

The backgrounds and biographies of both Bernadette and Herman typify the unfulfilled potential, broken dreams, and violent tendencies of so many young black persons on the low end of the social ladder. Bernadette, born in Binghamton, New York, was pretty and vivacious. Her mother quit school at the age of seventeen to marry and gave birth to Bernadette at the age of eighteen. The marriage didn't last long, and the father dropped out of Bernadette's life entirely. The mother, chronically ill and irregularly employed at menial jobs, left Bernadette and a younger brother with relatives who looked after them until she could find work and provide for them. Bernadette did well in school. She aspired to attend college and become a journalist. Although she got grades of A or B in all her high school subjects except math and

French, she was channeled into a curriculum for poorer students. One of only nineteen black students in a class of twelve hundred, she was placed in a commercial rather than academic course. By age seventeen Bernadette, already pregnant by Herman, quit school. She gave up the child, continued to see Herman, and terminated two more pregnancies. She returned to high school and graduated. She enrolled in a business college hoping to become an executive, but did poorly. In the meantime Herman was ardently pressing his suit. In order to keep him she quit school and married him. For a short while the marriage thrived. Bernadette gave birth to a boy. They bought a house which Herman improved and Bernadette proudly kept immaculate.

When Herman's auto reconditioning business began to falter, the beatings began and continued to the point that Bernadette sought legal relief. Undeterred by court orders to stay away from Bernadette, Herman returned to the house, severely beat her and smashed furniture. Soon thereafter the court dissolved the marriage. Bernadette, with her child, relocated from Binghamton to Ithaca, New York and went on welfare which provided a rent subsidy and payment of $377 per month. She obtained work at the IBM plant, but failed to notify social services and continued to receive welfare checks. She enjoyed entertaining; her parties at times got raucous. A fight at one of them resulted in her arrest for "menacing." She moved again, this time to Oswego, where she continued employment with IBM.

Herman, an amiable, apparently easy-going young man, started life in Biloxi, Mississippi. A high school athletic star, he won a scholarship to a college in Texas. He quit after one semester, then moved to Binghamton, New York where the paths of the two young people would cross. In the course of an irregular employment history, he acquired a criminal record, including an arrest and conviction of burglary. In a drunken brawl, he fired a shot at his adversary. What might have been prosecuted and punished as *assault with a deadly weapon,* a severely punishable felony, resulted in a conviction of simple assault and release.

Then he met and married Bernadette. They shared a desire for a better life. For a brief while their hopes seemed within reach. Herman settled down to running his business and they were able to accumulate the material things they wanted. Their troubles began when their bills outran their ability to pay. Herman drank incessantly and began to beat Bernadette, so severely that the police intervened. The beatings continued and she sought the protection of the court. After a divorce his life moved into a new phase as a procurer. He combined business with pleasure by assembling a stable of white girls for whom he pimped. He continued to drink excessively. Their child remained a link between him and his wife. Friends of Herman said he believed that she was not a fit mother, that he wanted to take the child back to the south to be raised, and that he accompanied her to the motel that fateful night for the purpose of resolving custody issues. Some thought that Herman wanted to die, and that he set Bernadette up to kill him.

Summary

Vulnerability is the prime mover of people like Herman and Bernadette in resorting to violence: Herman beat Bernadette to shore up a crumbling self-esteem; Bernadette shot Herman to get rid of a man who had shown himself to be a danger to her. But what of deadly outbursts in situations involving participants who know one another barely or not at all? The bewilderment commonly expressed at such occurrences cloaks a disingenuous denial of proclivities which the vast majority of people knowingly harbor. No special discernment is required to understand that when men fight over who is to sit on a particular bar stool, or are engaged in a stare-down, the situation for the antagonists is meaningfully not much different from the duels to the death of "gentlemen" of a discarded European tradition who, to prevail in disputes, were willing to sacrifice their lives. In claiming they are upholding their personal honor, they strive to meet a cultural standard of manly virtue, regardless of the cost.

Nor is any extraordinary knowledge required to recognize the self-serving interests at stake in street killings by inner-city children and youths. The situational context differs little, save for the availability of guns, from the fist-fights, bullyings, and gang fights of juvenile rough play a generation ago. Styles in street killings may change, but the purposes remain the same. In the 1950's newspaper readers were shocked by juvenile gang killings in street wars by means of hand made zip-guns instead of the usual killing and mayhem from fists, clubs, razors, and knives. That pattern has been raised to a higher level of efficiency by an abundance of handguns, and, for the boy drug merchants, high power assault weapons. The apparent dreary sameness of such events and the unimportance attached to the lives of the participants do not inspire writing book length true crime stories about them.

9

Recreational Murder

Murders directed to no apparent end other than the enjoyment of killing are the most baffling. The connection of killing and torture with the hedonistic side of human nature has been well documented by social historians, but has evaded the recognition of behavioral scientists. Serial murder has provided promoters of non-rationalistic explanations of homicide with a wide open field for just about every theory of morbid mentality. The seeming craziness of repetitive killing—inferred from the lack of a commensurate return, the indifference to the fate of the victim, the infliction of cruelty for its own sake, the bizarre sexual release usually sought, and the mutilation of corpses—has inspired the conviction that serial killing is a disease in the medical sense.

The extensive coverage given serial murder in the media and true crime literature and the popularity of the theme in horror fiction and films, obscure the fact that serial killings account for an insignificant fraction of all homicides. The history of crime in the western world for the past two hundred years shows a sporadic though dependable recurrence of sequential murders bearing the stamp of the same killer. The oft-repeated claim that the phenomenon is on the rise has heightened awareness and concern, but lacks substantiation beyond what can be attributed to improvements in inter-agency police communications. Trademark similarities in the killing or mutilation of murder victims found in widely separated localities, formerly unnoticed for lack of a national information clearinghouse service, are now more efficiently identified as the work of the same killer.

Clinical examiners of serial slayers cast their diagnostic nets over every factor thought to produce individual pathology—"patterns of child abuse, pathologically negative parenting, brain injuries resulting from physical traumas, inherited neurological disorders, chronic malnutrition, chronic drug and alcohol abuse, and toxic poisoning from environmental pollutants". (Norris, 35-36) While one or a combination of these states can be shown to accompany most serial killings, nearly all people who are diagnosed with any, or a combination of them do not kill, let alone serially.

In their search for the unobvious to comprehend the awfulness of serial murders, forensic psychiatrists who testify in the trials of serial killers overlook the obvious. For people who are deficient in the sentiment of pity, *killing other people can be fun, an exciting sport, or a garnish to sexual gratification.* England was shocked by the revelations of apprehended serial killers Ian Brady and Myra Hindley who, in the loneliness of the English moors, killed at least a dozen children and adolescents. They used their victims as sex objects and models for pornographic photos, then recorded their dying agonies adding Christmas music to the tape. John Gacy, alleged to have killed scores of young men while acting out his orgiastic fantasies, uncontritely regaled interviewers with accounts of the pederastic tortures he lecherously inflicted on them. Gacy lured his young male quarry by the promise of a job in his construction firm, cajoled them into sado-masochistic sexual acts involving role playing with handcuffs, which rendered them defenseless to resist strangulation, and interred their corpses, some thirty in all, under the dirt floor of his basement crawl space. When he had used up all of the burial space, he disposed of the bodies in a nearby river. Ted Bundy used his good looks and charm, while pretending to have a broken arm, to ingratiate himself with attractive young women and get them to help him lift or move objects. Disarmed of caution, they consented to accompany him on errands, in the course of which he drove them to a deserted spot, ravished, and killed them. David Berkowitz, better known as "Son of Sam," the urban huntsman, roamed the streets of the Borough of Queens, New York City at night armed with a revolver, searching out and shooting his preferred game, young women. If they happened to be in the company of a man, the hapless escort also would be shot.

Nations other than the United States have occasional serial killers. Russian Andrei Chikatilo is believed to hold the world record of fifty-three authenticated murders, committed over the period 1978 to 1990. Who would think that a middle-aged educator, with a master's degree in Russian literature, later a management functionary in industry, would have the wicked pastime of luring children and alcoholic drifters with the promise of chewing gum and vodka into secluded areas and attacking them from behind. The killings were apparently the means of a heterosexually impotent married man with grown children to pursue an alternate mode of sexual gratification. Two books on the case, one by a Russian and one by an American are in preparation and should have much to say about the psychiatric implications. The publisher of the Russian work commented that once the authorities realized that they were hunting a serial killer, the information was withheld from the public. "'We had a socialist country, and it was well understood that under socialism there were no killers— certainly not serial killers.'" (Treen & Richards, 1992)

The. infamous Dr. Marcel Petiot, a physician of dubious credentials, was convicted on twenty-six individual counts of murder by a French court in 1946. He insisted to the end that he was a patriotic resistance fighter and that his victims were traitorous collaborators and Germans. The facts and a police dossier which revealed him to have a vicious streak of sadism going back to childhood spoke otherwise. Since the issue of the trial was whether petiot committed the crimes of which he was accused. The question of motive did not arise, except that the prosecutor accused him killing for plunder. (Maeder, 1980)

Throughout accounts of serial murders run themes of adventurous risk in the stalking of human prey by stealth or deception, the excitement of the kill, and exultation in the secret knowledge that one has demoralized the community and embarrassed the police. Law-abiding people test fate by sky-diving, scaling sheer precipices with, or even without, mountain climbing equipment, bungee jumping, climbing skyscrapers, hunting ferocious animals with light weapons, walking a tight-rope without a safety net, or going over Niagara Falls in a barrel. The repetitive killer, lacking the minimal restraints imposed by empathic bonds, is free to find his sport in the terrorization and extermination of other humans.

It is reassuring to imagine a great psychic difference between ourselves and the sensation-seeker who defies peril at great personal risk, and an even greater gulf between us and the serial killer-adventurer. Surely, we think, the people who engage in such sport must be unstable. Psychiatrists give scientific respectability to this popular judgment by imputing to great risk-takers an unconscious death wish and, to serial killers, a hatred of some preferred category of victims, usually women, or self, or whatever other syndrome, the analyst thinks fits the patient's criminal behavior pattern and personal history. *That repetitive murder could be the nasty pastime of a mentally integrated human being overwhelms sensibility.* It is comforting, particularly in dealing with the demons within ourselves, to think, that anybody who destroys people for "no good reason" must be insane.

The common attribution of the serial killer's cruel abandon to the sociopathic personality syndrome is a high-sounding cover for ignorance. It is merely another way of saying that the killer lacks the quality of mercy, but doesn't inform how he got that way. The common traits of serial killers are shared by tens of thousands of men who don't kill. Unlike ordinary murderers, most of whom are lower class black males, the serial killer is a lower-middle class white male. In his study of mass and serial killers, bearing the whimsical title, *Hunting Humans*, Elliot Leyton ascertained that all of the twenty serial killers of recent decades, on whom relevant data were available, had unstable family backgrounds involving adoption, illegitimacy, institutionalization in an orphanage, juvenile home, or mental hospital, or mothers who had thrice married.

A common outcome of an irregular upbringing, is the inability to form an acceptable social identity which, Leyton believes, places the individual at a disadvantage in realizing aspirations for upward social movement. The failure to find a suitable niche in the social order and the resentment stemming from thwarted ambitions imparts a political flavor to serial killings. Leyton advances the provocative theory that erosion in the demarcations between social classes determine the class level from which serial killers are most likely to emerge at any particular stage of history. In the pre-industrial period the landed aristocracy, threatened by a restless peasantry and the burgeoning mercantile class, wreaked their sadistic fantasies on their social inferiors. During the industrial revolution the insecurities of change fell most heavily on functionaries of the new middle class—doctors, school teachers, and clerks, from whose ranks came the torturers and killers of prostitutes and easily engaged women. The early twentieth century ushered in a period of proletarian radicalism which fed the resentment of unsuccessful upward strivers at what they perceived as exclusion by bourgeois institutions. The usual contemporary serial killer overlaps the boundaries of the upper-working class and the lower-middle class. Kenneth Bianchi and Angelo Buono and Ted Bundy masked their resentment in friendly overtures toward middle-class women who paid a dear price for their responsiveness. (Leyton, 322)

The case of Wayne Williams is an exception to the rule. He is not white, comes from a stable family, and evinces none of the social or organic pathologies imputed to serial killers. Williams was the indulged only child of a closely knit black middle class couple. After quitting school at the age of eighteen, he immersed himself in a broad range of interests. He cruised about town in a vehicle that resembled an unmarked police car; sold advertising time for broadcasts from a homemade radio station, and studied television camera work. Presenting himself as a talent scout he lured young black males to interviews baited by the prospect of professional careers in entertainment. Williams was convicted of two of a string of thirty murders, mostly of youths, which plagued Atlanta between 1979 and 1981, and blamed for the remaining twenty-eight.

James Baldwin's essay, *Evidence of Things Not Seen*, takes an uncommon view of the Williams case. The allegations that the killings were a product of Williams' homosexual lust, Baldwin charges, were trumped up by the authorities and concealed the much profounder truth of the degraded status of the black man in American society. Baldwin uses Williams' case as grounds for an impassioned indictment of white racism as the cause of the black murder epidemic. Actually Baldwin says less about Williams' case than about the murderous climate established by the social and psychological, as well as physical, assaults of whites on a powerless black population. He joins the chorus that finds the evidence against Williams lacking the certainty to warrant conviction. The arrests, he noted, were for the murder of two adult men; the accusations of the murders of the twenty-eight children were an afterthought, tacked on after the trial started. After Williams' conviction, seven cases were closed as a prosecutorial convenience, rather than on the basis of evidence. The prosecution's case was weak, relying mainly on evidence consisting of Williams' being in the vicinity of a splash, heard by police, in a local river from which the body of a victim was shortly thereafter recovered, and the similarity of carpet fibres and dog hairs hairs found on some bodies and in Williams' house. Baldwin doubts, but believes worth considering, an "untidy" hypothesis for the child killings, advanced by the prominent black activist Dick Gregory, to the effect that the killings were part of a secret experiment. As Baldwin puts it, "I am being very deliberately vague, but the nature of the experiment was based on the possibility that the tip of the Black male sexual organ contained a substance that might be used to cure cancer." (Baldwin, 87)

Reading the Mind of the Serial Killer

The popular belief that serial killers must be crazy springs from the monstrousness of their crimes rather than any verifiable diagnosis. Vanity, more than practicality, accounted for the refusal of serial killer Ted Bundy to seek the protection of the insanity defense. The issue of insanity or psychopathology did not arise because he denied having committed any of the killings. Bundy took a mischievous satisfaction in playing a cat and mouse game with the crime writers who came to interview him, among them Stephen G. Michaud and Hugh Aynesworth. Bundy's answers to their questions about the killings contained in their book, *The Only Living Witness*, ooze a supercilious pretense. His account, constrained by care not to say anything that might provide the police with evidence against him or be construed as a confession, was overlaid by a tone of sly cleverness in reconstructing his "imagined" conception of the mind of the "actual" killer: the artfulness of his methods and the psychological complexity of his motives.

Yet there is a ring of candor in Bundy's roundabout way of expressing himself and in what he says of the hypothetical killer's intents and purposes. His musings, presumably projections from his own experience, contradict some of the stock thought about the absence of empathic capacities in persons labeled sociopathic and confirm other typifications. His surrogate admissions delineate the joys of killing. Taking the role of an astute observer he likened the bloody career of his "subject" to a hobby, an adventurous sport. The egoism of the hunter permits the degradation of potential victims to the level of wild game. The planning, excitement, and thrill of the hunt overrides all other considerations except eluding capture.

The interviewers' efforts to fathom Bundy's character turned up nothing remarkable in his childhood and adolescent history, other than the fact of his illegitimate birth, to blame for his murderous career. If anything, he had many qualities that augur for success in worldly pursuits. He was a college graduate and had attended law school. Women found him attractive. He spoke articulately, dressed tastefully, and ingratiated himself with those whom he wished to impress. Even at the height of his notoriety he attracted a sympathetic following of women, one of whom married him.

Most of the psychiatrists who examined Bundy found him legally sane. On the occasion of an earlier conviction for sexual assault, a psychiatric examination concluded that Bundy possessed an "antisocial personality" disorder and a tendency toward reclusiveness. The lack of any psychiatric disability severe enough to warrant a plea of insanity, prompted the diagnosis of Bundy as the archetypal sociopath, the personification of evil. An equivocal opinion delivered by Dr. Emanuel Tanay, in judging Bundy's competence to stand trial, agreed that he did not suffer from a psychotic disorder that met the legal standard of insanity, but he did "...suffer from an illness inasmuch as there is an impairment of a variety of psychic features." Dr. Tanay recommended a plea of insanity which Bundy declined. (Larsen, 298-300)

Michaud and Aynesworth held extensive interviews with Bundy spanning a period of more than a year, from January 9, 1980 to March 31. 1981. The data they obtained became the basis for their second book on Bundy. (1989) The sessions took place after his conviction in Florida of the murders of three young women and the imposition of the death penalty. Since his case was pending an appeal, it was agreed that Bundy's "conjecture" on the thoughts of the killer would be stated in the third person lest anything be said could be construed as a confession. Clearly, however, Bundy knew that his interrogators were morally convinced that he was guilty of these and many other killings.

The interviewers express disappointment with the incompleteness and evasiveness of Bundy's responses to some key questions, particularly those asking for details of various killings. His accounts of the killer's motives and attitudes, however, are deeply revealing, especially the inconsistencies, for what they say concerning his attempt to reconcile his monstrous crimes with an image of himself as an essentially decent person. Bundy had majored in psychology and evinced familiarity with psychological concepts pertaining to aberrant behavior. He glibly incorporated this vocabulary into his portrait of the hypothetical killer who tacitly represented himself, at times dropping the pretense that he was talking about someone else. When he spoke of having an *overpowering* urge to kill, he neatly, and self-servingly, fitted his thoughts to the language of the irresistible impulse doctrine of the insanity defense observed in some states. He denied any history of abuse by his mother or bad relations with other females that would justify the inference of a hatred for women, a common theme in psychodynamical theory of the repetitive killing of women. Rather, he explained, he was interested in a kind of sexual activity involving violence that dominated his fantasy. Soldiers are able to kill because they depersonalize the enemy. The same attitude appears in the person who kills indiscriminately. He is not killing a person, he is killing an image of a category of persons, in the case of Bundy's hypothetical subject, an abstraction of women "...created through the mythology of women and how they are used as objects."

In debunking scientific platitudes on serial killing, Bundy decried textbook labels that stereotype his sort of deviance; each case is unique. Contrary to the usual conception of sociopathy as a complete breakdown of character, Bundy argued that the sociopathic killer syndrome occupies a small region of the personality of the serial killer. The individual is quite normally socialized in other regards. He complained about a writer who, in describing his personality, failed to recognize "...that the great bulk of my personality is alert and vital and reality oriented and *normal* ...I *do* have a conscience. It may have gaps in it, but I have a very *strong* conscience." (Michaud et al, 1989, 264) Bundy may have been alluding to the judgment of true crime writer Ann Rule, one of his biographers, that he was a sociopath, an utterly conscienceless man. (Rule, 1980, 437) Yet when it suited his pose, Bundy contradicted his claims to conscientiousness by denying the reality of guilt which he regarded as an "illusion," a "control mechanism" that "does terrible things to our bodies." He contended that guilt over past misdeeds is not required to do the right thing in the present. He reduced the impulse to do right to a conditioned response: we conform because of the positive reinforcement from those whose opinions we esteem.

Bundy's description of the phases of a killing goes from its inception in erotic imagery to the death-dealing act. First there is the excitement and anticipation of the hunt. Then the approach: the killer engages the victim, limiting the conversation to small talk lest her personhood overshadow his image of her as an object of his fantasies. By removing her to a remote spot, the killer obtains complete control; the need for pretense ceases. The victim is taken sexually in what Bundy calls a "perfunctory" sex act, followed by the killing. In the aftermath there is remorse (uncharacteristic of the sociopath) mixed with anxiety. The killer did not relish the act of killing; it was simply a means to avoid detection.

Brian Masters' portrait of a serial killer in *Killing For Company* takes the reader on what may be the most thorough exploration of the mind of a murderer in modern true crime literature. His subject, Dennis Nilsen, a highly literate young man, who racked up a score of fifteen killings and eight attempts to become the record holding serial killer in Britain, was as forthright in admitting his killings as Bundy was circuitous in denying his. Yet there is a haziness in Nilsen's revelations that contrasts with the precision of Bundy's reconstruction of the motives for the killings he denied. Nilsen provided Masters with the data of fifty exercise books of floridly written self-analysis and many hours of interview. Masters' editing and interpretation of these materials—the details of the killings, the aftermath, and the disposal of the bodies—did not screen out the dream-like quality of Nilsen's prose which infuses some of the most gruesome reading in the annals of serial crime.

Nilsen followed a consistent pattern in his killing behavior. He sought relief from loneliness through sociability in pubs frequented by gay men. He would invite acquaintances to his flat to continue the evening. The guest, stupefied from excessive drinking,was invited to stay the night and share Nilsen's bed. Some perfunctory sex-play usually followed. Aroused from sleep, gazing upon the inert form of his guest in a deep alcohol-drugged sleep, Nilsen abandoned himself to his murderous impulses by tieing up and strangling his prey. If the luckless victim showed any sign of life, Nilsen would complete the job by drowning him in the bathtub.

Since strangulation may be accompanied by a bowel movement or urination, Nilsen would undress the newly dead, and bathe and dry the body "...to make it clean and comfortable." He would treat the body as a companion, taking it to bed, propping it up in a chair and talking to it. "The stark, unpalatable fact", as Masters saw it and made the title of his book, is that Nilsen was "killing for company." The dead bodies were like dolls in a child's make-believe tea-party. Nilsen explained that all he wanted was "...a warm relationship and someone to talk to...to be a material provider and give hospitality." Sex, according to Nilsen's notebooks, was secondary. He did not always seek sex, nor did he force sex on any of his guests; there was no penetration of the body in any of the corpses. He frequently masturbated, however, over the bodies of the victims.

Nilsen had a problem in disposing of the corpses. They were stored in a garden shed, or cupboard, or under the floorboards of the kitchen where they might be easily accessed. When he had used up the storage space, he got rid of the bodies by cutting them up and burning them in a bonfire or by removing the flesh from the bones, cutting it into little pieces, and flushing them down the toilet. This mode of disposal led to the end of his avocation in murder when a back-up of water from the toilets in all of the flats in the building caused by wads of human flesh caught in the plumbing was traced to his apartment. The police were called. Nilsen admitted his crimes. He confessed to everything, offering more information than was demanded. His barrister mounted a defense aimed at a verdict of insanity or diminished responsibility. The jury was not persuaded of any mental incapacity and found him guilty of first degree murder. The judge imposed a life sentence requiring that he serve at least twenty-five years.

Masters confronts a more difficult task than most true crime writers in explaining his subject's conduct since there is nothing in Nilsen's background or developmental experience that portends the murderous spree begun in his late twenties. Master's probe ranges more widely and deeply than the whimsical title of the book suggests. Following a standard practice of true crime writers,

Masters takes us back into the life of the killer—his origins among the poor but proud fisherfolk of the east coast of Scotland; the indifference of his father who was away from home for long periods of time and eventually left Nilsen's mother and the three children she bore him; his mother's remarriage to a man with three children of his own; and at the age of fifteen, his departure from home to join the army. He served for nine years, mainly as as a cook, acquiring the butchering skills he used later to cut up his victims. After release from the army, he was a policeman for a year, a job he found not to his liking. He resigned, and entered the civil service in the Department of Employment. His contentious, rule-bending manner incurred the displeasure of supervisors and kept him in a routine clerical niche for eight years before he was promoted to a more challenging position. His work associates esteemed him for his support of union causes, but found him boringly garrulous at times. It was not until after he became a civil servant that the killing began.

Nothing in Nilsen's social background, as reported in his notebooks, distinguishes him from the millions of other British working class males whose careers in criminal violence seldom involve more than adolescent ventures into rowdyism, minor theft, a pub fight, or wife beating. A clue that appears repeatedly in Nilsen's reflections is an obsessive imagery with death, which goes back to the viewing at the funeral of his grandfather. Attaching great portent to the experience he describes how gazing at the wrinkled countenance of the old man, "...immeasurably content, blandly satisfied", filled him with a sense of elation rather than sorrow. In the next sentence he says that "...a baleful malignant influence that seemed to emanate from the corpse itself held [him] with magnetic fascination." (Masters, 272) His preoccupation with death is expressed in remembered dreams, poetry, a narcissistic viewing of his nude body in the mirror with makeup on his face to simulate the colors of death, and eventually the series of murders which did not begin until the tedium of his civil service job had settled in upon him. His notebooks contain sketches of the victims lying dead. One shows Nilsen standing in an attitude of sad reflection by the bed on which the victim is laid out. The act of killing itself brought him a strange solace which he did not define as pleasure, but rather, relief at avoiding some calamity to himself and the victim. (Masters, 143)

Given the voluminousness of Nilsen's statement, some inconsistencies are bound to occur. Nilsen never denies that by common standards of morality his conduct is abhorrent. In one phase of his confessions he concedes the probabilty that he did the killings for the thrill it produced. Yet though he fully grasps the objective monstrousness of his conduct, he continues to insist that the subjective truth is different, that his true nature is not evil, that somehow the real Dennis Nilsen stood aside and observed while something over which he had no control took over and forced his actions. His contrition is flavored with the vocabulary of the dualism of the human moral state. He identifies himself as a "creative psychopath" (a reference to his literary and musical talents) who, under the influence of alcoholic drink, "lapses temporarily into a destructive psychopath." He disavows blame by attributing this disorder to a subconsciously rooted "sense of total social isolation" and a "desperate search for sexual identity". In a final statement after his life sentence began, when there would no longer be anything to gain by dissembling, Nilsen admits that the whole experience in which a kill was embedded— "...the drink, the chase, the social seduction, the getting the 'friend' back, the decision to kill, the body and its disposal..."—was enjoyable for its own sake. At the same time he believed that the wish to kill was present long before he started to kill and that his fantasies of himself being killed, as enacted before the mirror, were substitutes for the real thing.

On trial, Nilsen became the subject of a medley of theories and diagnoses invoked for or against a diminution of responsibility. His defense pleaded that he was suffering from a mental abnormality that prevented him from forming the specific intent to kill. Friendly psychiatrists attributed his killing state of mind to destabilizing elements in his personality, including schizoid and paranoid elements, dissociativeness, and a condition extravagantly termed, "Borderline False Self As If Pseudo-Normal Narcissistic Personality Disorder"—for short, "False Self Syndrome." According to a footnote, the notion of the False Self originated in the works of existentialist philosopher Jean-Paul Sartre and signifies "...an artificially created self-image designed to concur with expectations, while the true self remained hidden and protected." This construct was put forth to explain the apparent lack of a motive for the killings. The False Self can maintain itself when supported by affectionate relationships, but breaks down when the there is the threat of their withdrawal. The defense brought forth additional blame-disavowing formulas of forensic psychiatry—the acts of killing were a defense against going insane; Nilsen did the killings in a zombie-like state; and, the last ditch of the insanity defense: the perpetration of such horrendous crimes proves the insanity of the killer.

Masters, unrestrained by the rules of legal evidence, combed the literature of psychiatry, religion, and literary allusion to seek clues to Nilsen's homicidal tendencies. He concluded that they were the deadly expression of the common run of human foibles: egocentricity, overdeveloped fantasy life, and the perversion of normal aggressive and sexual tendencies. Masters does not implicate sociological factors in Nilsen's behavior. Britain's very small homicide rate, the lack of a homicidal subculture as in the United States, and a social system which offers fewer incentives for materialistic crime by elevating class loyalty above upward mobility, has contributed to the emphasis on individual factors characteristic of European criminology.

Elliot Leyton's insightful observation, that "[T]he...[serial killer]...of the modern era is the man who straddles the border between the upper-working class and the lower middle class" cogently applies to Nilsen, who occupied that transitional status. Leyton notes that although most serial killers "punish" those above them in the system, such as unambiguously middle-class figures represented by university women, "[o]ccasionally, as with Robert Hansen in Alaska or cousins Kenneth Bianchi and Angelo Buono in Los Angeles...they continue a metaphor from the earlier era and discipline unruly prostitutes and runaways." (Leyton, 322) Nilsen fits the more traditional type in his selection of victims: they were all homeless men younger than himself.

Masters refers to a psychological profile of the sadistic mass murderer constructed by Dr. Robert Brittain (Masters, 246-7) which remarkably fits Nilsen. The composite describes a person who is introspective and withdrawn, studious and pedantic, shy, inadequate, uncommunicative, sometimes presents himself as a pseudo-intellectual, rarely shows his temper, does not relate to violence, and feels inferior to others except in relation to his offenses. Success in crime accords him an arrogance, and a feeling of superiority to the police, which his desire to exhibit may render detection and apprehension acceptable for the limelight afforded by the publicity. Another feature of Brittain's profile, "He is at his most dangerous when he has suffered a loss of self-esteem, such as might happen if he were demoted at work," (Masters, 246) aptly applies to Nilsen who complained of criticism and unappreciation of his work by supervisors. The fact that the killings did not start until after he began his career in the civil service suggests a connection between the klllings and the disparagement he suffered, although the nature of the link is unspecified. A psychodynamically oriented analyst could invoke the stock frustration-aggression theory, that setbacks to Nilsen's ego generated a free floating hostility which he displaced onto his unsuspecting drinking companions. But such an analysis would require additional links to account for the willingness to use so extreme a means of catharsis as murder.

The traits in Dr. Brittain's composite portrait imply a sensitivity not apparent in the general run of American serial murderers. Most of the American variety, with the exception of Ted Bundy and later, Jeffrey Dahmer, are doubtfully studious, pedantic, or shy, and seldom make intellectual pretensions.

John Wayne Gacy had neither the suaveness of a Bundy nor the intellectuality of a Nilsen; he comes across as an uncouth boor, the quintessential sociopath intent on gratifying his own needs regardless of the cost to others, which came to thirty-three known deaths and the possibility of yet undiscovered victims. His conduct provided his psychiatric examiners with a striking example of narcissism and sado-masochism.

From extensive interviews with Gacy, author Tim Cahill acquired information that gives some indication of how Gacy perceived his victims, himself, and his conduct. His two marriages were not successful. He sought fast sex from young males he picked up. He denied being a homosexual; he preferred to think of himself as bisexual. He explained that he was a workaholic and didn't have time for the foreplay required in sex with females; he wanted only release.

Because he used the name of "Jack Hanley" when he was out on his "chicken hunting" forays, the medical examiners and his lawyers suggested to Gacy the idea of a dual personality. Gacy took the cue and played the role to the hilt. While under psychiatric examination, Hanley and Gacy came together in confrontation.

Gacy was interested only in consensual sex with boys; Hanley was the killer. Later Gacy repudiated the pose of a dual personality.

Gacy got control of the situation in which he killed by playfully showing his intended victims a handcuff "trick", from which escape was possible if they could figure it out. When the unsuspecting "guest" tried the trick and could not free himself, Gacy would jocularly inform him that the trick was that a key was needed to remove cuffs. Gacy would then subject his captive to a variety of torturous pederastic activities. A "rope trick" involved tying a complicated series of knots in a noose placed around the neck to constrict the carotid artery in order to induce a more intense orgasm, a practice known to produce an annual accidental death toll of young males while masturbating. Gacy, however, used the procedure on his helpless victims to kill them. Their death gurgles would accompany his orgasm.

Once Gacy put the handcuffs on a young man, and when he refused to remove them, the intended victim, an athletic type, kicked Gacy in the head and recovered the key. The "other guy", "Hanley," Gacy's co-personality, was watching and learning from Gacy's mistakes. Next time he would put the cuffs on with the victim's hands behind his back, which would prevent such a maneuver.

Gacy rationalized his attitude toward the victims by casting them in the role of low-life male-hustlers, *jack-rollers*, intent on getting payment and then fleeing without rendering service; they deserved punishment. Actually none of the victims solicited him. He took the initiative, targeting hitch-hikers, arrivals at an interurban bus terminal, or job applicants for his construction business. In some instances he would flash a counterfeit police badge at a pickup, demanding to see identification, force the "arrestee" into his car, and eventually bring him to his house where the sex play occurred. He liked slender, blond, nicely, but not overly muscled youths. To disarm any suspicions he would often take a fatherly role toward his pickups giving them advice on how to live their lives and be a man.

Gacy so disvalued the lives of the young men who entered his deadly orbit that he killed them for minor economic gain as well as for pleasure. One of his pickups had a car he wanted to sell. Gacy expressed interest and asked to see the title. After killing the boy, he took the title, forged his name to it, and sold the car to one of his young employees, allowing the buyer to pay off the car by making payments to Gacy.

Gacy was a heavy drinker, took an inordinate number of valium pills, and smoked marijuana frequently. He was a braggart, posing as a big shot with important political connections and ties to the underworld "syndicate," and claimed to have degrees in sociology and psychology. Despite his instabilities of character, he operated a successful contracting business which enabled him to influence youths by promises of jobs, maintained cordial business relationships with other contractors and suppliers, organized neighborhood festivals, and was recognized for his services to the Democratic Party.

The defense psychiatrists declared that Gacy was temporarily insane during the killings, that his crimes were the product of an irresistible impulse, originating in childhood relationships with a strict, harsh father who found his son lacking in qualities of manliness, an attitude which Gacy turned onto his teen-age victims. The defense experts perceived in Gacy every textbook manifestation of a dangerous personality. As one of them put it, "...he has a personality disorder called a borderline personality organization with a subtype of antisocial or psychopathic personality manifested by episodes of an underlying condition of paranoid schizophrenia [as a result of which, Gacy] did lack substantial ability to conform his behavior at the time of each of those crimes...to the requirement of the law." (Cahill, 341)

The prosecution psychiatrists completely disagreed with their defense colleagues. To them Gacy was a liar. He was too well organized to be insane. He ran a business. He participated in politics. He was too well connected to reality to qualify as a psychotic. His handcuff and rope tricks—the conning of the victims to allow these tricks to be played on them—required a calculatingly playful manner. Getting one of his employees to dig holes under the crawl space to accommodate prospective victims bespoke planning and rationality. "I don't think," acerbically commented one of the prosecution psychiatrists, "that a person who plans to have an irresistible impulse in the future could be having irresistible impulses." His remark referred to thirty-three irresistible impulses for which a plea of temporary insanity was entered. The death penalty imposed on Gacy and confirmed on appeal in 1984, has yet to be applied in 1992.

The career of serial killer Jeffrey Dahmer, himself white, who in 1991 confessed to killing seventeen young men, most of them non-white, over a thirteen year period will undoubtedly generate a spate of true crime books—at the time of this writing three have already appeared (Davis, Norris, Schwartz)—which speculate luridly on Dahmer's motives. Defense psychiatrist Dr. Fred Berlin, a Johns Hopkins University specialist in sexual disorders, was more specific. He declared that Dahmer knew right from wrong, but had uncontrollable urges to kill and have sex with dead bodies. He proclaimed a novel diagnostic metaphor which will doubtfully become a staple of forensic psychiatry: Dahmer suffers from a "cancer of the mind," which deprives him of the will power to stop. (Associated Press Wire Report, *Sarasota Herald Tribune*, Tuesday, February 4, 1992)

Dennis Nilsen's chronicler, Brian Masters, has drawn a parallel between the killing career of Londoner Dennis Nilsen and Milwaukeean Jeffrey Dahmer. Masters' article in the American magazine, *Vanity Fair,* is more interesting for what more it reveals about Nilsen, his affability and sense of humor, than for what it tells about Dahmer. Both had troubled childhoods, were loners, and sought companionship and sex with men. Each came from a home broken by divorce. Nilsen's parents were poor people; Dahmer's were well off; his father was a chemist with a doctor of philosophy degree. They employed the same *modus operandi,* roaming bars (or pubs) in search of quarry. Both brought their unsuspecting "guests" to their apartments for a drink, got them drunk and strangled them. Each admitted to having sex with the dead bodies and admitted to having eaten the flesh of victims. Like Nilsen, Dahmer had a body disposal problem: the police found dozens of body parts in his foul smelling apartment.

To help develop insights into Dahmer's thinking, Masters called upon Nilsen, in prison, who willingly projected himself into Dahmer's situation to psychologize on his motives. Nilsen's analysis has more of a sociological than psychological flavor. He speculates that growing up in a female-headed family with no adult male present during his later childhood years, deprived him of a role model for the interpersonal skills needed for worldly success. He was an oddball among the children with whom he grew up, striving for attention at school by doing unseemly things. He was kicked

ıe United States Army for drunkenness. The killings, Nilsen
ıes, taking a trendy perspective in American thinking, were
an expression of power, an attempt to compensate for being a
nobody. He could not command the esteem of people in the real
world, so he obtained it in fantasy, in the reduction of his
companions to utter passivity by killing them. Eating the flesh of his
victims proclaimed the ultimate power over them by the literal act of
possession. Dahmer's inability to relate to people made him both
victim and predator. His disorder lay in the paradox that the
fulfillment of his need for love required the death of his love object.

Masters, taking over from Nilsen, perceives Dahmer after his
arrest, in a state of abject remorse, evidenced by profuse apologies
to the families of his victims. Anguish, he muses, may be too mild a
word to describe "the depths of introspective horror which now
afflict him." (Masters, 1991, 84)

The reader is impelled to ask: Where was this empathic capacity
when he was on his killing spree? To ask why it suddenly
materialized only after he was apprehended is to imply that Dahmer
was cynically trying to arouse in others a sense of pity whereby to
mitigate the gravity of his crimes. Yet there are grounds to believe
that Dahmer was genuinely contrite, but not because of any sudden
moral conversion. The existence of contradictions in thought within
the individual is a common human experience and need not signify
deception or mental disturbance. An explanation uncomplicated by
flights of psychological speculation rests on two assumptions. First,
there is no reason to think that Dahmer, or any other serial killer,
approves of killing in the abstract. They know that they depend on
an orderly society in order to pursue their sport and they certainly
wouldn't want the fate they inflict on others for themselves. Indeed,
they manifest their recognition of the awfulness of killing by
becoming, like Ted Bundy, staunch opponents of capital punishment when they face death themselves. Or, like Henry Lee Lucas,
self-proclaimed killer of over a hundred women, they offer to pay
the supreme penalty as the only means of expiating so monstrous a
crime, no doubt aware that there is little probability that it will be
exacted.

The second assumption relates to Dahmer's motives. Once
Dahmer was apprehended killing became an irrelevancy, no longer
available to serve the end to which it had been directed, whether
power or sensuality. The source of tension between moral

sentiments and homicidal desires was removed. He could now in all honesty display the remorse appropriate to the horror of murder and thereby win from his keepers and examiners the approval that had eluded him in his previously unfulfilled life.

Nilsen's judgment that Dahmer's killings were primarily an expression of power to shore up a stunted self-esteem reiterates the widely diffused cliché that sexual assaults or murders, whether heterosexual or homosexual, are aimed at domination over the victim rather than sexual gratification. But like many clichés of behavioral analysis, it has a circular quality, explaining the motive for an assault by the inherent necessity of exercising physical power in order to effect the assault. This illogic fails to distinguish between means and ends, between instrumentality and consummation. The advocates of the power explanation argue the obvious, that violence is unnecessary because sex is readily obtainable non-violently. But the "obvious" is not true for everyone. Loners like Nilsen and Dahmer, perhaps Bundy, or even extroverted types like John Wayne Gacy, find in the achievement of absolute control over their victims, the most direct route to sexual gratification. They lack the sensitivities, the skill, the time, or the patience for the usual overtures leading to negotiation and agreement.

The situational backdrop of Dahmer's killings suggests that his motive in killing was similar to Nilsen's, characerized by Masters as "Killing For Company." A socially inept person from early childhood, Dahmer sought sexual gratification in non-human objects or with humans whom he could control totally. Killing people was one way of achieving that control, although he sought alternative means, such as using a power drill to lobotomize a "guest" whom he had disabled with drugs. He retained parts of those whom he killed, using portions of the viscera with which to have sex and flesh which he cooked and ate. Dahmer sought his sexual pleasure in lying next to the bodies of his "partners" and doing the things that lovers normally do—hugging, kissing, and obtaining sexual release.

The sexual preference for inanimate things or non-consenting persons—in the case of Nilsen or Dahmer, dead persons—is known as paraphilia, a condition familiar to clinical practitioners, and not in itself proof of cognitive impairment. For people of lively erotic imagination who have difficulty with interpersonal relationships, paraphilia makes sense and can take different forms. The case of London serial killer and necrophiliac, John Reginald Christie, convicted of the murder and rape of thirteen women, including his wife, exemplifies a heterosexual serial killer in a hurry for sexual consummation. Seen by acquaintances and associates as shy, maladroit, and as his trial revealed, sexually inept, he kept the courtship preliminaries to a minimum. He invited women to his house, got them drunk, gassed them, copulated with their corpses, and like his homosexual counterparts, disposed of the bodies on the premises of his residence. He went to the gallows in 1953. (Cox *et al*, 176)

Summary

A close inspection of the twists and turns in individual cases puts a damper on the attempt to draw a profile of serial killers based on experiential or demographic traits. The common denominator of serial killers is less a bundle of traits than an ego-inflating self-conception: *the bold lone adventurer into uncharted areas of human experience: the secret agent of one's darkest desires, the holder of astounding secrets straining to be known. Keeping them is test of strength of character; telling them is a revelation of superiority.* As a practical matter they seek their victims in the type of persons whom they feel able to manipulate socially.

The rationalizations advanced by the more articulate serial killers to account for their villainy exemplify the application to oneself, in a form of dramatic self-display rather than absolution, of themes which the rich literary culture makes available to those who transgress the most inviolate rules. Nilsen's were couched in Dostoevskian phrases of the tragedy of the human condition. In the manner of Raskolnikov he racked his thoughts and feelings in an attempt to understand himself. He was an angel and devil united in one; his good self protected the bad self. The good part couldn't turn in the bad part without destroying himself. Bundy, in making his surrogate "confessions" took his cues from the media casting of him as the well educated, urbane, irresistible womanizer. He adopted a philosophical pose to couch his "impersonal" assessment of the serial killer in the rhetoric of social behavioral science which his college education afforded him.

10

Murder For High Principle

Killing to "right a wrong" may offend sensibilities more or less than than any other category of motive because on issues of morality, one person's right may be another's wrong. The action films in which lawmen or decent citizens, as played by Clint Eastwood or Charles Bronson, take extra-legal means to obliterate the scum who prey on innocent people play to sympathetic audiences. Obversely, the hero is the lawman who prevents the vigilantes from lynching a suspect who, to drive home the point, is actually innocent. The lynch mob, the political assassin, the terrorist, the mercy killer, and the self-appointed dispenser of deadly retribution justify the breach of laws of institutional order by an appeal to some higher moral authority than enacted law—the will of God, or some abstract principle such as justice, national honor, inalienable rights, or the wickedness of the victim. The Iranian ayatollahs declared themselves the magistrates of God in placing the blasphemer, Salman Rushdie, under a death sentence.

In rare instances the appeal is to principles of evil institutionalized in the worship of Satan, although most Satanic devotees deny that Satanism involves a commitment to evil acts. Richard Ramirez, "The Night Stalker," claimed that the thirteen murders for which he was tried were rites of Satanic worship. (Kahaner)

Morally justified killing finds its most exalted expression in the wiping out of one people by another. In antiquity, wars were often concluded by the victor razing the enemy's cities and slaughtering its inhabitants. Hordes led by Attila the Hun and Genghis Khan obliterated hundreds of communities in their westward migrations. The practice continued in the medieval period in Europe and Asia. Crusaders on their way to redeem the Holy land from the heathen Muslim tarried to plunder and slaughter Jews and non-conforming Christian sects of Albigensians and Hussites.

Neither biological evolution nor progress has lifted humanity above the genocidal solution to political problems. Colonization provided the cover for deliberate policies of extermination. The natives of Tasmania were hunted as animals by the English colonists and driven to extinction before the close of the nineteenth century. The twentieth century has witnessed the elevation of the mass killing of defenseless populations to a science by means of modern technology and organizational efficiency. Leo Kuper's book, *Genocide*, details the depletion of whole ethnic populations including the Jews of Europe, the Armenians in Turkey, the Bengalis in Bangladesh, and the mutual slaughter of the Hutu and Tutsi in Burundi. In Uganda religious, political, and ethnic minorities were subjected to random, whimsical, indiscriminate slaughter by security forces made up of Sudanese mercenaries and members of Idi Amin's tribal group. (Kuper, 167) An update of Kuper's book could show the continuing strength of the genocidal impulse, even after the horrible lessons of recent history, by detailing the carnage attending the "ethnic cleansing" by Serbian forces in areas of what was Yugoslavia.

Mass Murder as a Political Solution

The normality of mass killing is nowhere more authoritatively shown than in the minutely documented recent historical record of genocide as a deliberate policy of nations notable for their contributions to science, art, philosophy, and religion. The German Third Reich combined modern technology, logistical science, and opinion management to plan and carry out the annihilation of the Jews. The policy-makers manufactured false accounts of crimes against the national security which they blamed on the victim population, and appealed to sentiments of racial purity and the fear of cultural contamination to justify the removal of the "cancerous" Jewish population.

The killers exhibited all of the sensibilities, sentiments, and outward signs of decency. When called to account for their crimes, they excused themselves by blaming higher authority: as befits a good soldier, they were only carrying out orders. Studies of the careers of Hitler era German death camp warders whose extermination of thousands of prisoners unquestionably met universal standards of the definition of murder, attest to the psychologically unexceptional nature of homicide.

Christopher R. Browning's book, *Ordinary Men* is an intensive case study of a German killing unit stationed in occupied Poland during World War II. The complement of the ostensible "police" force consisted of men in their thirties and forties, too old for conscription in the army, who in civilian life had been a cross-section of petty professionals and bureaucrats, skilled and semi-skilled workers. Some were revolted by the job of shooting thousands of Jews in the back of the neck. For many it became routine, and for some, amusing. Ethical qualms at killing defenseless men, women, and children were put to rest by their commander's assurance that the Jews were enemies who deserved their fate.

Hannah Arendt's controversial essay on the trial of soldier-bureaucrat Adolph Eichmann who directed the round-up and dispatch of Europe's Jews to the killing camps, pleading that he was merely an obedient soldier carrying out orders, is appropriately subtitled *The Banality of Evil*. The Nazi experience shows that the latency for genocidal mass murder abides in culturally ingrained traits that we find admirable in a people. A German journalist chararacterizes what is typically Prussian: "Punctuality, precision, order, thrift, discipline, diligence and dedication to duty. These qualities were perverted into the service of a bureaucratically organized mass murder that became part of German history." (Kinzer) Officers in the Nazi SS, Hitler's private army, entrusted with the day to day processing of the slaughter would return to their homes after a hard day's work to take up proper familial roles. SS head, Heinrich Himmler, under whose direction the death camps operated, gave pep talks to the warders to help them overcome their job stress. He praised them for their courage and decency in the face of the painful, but necessary, job of bringing about the final solution to the Jewish problem.

The moral onus for the holocaust does not rest exclusively on the Germans. The removal of total civilian Jewish populations in

Nazi occupied or Nazi-allied territories including France, Poland, Hungary, Croatia, the Ukraine, and Italy, was aided and abetted by local people, many of whom lived in communities near the slaughtering grounds or death camps. They knew of the fate planned for the victims, and benefitted materially, taking over the houses and possessions of their former neighbors. There was also silence from religious leaders and indifference from political leaders who knew what was happening, and even exhortation by clerics in countries with long histories of animosity toward Jews to hasten the evacuation.

Regarded as an act of war when done by nations, or a blow for freedom when done by terrorists or guerillas, mass killing becomes an individual pathology or a social problem when commited by a gang of miscreants as execrable as Charlie Manson's family. In a riot of bloodletting, shooting and stabbing, they killed film actress Sharon Tate, wife of Polish film director, Roman Polanski, and four guests in the Polanski home. The next day they killed Leno and Rosemary LaBianca, a wealthy couple who resided in the same area. Yet the Manson folk, believed responsible for twenty or more murders in southern California, were moved by a sense of mission kindred to the zeal that sustains terrorism and genocidal warfare. Vincent Bugliosi, the district attorney who prosecuted the Manson family, relates in his book *Helter-Skelter*, how he arrived at his assessment of the attitudes and sentiments that motivated the killings.

Manson's background has Hitlerian parallels. He emerged from prison at the age of thirty-two in 1967 having spent most of his life in penal instututions. He headed for San Francisco's Haight-Ashbury district, then a fertile recruiting ground of alienated young people whose lives centered around drugs and sex. He assembled a coterie of impressionable, poorly educated, young women who had run away from home and a smaller number of equally rootless young men and bent them to his will. He promised to provide for their material needs, and to to lead them to sanctuary and spiritual salvation out in a California desert retreat.

Manson was self-educated. What he taught himself coalesced into the messianic message he preached. Posing as more than a religious leader—prophets abounded in Haight-Ashbury's hippy world—he proclaimed himself Christ-Manson and awed his followers with the recollection of looking down at his mother, Mary, from the cross to which he was nailed. His preachments differed sharply from the conventional Christian message. He denied the wrongness of killing; whatever happened was right. A reading of the German philosopher, Nietzsche (also an inspiration to Hitler) imbued in him a belief in the master race with its corollary of the inferiority of the black race.

For Bugliosi the key to understanding the Tate and LaBianca murders is in the term "Helter-Skelter," the title of a Beatles song, endowed by Manson with the connotation of doomsday. According to information given by followers, Manson prophesied that there would be a terrible struggle between blacks and whites. The revolution would start with blacks invading the homes of wealthy whites, then move out into the streets as whites retaliated in anger. Millions would die and the blacks would prevail. While all this was going on the Manson people would be safe in their desert refuge. Once in power the blacks wouldn't be able to administer things, so they would gratefully relinquish management to superman Charles Manson who would take over and become the ruler of the world.

The LaBianca and Tate killings, Manson reasoned, would transform the apocalyptic vision into reality. The words printed in blood on the walls of the murder site—"Pig" and "Death to Pigs" were intended to mislead the world into thinking that the black assault on whites had commenced. The circumstances of the killings closely followed Manson's prophecy, preached to his followers six months before the event.

As preposterous as Manson's plan for world domination may seem from a hindsight of twenty-five years, it bears remembering that Adolph Hitler's *Mein Kampf* was steeped in an equally asinine imagery. The testimony of the killers in Manson's entourage clearly shows that any guilt or regret over the killings was submerged by their obedience and dedication to the leader and his cause. A willingness to kill inoffensive defenceless people on command is a common historical event. The implantation in normal people of an unquestioning response to orders from authority to hurt others appears in the classic psychological experiment by Stanley Milgram and David Rosenhan. The subjects of the study, believing themselves to be participants in a psychological investigation into the effect of pain on learning, were told by "scientists" wearing white laboratory smocks, to administer painful electrical shocks to people being tested. The "learners" were actually confederates of the researcher posing as subjects. Despite the anguished cries of pain of the "slow learners," even after the discrediting of the person posing as the authority figure in the experiment, the subjects persisted in delivering the shocks. (Milgram)

Terrorist Murder

Terrorism as practiced in recent times by the Irish Republican Army, the Baader-Meinhof gang, the Red Army, a number of Palestinian organizations, and allegedly covertly by some governments, involves the use of impersonal murder as a political tool. Abandoning any pretense of observing civilized rules of warfare, terrorists kill indiscriminately to impress the enemy that no one is safe from them. Some of their most notorious activities include the kidnap and torture of governmental, business, and educational officials; machine-gunning crowds in airline terminals; slaying the members of the Israeli Olympics team in 1972; high-jacking the cruise ship *Achille Lauro* and passenger planes and killing passengers. The greater the fear and outrage they evoke in the target population, the more successful the venture. Terrorists are not drawn from the impoverished and disinherited masses. The European, American, and Japanese activists, and the leadership of the Middle Eastern terrorist societies are of middle and upper class background, well educated, often professional, with pretensions to intellectalism. They feed on one another's discontent, and pool their radical ideologies into a nihilistic philosophy that permits a no-holds barred assault on conventional values to achieve their goals.

Killing to "Enforce" the Law

Lynch law, really the revocation of law, takes different forms. Less malign is the informal suppression of crime under frontier conditions before police and courts arrive on the scene. Much worse, a callous regard for whole groups, which makes it possible to tolerate the unwarranted killing of their members, is not alien even to societies with a democratic ethos. Until the strengthening of civil rights laws in the United States beginning in the nineteen-fifties, officialdom reacted feebly or indifferently to lynch mobs. Participants in lynching parties justified their appropriation of the judicial function by charging the courts with failure to properly exercise it. Ralph Ginzburg has documented from newspaper accounts over five thousand lynchings in the period of American history from 1859 to 1962. Nearly all occurred in the American south, and were justified by the lynchers as necessary to keep the Negro in his place or, in cases of alleged rape, to vindicate the honor of southern womanhood. Many were committed on the basis of unverified charges or false information.

The informal executions generated a festive atmosphere as the executioners indulged a monstrous cruelty. In a typical instance, a nineteenth century Georgia mob burned alive a Negro, Sam Holt, for the alleged murder of a white farmer and an assault on his wife. Before setting him afire they cut off his ears, fingers, and genitals. Appeals to the mob to let justice take its proper course went unheeded. The victim was brought before the mother of the rape victim who recognized him as being from the area. He was not identified by the rape victim herself since she was considered too ill to be disturbed. The next day the *Atlanta Constitution* editorialized on behalf of the lynch mob that an evenhanded evaluation of the event required taking into account the heinous crime of Sam Holt: "Remember the slain husband, and, above all, remember that shocking degradation which was inflicted by the black beast, his victim swimming in her husband's warm blood as the brute held her to the floor." (Ginzburg, 18) Before Sam Holt was burned, his killers said that he confessed, implicating Lije Strickland, a Negro preacher, who paid Holt twenty dollars to kill the farmer. As the mob was about to lynch the terror-stricken man of the cloth, The owner of the plantation on which Strickland lived, intervened assuring them of Strickland's innocence and expressing doubt that the man ever had twenty dollars. The mob voted not to hang Strickland, but rather than see their afternoon's sport interrupted, changed their minds and hanged him anyway. Before allowing him to die they cut off his ears and severed the small finger of one hand. Attached to his dead body was a piece of paper with the words, "We must protect our ladies." (Ginzburg, 12-21)

Lynching, a rare occurrence anymore, is associated with semi-literate, poor, rural and semi-rural white populations in the American south. The blacks learned, however, from the whites; Professor Ira Wasserman, an authority on lynching informs me that blacks were themselves responsible for ten percent of the total number of lynchings.

The sentiments that prompt lynching extend into the upper reaches of the social pyramid, as the sensational murder trial of naval Lieutenant Thomas Massie, his socialite mother-in-law, Mrs. Grace Fortescue, and two Navy enlisted men attests. Theon Wright's book, *Rape in Paradise*, details how sympathetic officials made sure that the defendants would receive no punishment if convicted.

The setting was Hawaii which, in the pre-statehood period of the early nineteen-thirties when the crime occurred, was a virtual fiefdom of the United States Navy. Aggrieved by the mistrial and release of five men accused of raping his wife, Thalia, Lt. Massie, exhorted by his mother-in-law, led the two enlisted men in kidnapping, shooting, and killing one of them, Joe Kahahawaii.

Thalia Massie came from a well-connected old Kentucky bluegrass family. Her husband was a Naval Academy graduate. The alleged rapists were racially mixed native Hawaiian and Asian working class "boys." The celebrated trial attorney Clarence Darrow, by then in his declining years, led the defense for the alleged killers. For what it might be worth, Darrow injected the insanity issue proposing that Lt. Massie was so upset by vicious rumors circulating around the island—his wife actually had not been raped, she was unhappily married, and her husband had broken her jaw—that the vindication of her character and the integrity of their relationship became an obsession for him, culminating in his mental breakdown at the moment of the killing. The rumors may not have been ill-founded. Two years after the trial, Thalia Massie was awarded a divorce decree on the grounds of unbearable cruelty.

Checked by the prosecution in his attempt to construct a defense of insanity, Darrow appealed to the "unwritten law," that all else failing in achieving the vindication of a woman's honor, the husband is justified in taking the law into his own hands. The real issue, argued Darrow, was not the guilt or innocence of Joseph Kawahawaii, but whether Massie truly believed that Kahahawaii had raped his wife. The defense also argued that, although the victim was held at gunpoint, Massie did not intend to kill his captive; Kawahawaii lunged toward Massie, and in the ensuing fracas Massie shot him.

Although the rape issue was unresolved, the case having ended in a mistrial, Darrow's closing argument for the "unwritten law" leaned heavily on the presumption that Mrs. Massie had been raped and that the victim was one of the rapists. In arguing that there was no evidence to contradict her version, Darrow ignored the powerful alibi testimony produced by the defense in the rape trial.

The jury did not go so far as to grant Darrow's plea for an acquittal, but they agreed that the facts of the killing warranted a conviction of manslaughter rather than second degree murder. The convicted killers were given mandatory ten year prison sentences. The disposition had no practical effect. The trial had heated up racial tensions on the island and the mainland. High naval and governmental officials decided that no prison time would be imposed. After the elapse of one hour, spent with attorneys and well-wishers in the judge's chambers, Lt. Massie, Mrs. Fortescue, and the two enlisted men were freed under a secret pre-arranged order of commutation of the sentence by the governor.

Minority Terror

The "zebra" killings represent an exceptional instance of racially toned, politically motivated, impersonal murder by a minority group. Over a period of one-hundred seventy nine days in 1973 and 1974, a group of black men, proclaiming themselves soldiers of Islam in a war against the "blue-eyed devils," terrorized San Francisco whites by random shootings. The motives of the terrorists were not purely political. Killing the victims would have sufficed to make their point. These assassins, however, were not the ostensibly idealistic Middle Eastern or European varieties, driven solely by the desire to convince their oppressors that further denial of political independence is too costly. They had serious records of violent predatory crime before embarking on their killing spree and acquired the virulent anti-white slant of the early Black Muslim movement while doing time in prison. They spiced their "protest" with predatory diversions of rape and robbery, and gratuitous mutilation. Twenty-three people were attacked; fifteen did not survive.

Information from survivors and witnesses that the killers were black instigated an unprecedented police manhunt. Young black males were stopped on the streets, questioned, and searched for weapons. The police were condemned by civil rights and black activist organizations protesting alleged infringements of civil rights. The police responded that in cases where the offender was known to be white, they treated white possible suspects in the same manner. The case was finally broken when one of the gang saw a police sketch in a newspaper of two suspects, one of whom looked very much like himself. Propelled by fear of identification and lured by a $30,000 reward, he became the state's star witness. Four of his associates were tried and convicted in a trial that lasted over a year, the longest in California history. (Howard)

Murder for Salvation

A remarkable criminal defense based on the Christian tenets of sin and grace was constructed in the case of John List, accused of coldbloodedly murdering his wife, three children, and mother. Mary S. Ryzuk's book, *Thou Shalt Not Kill*, shows how oppositely a killing can be construed: by the defense as a prayerful act, and by the prosecution as a fiendish expression of rampant egoism.

The motive for the killings, List's attorney pleaded, stemmed from his client's deep religious convictions. The killer really intended to save his family from a fate worse than the death he inflicted upon them. List, an accountant, was faced with serious financial problems. He felt he could no longer support his family. He feared the disgrace of bankruptcy, losing the house and moving to a bad neighborhood where the children might be corrupted by drugs. By his beliefs concerning sin and redemption, John List had license to kill all the members of the family. Mrs. List did not share her husband's religious convictions; she no longer accompanied him to church and had asked that her name be stricken from the church rolls. His relations with her were further abraded by the fact that she had syphillis, contracted in a previous marriage, which was affecting her brain. His mother, whom he esteemed as a good Christian woman, was old and had few resources of her own. The Lists' high school age daughter was interested in a career in the theatre which, List thought, would undoubtedly corrupt her soul. The two younger children were still innocent; would that he could keep them that way.

The options? Desert his family; but that would not discharge his responsibility to them. Suicide offered no solution because in the Lutheran religion it would guarantee his going to hell. But if he killed them a loving God would receive them into joyous salvation and he would still have a chance through sincere repentance to get to heaven.

So on December 7, 1971 List shot them all to death, doing it, he said, as painlessly as he could and without warning to spare them a moment of dread. He wrote notes to the milkman, to discontinue delivery, and to the childrens' teachers informing that they would be out of school since the family was going away to be with a sick relative. He left a number of letters where they would be easily found: one to his pastor explaining the deed; others to those who would have the task of cleaning up and disposing of the bodies and the property.

The letters were the last traces of John List in Westfield, New Jersey. Twelve days later he applied for a social security card under the name of Robert Clark and for the next eighteen years, made a new life living in Denver, Colorado and Richmond, Virginia. He found the happiness he missed in his former life. He remarried and maintained his ties with the Lutheran Church. The pastors of the various churches in which he worshipped later testified at his trial that he was a dedicated church worker and a person of fine character.

Eighteen years after his disappearance, List was featured on the television program, *America's Most Wanted*. A neighbor who viewed the show reported him to the police. He was arrested in Virginia and extradited to New Jersey to stand trial. Since the reason List gave for the killings might stretch the credulity of jurors or smack of religious fanaticism, his attorney, Elijah Miller, did not insist on its truth in any objective sense, but rather presented it as the defendant's definition of his problem. Call List's solution crazy or insane if you will. This is exactly what Miller did; he entered a plea of not guilty by reason of mental defect. He summoned two psychiatrists who had examined List and found that he suffered from an obsessive-compulsive personality disorder, which, one of them testified, refers to a tendency to be "excessively conscientious, moralistic, scrupulous, and judgmental of others, as well as [oneself]." They agreed that the pressure of financial problems coupled with his religious beliefs set him on a murderous course from which he could not deviate. A psychiatrist for the prosecution agreed essentially with the defense psychiatrists assessment of List's character but disagreed on the extent to which he was out of control. He regarded the obsessive-compulsiveness as a trait rather than a disorder, observing that List had the capacity to review his options and had premeditated the crime.

In the summation to the jury, Miller asked for a verdict of something less than first degree murder because the defendant, however warped his judgment, had acted on sincerely held religious beliefs. The prosecution depicted John List as a calculating killer who sacrificed innocent lives to satisfy egoistic desires. The jury found him guilt of first degree murder on all five counts. The judge, in sentencing him to five consecutive terms of life imprisonment, condemned him as a man without honor. He granted that List's relations with his wife were difficult, but not an excuse for murder. There was no reason for killing his aged mother who found satisfaction in her life or in denying the children the full sweep of their years. In deciding that he was God's surrogate, List preempted the roles of jury, judge, and executioner.

The Mass Killer: Getting Even

Vengeance is the dominant theme in the motives of mass murderers. Provoked by long standing grievances against former employers or work associates, wives and in-laws, or by hatred of minorities, they whip themselves into a cold rage that can be relieved only by the wholesale killing of their tormentors, even if it means paying with their own lives. Their rage spent, they commonly turn their weapons on themselves. Rapid fire weapons with large ammunition capacities are so efficient that Charles J. Hennard, in October, 1991, was able to kill twenty-two people and injure fifteen others in a cafeteria line, then kill himself before he could be stopped.

What appears to the horrified observer as rampant vindictiveness, for the killer, is justice. Mass killers for the most part are mature men, generally past thirty, who have not made their mark in the world. They attribute their defeated aspirations to the machinations of others and target them, or people like them, for death. Mass killers do not have serious records of prior criminality. They are often disagreeable in their relations with others and frequently have strong dislikes of certain categories of people whom they believe responsible for their woes. Hennard's nemesis was women; Camden killer Howard Unruh emerged from the hermetic fastness of his house to kill Jews; chronically unemployed James Oliver Huberty blamed his frustrations on Chicanos.

Mass killers seldom have histories of mental illness. An exception was Laurie Dann who had been in and out of psychiatric therapy for years. Also exceptional among mass killers, was the fact of her sex. She entered a classroom in a public school in Winnetka, Illinois and shot five children, one fatally. While trying to get away, she killed a man who tried to disarm her before she killed herself.

A canvas of experts by the *New York Times* (Oct. 19, 1991) on the causes of mass murder carried out shortly after the Hennard killings, brought forth random hypotheses including fantasies derived from media stories, a sense of failure blamed by the killer on others, the lyrics of popular songs, and the increasing violence of pornography. Two suggested that the Senate hearings on the nomination of Clarence Thomas to the Supreme Court may have stirred up Hennard's feelings. Of all the expert opinions, the one by Dr. James A. Fox was pragmatically closest to the mark. Observing that high tech weapons are the principal factor, he stated, "It's hard to kill 22 people with a knife." Fox's comment takes on added importance in light of the inverse relationship internationally between homicide rates and the strictness of gun regulations; also the fact that the American states with the greatest frequency of mass murders—Texas, Florida, and California— are those in which the values and sentiments of the gun culture are most ardently proclaimed.

11

Interpreting The Facts

A killing is not a crime until the court says it is. The law requires the court to make two kinds of judgments in order to arrive at a verdict in a criminal case. The first, on the allegations regarding the physical element of a crime, including the facts and inferences which connect the accused to the crime; and the second, on the charges set forth to establish the requisite malicious intent.

Death by homicide is a physical fact attested by witnesses to the killing or by the condition of the corpse. Deductions from physical evidence linking a suspect to the killing, the *circumstantial evidence*, are not facts; they are inferences, but may be as compelling as any facts. Nor do pronouncements concerning the intentions of the killer constitute facts. They, too, are inferences based on the assumption that, in the absence of evidence to the contrary, the killer intends the foreseeable consequences of his act.

The conversion of the fact of a slaying into a murder, a manslaughter, an accident, or a justifiable homicide entails a judgment based on a reading of the killer's mental state. The transformation is effected in a secular rite of trial by debate. The adversarial format of the criminal trial is justified by the pious belief that out of the crossfire of disciplined argument, truth and justice will emerge. Trial lawyers, ironically, are the foremost subverters of this ideal, cynically bending the "truth" in the interest of winning, or cushioning a loss.

The obfuscation of fact and reason apparent in criminal trials is an inevitable consequence of the flexibility of the written law and the adversary relationship between prosecution and defense. Seymour Wishman, a criminal lawyer who spent years defending violent offenders, writes in his penitential *Confessions of a Criminal Lawyer* that the generality of the rules enables lawyers to obscure the truth by means of innuendo, ambiguity, and the phrasing of questions to shade the facts, demean hostile witnesses, and show exaggerated respect to friendly witnesses. Lawyers claim that none of these practices, short of outright lying, is a violation of professional ethics since they have a disinterested obligation to serve their clients with every procedural device permitted by law. If rebuked over their fanciful reconstructions of reality, they can invoke philosophical platitudes about the elusiveness of truth.

The case of serial killer Albert DeSalvo models the process whereby the facts of a murder fed into the maw of the criminal justice system have little bearing on what goes into the official record or on the outcome. Gerold Frank's detailed documentary, *The Boston Strangler*, describes how DeSalvo ran up a tally of thirteen murders and hundreds of sexual assaults on women to terrify the Boston metropolitan area and mobilize the police in a costly fruitless manhunt, and how the disposition of the case rode more on political and legal exigency than on the facts.

DeSalvo had an insatiable sexual appetite. His wife reported that he insisted on having sex in the morning, at noon when he came home for lunch, and at night. Albert complained that she was frequently unobliging and contemptuous of his needs. He was arrested in 1961 for being the elusive "measuring man" who, pretending to be from a model agency, approached women in their homes and offered to measure them for a possible position with the agency. The police didn't know quite what to make of him: a pathetic figure who got his sexual gratification from touching strange women, or a burglar who used this approach to disguise his true intentions when observed lurking in the hallways of apartment houses. He was sentenced to two years on charges of assault and battery and was released after serving eleven months.

The stranglings took place during the next three years. In November, 1964 DeSalvo entered the apartment of a woman, attacked her, tied her down on the bed, sexually abused her, and left without killing her. From an artist's sketch he was recognized by detectives as "the measuring man." Surviving victims of other

sexual assaults in a tri-state area came forward and identified him as
their assailant. He was dubbed the "Green Man" for these offenses
because he wore green trousers when committing his crimes. He
denied knowing anything about the stranglings and was not
seriously regarded as a suspect.

A pre-trial psychological assessment found that DeSalvo suffered from "a sociopathic personality disorder marked by sexual
deviation with prominent schizoid features and depressive trends."
(Frank, 233) He was found not competent to stand trial and was
committed to a psychiatric institution as mentally ill. There he
bragged to another inmate, charged with murder, that he was the
Boston Strangler. His new friend promptly advised his own
attorney, F. Lee Bailey, who talked to De Salvo, became his lawyer,
and obtained confessions to thirteen murders.

Bailey was convinced that DeSalvo's confession was genuine,
but the Attorney General's office was skeptical. In a series of
meetings with an assistant attorney general, DeSalvo described two
of the killings in sufficient detail to convince the authorities that he
was indeed the Boston strangler.

Bailey sought to save his client from execution by having him
declared insane and incarcerated in a mental institution. A tactical
problem was how to avoid a murder trial with its inherent possibility
of a death sentence. The Attorney General of Massachusetts,
Edward Brooke, was not averse to a deal, but had reservations
based on the lack of witnesses or physical evidence. All the state
had was DeSalvo's confession, which in the light of DeSalvo's
claim of mental instability could not be accorded much credibility.
Also Brooke was a candidate for the United States Senate and did
not wish to give the appearance of using the tragedy to advance his
own political ambitions.

In what seemed like a "no lose" strategy, Bailey worked out a
compromise acceptable to the state whereby DeSalvo would be
tried on charges pending against him as the assaulting, but not
killing, "Green Man." Psychiatric evidence could then be introduced. If the psychiatrists said that DeSalvo was insane, Bailey
would permit him to confess to the murders. If they said he was
sane, Bailey would ask each psychiatrist if he knew the complete
history of the defendant and if his opinion took into account the
killings of thirteen women. Presumably the answer to both

questions would be no. Whereupon, Bailey would subpoena the investigators assigned to the case to corroborate DeSalvo's confession and the detailed supporting physical evidence with the expectation that their testimony would convince the psychiatrists of DeSalvo's insanity.

Although the strategy did not work as expected, Bailey managed to save DeSalvo from execution. A hearing was held to determine DeSalvo's competency to stand trial. Three psychiatrists, two in private practice and the third, Dr. Ames Robey, the head of a state mental institution and prominent in forensic circles, testified. The two private practitioners agreed that DeSalvo had a mental disease, but that it was not so disabling that he could not stand trial. One described his condition as a "'chronic undifferentiated schizophrenia [which] would make it difficult for him to accept a world of reality as most people know it.'" The other described him as a "'sociopath with dangerous tendencies.'" (Frank, 358)

Dr. Robey disagreed with his colleagues' judgment that DeSalvo was competent to stand trail. He described DeSalvo as a "'schizophrenic reaction, chronic undifferentiated type [with] very extensive signs of sexual deviation.'" He buttressed his diagnosis with observations of the swings in DeSalvo's mental states, which another observer could just as plausibly have interpreted as a normal reaction to the anxiety produced by the prospect of a death sentence. Robey found DeSalvo, variously, sociopathic, in a state of acute anxiety hysteria, obsessive and compulsive, or appearing very close to wild overt psychosis. He pronounced him in a state of "'homosexual panic or sexual panic of some sort,'" a judgment that DeSalvo denied by an emphatic shaking of his head. Robey deemed DeSalvo a "'compulsive confessor.'" If put on trial, he testified, DeSalvo might become violent, but gave no reason for such a reaction nor ventured the likelihood that it might occur. Robey purported to know better than Desalvo what was in DeSalvo's mind. He took issue with an admission by DeSalvo that he had faked hallucinations in order to be sent to the mental institution. The hallucinations, Robey insisted, were real.

Under direct examination in the competency hearing, Bailey led DeSalvo through questions designed to elicit answers favorable to a finding of insanity. The responses, however, bespoke self-possession and a commendable striving for redemption rather than a verdict of insanity. Yes, DeSalvo understands the proceedings; he is ready to go to trial and desires to "'[do] only what is right, no matter what the consequences may be.'" No, he's not concerned about going to prison as long as he can get the treatment he needs, although he believes he is more apt to get it in the state mental hospital. Yes, he is concerned about the possibility of conviction, but he is willing to take the risk in order to resolve the matter. Asked if he knew what his defense would be, DeSalvo said, "not guilty by reason of insanity." In response to the question, did he feel himself to be sick, DeSalvo said, "'I feel that I am in a mental condition.'" He believed that his "condition" could have started in childhood and erupted violently in later stages of life. For one relying on a plea of insanity to save his life, Desalvo could not have appeared more rational. He maintained a posture of earnest repentance during the cross examination and repeated his avowal to make a clean breast of the whole affair in the interest of justice.

The judge in the proceedings was unconvinced by Dr. Robey's scattergun diagnosis and found DeSalvo competent to stand trial. DeSalvo pleaded not guilty at arraignment. The court remanded him to Bridgewater State Hospital, where, presumably he would get treatment for his "condition" to await trial. The defense plan, to keep DeSalvo at Bridgewater indefinitely, was derailed when, in 1967, he was convicted of the "Green Man" offenses and was sentenced to life imprisonment in the state penitentiary. He was never called to account officially for the thirteen killings. Six years later he was killed in a fight with another inmate.

Bailey had succeeded in creating an aura for his client that required going beyond the compass of the facts. His plea for not putting Desalvo on trial for murder, the platitude that commitment in a mental institution would enable mental health specialists to study deranged personalities like his in order to advance understanding of the causes of such terrible crimes, has no support in clinical experience with incarcerated murderers. The evidence of DeSalvo's personality and criminal career justifies no more than that he was a cunning, ruthless person with an impressive sexual capacity who congratulated himself on fooling his victims and leading the police on a merry chase. His conceit was justified, for the police never did get any evidence to connect him to the killings until after he confessed. Neither his arrogance in bragging about his crimes to fellow inmates nor the match between his knowledge of the crime scene revealed in his confessions and the physical evidence obtained by the police investigation sufficed to warrant an arrest for the strangulation murders. Even when he confessed to the appropriate authority, there were reservations that the admissions might be attacked on the ground that he was only trying to get attention or that he was a compulsive confessor.

The Less You Know....

The typical murder trial brings forth two opposing reconstructions of the physical facts of the tragic event, either of which, or a compromise between them, prevails. The resourceful defense attorney may hedge his case with a story that is truthful, but incomplete, or sketchy enough to permit change in case the fortunes of debate call for revision. Under some conditions ignorance can be strategically benign. Alan Dershowitz' book *Reversal of Fortune* dramatizes events in the appeal by the aristocratic Claus von Bulow of his conviction for the attempted murder of his enormously wealthy wife by insulin injection. In the film version von Bulow's offer to tell his newly retained attorney, Harvard law professor Alan Dershowitz, "the truth" is flatly rebuffed. Dershowitz instructs the astonished von Bulow that the less his client tells him, except for what he asks, the less likely he is to be ethically encumbered by knowledge harmful to the client.

Joe McGinniss's true crime book, *Cruel Doubt*, documents the painful cost of violating this maxim of defense strategy. It tells of the killing of wealthy Leith Von Stein and the near killing of his wife, Bonnie, by an intruder who broke into their house and attacked them while they slept. Suspicion fell on Bonnie's twenty year old son by a previous marriage, Chris Pritchard, who had told friends about his step-father's money and of his longing to get his hands on some of it. The police knew that he regularly exceeded his allowance and was bailed out of debt by his mother, but this information hardly sufficed to press for an indictment.

Months after the crime, Mrs. Von Stein, exasperated at the inaction of the police and indignant at rumors which linked her and her son to the murder, retained separate legal counsel for herself and her son. Chris Pritchard's attorney, wanting a better grip on the facts of the case should an arrest materialize, had brought in a private investigator to try and get at the truth of what happened. Chris's lawyers sized up their client as an unsavory character. He used drugs and alcohol excessively, was a complete academic failure at North Carolina State University, displayed emotional indifference to his step-father's murder, and treated his mother with little respect or affection. In short, they didn't like him and doubted his innocence.

In breaking the rule, as laid down by Dershowitz to von Bulow, Chris's lawyers ran into problems they hadn't anticipated. Their private investigator subjected Chris to a harsh line of questioning and succeeded in getting more than they had bargained for—an admission that he had enlisted two of his friends in a conspiracy to kill his step-father, promising them handsome rewards, and that one of the friends had actually done the killing. The lawyers then confronted the dilemma that they were bound by the rule of lawyer-client confidentiality and by the obligation to accord their client the best defense they could. But if their efforts led to an acquittal, they would be turning loose a killer who might seek the death of his mother to obtain the money left by the step-father. They resolved the moral quandary by working out a negotiated plea with a willing district attorney who had been having problems in forging a binding chain of evidence against Chris. The deal saved Chris from the death penalty, but assured him a stay of twenty years in the penitentiary before becoming eligible for parole.

Measuring the Gravity of Homicide

What makes a homicide more or less legally serious is not the fact of the killing—dead is dead—but the degree of malice embodied in the intent to kill. To make that determination the court instructs the jurors in the legal definitions of the various degrees of homicide, first and second degree murder or manslaughter and orders them to apply the law to the facts as they understand them. In general practice, the charge in the formal accusation consists of the highest offense sustainable by the allegations, but the jury may bring forth a verdict of guilty of a lesser offense. Since the "facts" relative to *intent* may be in dispute, and the meaning of malice may be conceived differently by the various jurors, the verdict is often a compromise.

First degree murder is typically one of two kinds. The commonest is felony murder: the killer, whether deliberately or unintentionally, slays the victim in the course of a serious crime—robbery, kidnap, rape or arson. For a homicide, other than a felony murder, to qualify as first degree murder the prosecutor must prove *beyond a reasonable doubt* that the killing was willful, the result of a premeditated, deliberate intent to kill. Relatively few defendants are found guilty of first degree murder, other than felony murder; most are convicted of second degree murder or manslaughter.

Second degree murder is an intentional killing committed in a state of mental or emotional agitation without premeditation. Voluntary manslaughter, in the typical case, lacks the element of *malice aforethought*, which means that the homicidal assault is committed in hot anger or results from a provocation that would cause a hypothetical "ordinary person" to act impulsively. Involuntary manslaughter, also known as manslaughter by negligence, refers to accidental killings resulting from the failure to exercise due care, mostly cases of drunk or reckless driving. Not all homicide is criminal. Killings may be excused on grounds of self-defense, coercion, or mental incompetence.

The judge guides the jury in arriving at their verdict by instructing them in the requirements for a finding of guilty of each of the various forms of homicide. His explanation of the key terms for making their determination is an exercise in redundancy. The inexplicit concepts of law are defined by equally murky terms. In the language of judicial instruction, *premeditated* means *designed or planned beforehand; deliberate* means that the killing must be the result of *real and substantial reflection*, or that the defendant must have considered the *pros and cons* of that design and have *measured and chosen* his actions. The intent must be formed by a mind that is *free from undue excitement* ; this excludes acts done on sudden impulse, without reflection, or as a result of sudden fright. There must be a lapse of time sufficient to think about the purpose and intent of the killing. How long a lapse of time, is left to the discretion of the jury equipped by the judge with the standard of whether there is *sufficient pause* to afford a *reasonable man* time to reconsider his intentions.

The triers of fact—the jury, or the judge if a jury trial is waived— are expected to factor an equation consisting of measures for each of the following highly subjective standards for assessing the gravity of the homicide.

(1) *The extensiveness of planning.* The facts concerning the length of time or the amount of preparation devoted to planning the killing weigh heavily, but not necessarily decisively, in appeals to the jury. Appearances can be deceptive. A killing might be carefully planned, resolved upon, and executed within a very short span of time. On the other hand, the grievance that incites a killing may have a long history, but may have only suddenly come to a head of violence. The absence of any doubt of a deliberate intent to kill is most clearly indicated by cases in which a principal hires others to do the dirty work.

(2) *The extent of the reflection and the amount of time for a reasonable man to reconsider his plan of action once the intention is launched.* The stickler in this part of the equation is the "reasonable man." What is reasonable in this context is hardly a settled point. The law resolves the issue by assuming a community standard which it leaves to the jury to define. But in a pluralistic society whose institutions, laws, and social policies increasingly accommodate differences in outlook and experience among persons differing in age, sex, education, social class, and ethnicity, there are many standards of the amount of time that is reasonable for the reconsideration of a homicidal intention.

The behaviorally sophisticated criminal trial lawyer will organize his argument to take into account the findings of social-psychological studies which show significant cultural differences in temporal orientation among different categories of people. A short-run hedonism manifested in impulsive gratification is most common to young underclass males, precisely that demographic element which produces the highest murder rates. For persons whose time frame is bounded in the near past and close future, the unremitted fully formed determination to kill without regard to the conse- quences and the act of killing may take as little as a few seconds. The temporal orientation of the middle classes, more favored by selection procedures than the lower classes, to occupy the jury box or the judicial bench, extends far into the future. To the middle class mentality, the typical lower class homicide, from provocation to act, seems so precipitous as to hardly qualify as first degree murder.

Even within culturally homogeneous communities the indefiniteness of what is considered *reasonable* leaves a wide hole for a hardened jury to convict of first degree murder or a softened jury to convict of a less serious offense, or even to acquit. Robert Travers' celebrated novel, *Anatomy of a Murder,* reflecting the author's years of experience as a prosecutor in the Upper Penninsula of Michigan, illustrates the flexibility accorded the jury in evaluating the time factor. The defendant, learning the identity of the man who raped his wife, took a gun and drove a half-hour before finding the rapist and killing him. The crucial issue was whether the defendant, who pleaded the defense of "irresistible impulse," had sufficient time to reflect upon his intentions. Measuring the sufficiency of a half-hour's reflection by the yardstick of sympathy for the outraged husband, the jury concluded, to the astonished relief of the defense, that he did not have sufficient time for reflection, that there was no break in the impulse to kill from the time of incitement to the deadly act.

In effect the instructions of the judge to the jury are an order to take measurements on dimensions for which there are no uniform scales. The law, for example, provides the jurors no standard of *malice* by which to differentiate reliably between first and second degree murder. The product of the jury deliberations will consist presumably of an "average" of the subjective scales of all of the jurors.

Since the people who become jurors have likely never before had the experience of applying judicial instructions to a mass of information, varying greatly in specificity or generality, concreteness or abstractness, for the awesome purpose of judging a person accused of murder, each jury must create its own scale to fit the case. In trials where the jury is waived, judges who decide the verdict have the benefit of a more sharply calibrated subjective yardstick acquired from the experience of hearing cases of a wide degree of gravity. Jurors, lacking this experience, construct their scales from scratch out of a background of attitudes shaped by a mixture of media accounts of local homicides, unusual killings accorded wide publicity, and personal experience.

Nevertheless, the law sanguinely expects that a community standard for judging particular criminal events will emerge out of jury deliberations. The optimism of the law is more apt to be justified for the worst cases of deliberate ruthless killing or, at the other extreme, homicides for which there may be a moral justification shared by large segments of the community. Cases midway between these extremes are more difficult to resolve; they are the ones most apt to result in a hung jury.

Studies in experimental psychology show that the scales by which individuals make judgments in the physical, social, moral, or aesthetic sphere are constructed out of the experience of individuals with percepts or concepts of the kind under consideration. To illustrate, a temperature of sixty degrees Fahrenheit is delightfully mild to an Arctic dweller; to a resident of the tropics, it is uncomfortably chilly. Whatever the dimension—temperature, noise level, beauty, fairness—judgments of too much, too little, or "just right" reflect the range of intensities to which the individual has become accustomed.* Thus individuals who share a common background are more likely to have have experienced the same range of stimulation and, therefore, can be expected to share a common frame of reference for making judgments.

To extend this principle to the judgment of the seriousness of murder, consider the typical large American city—Detroit, Baltimore, Los Angeles, Houston, or Washington, D.C.—in which killings of all gradations of gravity, including many deliberate execution-style and felony murders clearly qualifying as first degree, have become monotonously commonplace in daily news reports. For residents of these communities, the closer they live to the areas of highest incidence of murder and the more habituated they are to the daily carnage, the bulk of killings would seem to lack the degree of malice

---

* Laboratory studies show that it takes repeated exposure to a particular kind of stimulus of varying intensity for an individual to establish a standard of judgment. In making physical judgments of weight, sound, or brightness, the intensity and recency of the stimuli to which the individual has been subjected strongly influences the midpoint and the endpoints of the individual's subjective scale. For example, in judging a ten-pound weight as "heavy" or "light," it makes a difference whether the subject has just completed lifting a series of four to eight pound weights or a series of twelve to sixteen pound weights. If the subject has been hefting weights of both ranges, the ten-pound weight will be experienced as neutral, neither heavy nor light. The same processes have been found to hold in the development of collective scales of judgement on moral or esthetic dimensions. (Sherif and Hovland)

to qualify as first degree murder. In a community with a low homicide rate and very few, if any, killings of the most savage kind with which to make comparisons, the same crimes would likely rank higher on the communal yardstick of malice.

The principle can be applied also to the issue of premeditation. Attorneys know that the jury's subjective judgment of the amount of time, long or short, elapsing between the inception of the intent and the act is vital to the determination of whether a murder is of the first or second degree. The usual defense ploy is to argue for the impulsiveness of the act, in effect relating a chronology of the defendant's mental process which puts the time span at the shortest credible estimate. The desired measure could be more favorably impressed in the juror's mind by juxtaposing it with a series of measures from comparable crime scenarios involving chronologies with longer spans. The prosecution, conversely, should supply a range of examples that place the alleged amount of time at the high end of the scale.

Assessing Intent: The Case of Mrs. Jean Harris

However clearly drawn the facts of a case, observers of unusual discernment, let alone jurors, may arrive at different opinions on the quality of the same homicidal act. Literary critic Diana Trilling and journalist Shana Alexander, both respected commentators, wrote books about the case of Jean Harris, headmistress of the fashionable Madeira school for girls, who shot to death her erstwhile lover, the sybaritic bachelor, Dr. Herman Tarnower, who had achieved national fame with his book on dieting. His ardor for her had cooled and he had shifted his attention to another woman. The spurned Mrs. Harris, in an emotionally agitated state, drove from her home in Virginia to Dr. Tarnower's Scarsdale, New York residence, arriving in the middle of the night, to plead with him to take her back.

As Jean Harris reports the encounter, Tarnower expressed annoyance that she had come at this untimely hour. Her entreaty did not soften his displeasure. Looking into the bathroom she saw a negligée, not hers, a bitter reminder of the end of her romance with Tarnower. Exactly what ensued is uncertain and became a key issue in the trial. What is certain is that they argued. She pulled out her gun. One shot grazed Tarnower's arm. He went to the bathroom to attend to the wound. When he returned there was another shot, and Tarnower lay mortally wounded. Mrs. Harris protested that the killing was accidental; that the gun she had brought with her on a trip that took four hours was intended for her own demise in case her mission failed; that in a struggle with Tarnower over possession of the gun, as she was attempting to kill herself, it was inadvertently pointed in his direction, not her's as she thought, and accidentally discharged. (Harris, 124-141)

Diana Trilling's dispassionate dissection of the case in her book, *Mrs. Harris: The Death of the Scarsdale Diet Doctor*, concludes that the killing was the hellish retribution of a woman scorned, the loser in a love triangle. Her interpretation puts the crime squarely under the rubric of *murder*. Shana Alexander agrees with Mrs. Trilling's view of Jean Harris's motive, but believes that Trilling's account does not give sufficient weight to crucial events leading to the emotional disintegration of Jean Harris. Her sympathies are implicit in the title of her book, *Very Much a Lady: The Untold Story of Jean Harris and Dr. Herman Tarnower*.

In Ms. Alexander's judgment Jean Harris was so emotionally upset at the time of the shooting that the killing qualifies as no more than manslaughter. She also sees Mrs. Harris as the victim of wrong trial strategy decisions. One was the failure to summon psychiatric testimony to vouch for the personality disrupting effects of the stimulant drug Desoxyn, prescribed by Dr. Tarnower for his paramour in increasing dosage over the years of their relationship. Another was Mrs. Harris's refusal to avail herself of a plea of insanity, or at least *extreme emotional disturbance*, to pave the way to a plea bargain for a reduction of the charge from murder to manslaughter. The lesser offense, with a minimum sentence of as few as two or as many as six years, could assure a timely eligibility for parole. It seems, however, to author Alexander that by the patrician code of Mrs. Harris, a plea bargain would amount to hypocrisy. For that reason she turned down an offer by the prosecutor to ask the judge to include the option of voluntary manslaughter in his charge to the jury.

There is reason to think that Mrs. Harris's determination to go for acquittal may have been influenced also by practical considerations. Conviction would have deprived her of the $220,000 that

Tarnower had left her in his will. Confronted with the limited choice of not guilty or guilty of murder, the jury convicted Mrs. Harris of murder which requires a minimum period of incarceration for seventeen years before becoming eligible for parole.

Most fatefully, in Ms. Alexander's opinion, was the misdirection of the defense strategy set in motion by Mrs. Harris's pride—her willingness to have put into testimony a letter in which she poured out her anguish to Tarnower. There was a risk that the letter could be interpreted either benignly, as a sign of the emotional turmoil that prompted suicidal intentions, or malignly, as the recrimination of a woman scorned. The jury opted for the latter meaning. Her unwillingness to admit to a jealous rage toward her rival for Dr. Tarnower's affection, his "office-girl," as spitefully labeled in the letter, lost for her whatever mitigating effect an admission of such emotional devastation might promote. To own up to so great a loss of self-control would be highly inconsistent with her self-conception as a lady.

Divining Intent: The Role of the Mental Health Expert

Where the physical facts of the crime are uncontested, and only the mental element is at issue, the prosecution has already won half the battle. Against these odds the defense can only dig for personality disorders or crises in the life of the killer which, arguably, diminish or altogether negate criminal responsibility.

The judgment of the mental state of the accused moves the jury farther away from tangible realities than the determination of the physical facts. Diagnoses based on the psychiatric or psychological examination of criminal offenders are no more than hypotheses or thinly disguised moral beliefs. The passage of the months between the occurrence of the crime and the opening of the trial encapsulates memory in layers of selective recall, rationalization, or outright evasion rendering the reconstruction of the defendant's state of mind as feasible as the proverbial recementing of Humpty-Dumpty. The courts and mental health specialists often regard the defendant as perhaps the least reliable informant concerning his thoughts and motives when he committed the murder, even if he confesses to the crime. They require that his utterances be screened through the analytic sieve of psychiatric examination and psychological testing, aided, where legally permitted, by truth drugs or polygraphic (lie detector) examination.

The wrangling over the determination of mental states extends to the certification of experts who make the assessment. At one time, the courts, influenced by pressures from the medical profession, excluded or restricted the scope of mental health workers other than psychiatrists in rendering expert testimony. Some states accord full recognition to clinical psychologists whose therapeutic role is similar to that of psychiatrists, except that they lack the authority to administer psychotropic medication. A growing belief in the non-medical character of most kinds of personal maladjustment has warranted the assignment of much routine psychotherapy to clinical or psychiatric social workers, for whom the terminal degree is the master's, whereas in the other two fields, it is the more prestigious doctorate.

The de-imperialization of psychiatry has been furthered by increasing dissatisfaction with the medical model of mental illness, which postulates that mental disease, like organic disease, is a clearly distinguishable diagnostic category. The countervailing view that much mental distress is a product of the strains of coping in a complex, secularized, impersonal, competitive, pluralistic society has bolstered the opinion that training in medicine is not needed by psychiatrists to diagnose and treat most of their patients. More germane to the understanding of non-organic behavior disorders is education in the humanities and social-behavioral sciences to increase sensitivity to the way people of diverse backgrounds and experience perceive and understand the situations in which they function.

Despite the growing recognition that much aberrant behavior is a psychologically normal response to social strain or to the norms of a deviant subculture, the education of the psychiatrist is still mainly in medicine. The embryonic psychiatrist does not necessarily get any but the most basic education in the social or behavioral sciences until the residency, which comes after the completion of medical school and the internship, and even then, not in the proportion or amount obtained by the doctoral or master's degree student in psychology or sociology, or even the master's degree student in social work.

A grounding in academic criminology is not required of forensic psychiatrists and clinical psychologists; nor is it reflected in their testimony, or their writings on criminal behavior. The remediation of this deficiency would correct the error of diagnosing much psychologically normal, culturally and situationally induced deviance as symptomatic of mental disorder.

The allure of consultation fees for expert testimony undermines the integrity of the fact finding process of the criminal trial. A reading of murder trials in which the main issue is the mental state of the defendant shows that having the money to obtain the friendly testimony of prestigious psychiatric experts reduces the odds of conviction or the gravity of the offense. Perhaps the reason that so few cases involving the insanity plea are successful is that in the vast majority of cases in which the mental state of the defendant is at issue, the assessment is left solely to examiners employed by the state who have no incentive to devise a basis for excusing the defendant of criminal responsibility. Few alleged murderers have the resources to shop for a second opinion.*

To authenticate their diagnoses with the stamp of scientific respectability, mental health experts routinely administer standard psychological tests to persons accused of serious crimes. Standardization means that a test has been administered to large numbers of subjects and that statistical measures of group performance—distributions, averages, deviations from the mean, and other indices—have been established. Test scores give an appearance of precision and objectivity. Although they have some value in

---

* The organization of psychiatric expertise for partisan purposes in an adversary proceeding is costly, and can be ethically dubious. Andrew Rosenthal, a New York Times reporter, tells how a Senate Republican supporter of Judge Clarence Thomas enlisted a nationally known forensic psychiatrist, Dr. Park Dietz, to provide information on mental disorders that could be used to undermine the testimony of Thomas's accuser, Anita F. Hill. Although the expert claimed that he did not offer any diagnosis of Miss Hill or offer advice on strategy, he did provide his client with information on possible interpretations, some adverse to Miss Hill's mental stability, which cropped up later in the Judiciary Committee's hearings. Another psychiatrist, Dr. Paul Appelbaum, indicated that Dr. Dietz in attempting to educate the Senators had not violated any professional ethics, but that he had problems with the Senators who took the information and did what Dr. Dietz refused to do. (*New York Times*, October 20, 1991) The degree to which the innuendo of psychological disturbance may have dulled the credibility of Miss Hill's testimony is problematic. Perhaps, as is often the case in actual criminal trials, it only hardened judgments already made by either side.

indicating the degree to which the subject differs from the average of the population tested, what they measure is problematical because the concepts to which the measurements apply are fuzzily defined. Psychology has yet to come up with personality tests which, like blood and urine tests in medicine, yield consistent results, and reduce to negligibility instances in which some subjects who test positive may indeed be negative and the converse.

Some of the most frequently used tests are the Minnesota Multiphasic Personality Inventory (MMPI), the Draw-A-Person test, and the Thematic Apperception Test (TAT). The MMPI, designed to ferret out signs of psychopathology, consists of 550 statements covering a wide range of attitudes, beliefs, and values pertaining to self-conception, politics, family, and sex, each printed on a separate card. The subject sorts the cards into three groups: *True, False,* or *Cannot Say.*   The subject is rated on a scale of 0 to 9 on each of nine clinical scales of deviateness. These include:

—*hypochondriasis*: excessive concern with bodily functions
—*depression*: a tendency toward chronic dejection
—*hysteria*: the tendency to use complaints of illness as an
          escape mechanism
—*psychopathic deviate*: trouble-proneness due to an
          absence of deep emotional response, disregard for others,
          and the inability to profit from experience
—*paranoia*: suspiciousness and feelings of persecution
—*psychasthenia*: excessive fears and compulsions of thought
          and action
—*schizophrenia*: bizarre thought and behavior, removed
          from reality
—*hypomania*: overactive, flighty mental and physical behavior
 —*masculinity-femininity*: sexual identification.

The scores resulting from this procedure are arranged into a profile which is regarded by clinicians as a useful adjunct to diagnosis. The test has some utility in differentiating persons with marked psychopathological tendencies from those adjudged normal. However, since most trials in which an insanity plea is entered involve defendants for whom it is claimed that the insanity was only a temporary aberration, the defense faces the ticklish task of finding credible evidence of past pathology in the results of tests administered long after the crime to a defendant who appears perfectly normal.

If tests based on words undependably communicate mental states, how reliable can tests based on drawings be? Projective tests, in which the clinician interprets the meaning imparted to pictures or inkblots by the subject rest upon a weaker foundation of fact, theory, and reliability of interpretation than standardized tests. In the *draw-a-person* test, the tester asks the subject to draw a person, without stipulating which sex. The resulting figure, if distorted, disfigured, or otherwise unusual in design, is thought to reveal a possible personality disorder. When the task is completed the tester asks the client to draw a figure of the opposite sex. The subject is asked to tell a story about each figure. From the data derived by this procedure, the analyst draws inferences about the subject's overall self-conception and attitudes toward his or her own and the opposite sex.

The Thematic Apperception Test (TAT) consists of thirty pictures, a number of which are picked by the clinician for viewing by the subject who is asked to make up a story for each picture about what events produced the scene, what it depicts, how the persons portrayed feel about it, and what the outcome will be. The analytical value of the TAT derives from features such as the recurrence of themes in the stories made up for the various pictures—the importance, power, and sex relationships imputed to the persons in each picture—and the outcome relative to the plot.

The results of the tests hardly speak for themselves. Along with the clinical interview, they form the basis for an opinion on the mental state of the accused killer. Success or failure in arguing for a mitigation of the charge, as we shall see, depends very much on how persuasively the attorney combines these materials and fits them to the legal standards of mental competence.

Summary

The convolutions in the handling of facts, inferences, opinions, beliefs, and judgments represent both strengths and weaknesses of the adversary system of criminal justice. Unsurprisingly, the stoutest defense and most searing indictment of the system come from the legal profession itself. Lawyers know better than anyone else the lengths of prevarication, short of lying, to which criminal lawyers go in the service of clients. Yet arguments for the radical reform of the fact finding process of criminal law, for example, to bring it more in line with the objective detachment of scientific inquiry— have not achieved much support on either side. For it *is* a fact that so many of the physical "facts" which the criminal trial seeks to uncover are not facts but inferences from circumstances or the projections of a witness's stale memory. Also, the mental state of the accused, required for a determination of guilt, is not a matter of fact but of opinion. The "truth" of any of these matters, say the defenders of the system, can not be assessed by direct inspection, but requires the lawyerly skills of argument and cross-examination.

physical illness. It did not take long to recognize the philosophical impasse of trying to accommodate contradictory conceptions of human behavior: the law's voluntarism versus psychiatry's determinism. Psychiatrists complained that only by artful equivocation could they fit their scientific concepts to the pre-scientific language of the McNaughton Rule.

More than a hundred years elapsed after the enactment of the McNaughton Rule before an attempt was made to redefine insanity congruent with psychiatry. The Durham Rule enunciated by Judge David Bazelon of the United States District Court of the District of Columbia in 1954, and adopted in Maine and New Hampshire, nullified criminal responsibility if the violation was the product of mental disease or mental defect. Hailed at the outset for its promise to create a common ground between law and psychiatry, it soon became evident that confusion in the language of psychiatric diagnosis made the Durham rule unworkable. In an attempt to remedy the difficulty, Judge Bazelon proposed what he thought would be a more readily diagnosable criterion: the impairment of the controls of mental or emotional processes or behavior to such an extent that the defendant cannot justly be held responsible. The language of the revision, known as the Brawner rule, doubtfully provides any more specific guidelines than its predecessor; indeed, it offers a loophole to bring practically every homicide into the orbit of insanity.

A third major effort to define insanity, formulated by the American Law Institute (A.L.I.) as part of its Model Penal Code, maintains the boundary between law and psychiatry while providing a means for psychiatry to inform the law. The A.L.I. definition, followed in the majority of states, removes criminal responsibility if, as a result of mental disease or defect, the accused lacks substantial capacity to appreciate the wrongfulness of personal conduct or to conform conduct to the requirements of the law. By substituting *appreciate* for *know*, relative to the wrongfulness of the act, the framers of the Model Penal Code felt that they were taking a long stride toward meeting the psychiatric community's objections to the McNaughton rule. A remaining flaw, however, is the vagueness of the term *mental disease*, defined, for example, in Michigan law, as a substantial disorder of thought or mood which significantly impairs judgment, behavior, the capacity to recognize reality, or the ability to cope with the ordinary demands of life. Although in the opinion of most experts, the A.L.I. rule is more compatible with psychiatry than the McNaughton or Durham Rule, some psychiatric critics object to its cognitive standard on the ground that one may appreciate the wrongfulness of an act and still be impelled to do it. To meet this criticism a number of A.L.I. states have supplemented their insanity statute with the qualification that an *irresistible impulse*, presumably originating in the unconscious recesses of the mind, could void criminal responsibility.

Irresistible or Unresisted Impulse?

The *irresistible impulse* formula as occasionally applied virtually dissolves the requirement of criminal intent. A Michigan case in the nineteen-sixties involving a federal prison worker who confessed to two sex murders illustrates the extreme degree to which a court may extend the notion of irresistibility. The victim of the first murder was a seventeen year old youth upon whom the defendant lavished expensive gifts in exchange for sexual favors. The alleged motive for the slaying was clear enough and certainly sensible. The boy had threatened to expose his homosexual lover unless he received more money. The second slaying, the defendant admitted, was to divert the police search for the killer to a distant area of the state. He picked up a hitch-hiker and after a sexual interlude, killed him in a way similar to the first murder. Hoping that the police would see a connection between the two homicides, he disposed of the body at a point considerably removed from where the first body was found. Despite the defendant's unmistakable intent, the court found him insane on the ground that he committed the killing under the irresistible goad of the sex drive.

A rationale for the application of the irresistible impulse standard to serial sex slayers is provided by Dr. Richard G. Rappaport, a defense psychiatrist who examined John Wayne Gacy, accused of murdering thirty-three young men in homosexual encounters. Dr. Rappaport concludes, "...that if Gacy did commit the murders, he was responding to an irresistible impulse which was allowed expression by a loss of ego controls under the influence of alcohol, drugs, extreme fatigue, and the stress of psychological conflicts within him. His victims were representations of these conflicts. It was at these particular instances that he was unable to conform his conduct to the requirement of the law." The "conflicts" in Gacy's life, Rappaport testified, arose out of relationships with a brutal father whom he could not please. Gacy introjected his father's negative attitudes toward him. The attempt to expunge the resulting self-conception lie at the roots of his murderous impulses. Gacy could not see himself as having a combination of good and bad qualities. He split off the bad from himself—the rage toward his parents, oedipal incestuous thoughts, and embarrassment over his homosexuality—and projected them onto the boys he brought home. He perceived them as degraded and dehumanized as his father had made him feel. "'He is so convinced that these qualities exist in this other person, he is completely out of touch with reality...and he has to get rid of them and save himself...he *has* to kill them.'" (italics supplied; Cahill, 322) Asked on cross-examination whether the irresistible impulse recurred thirty-one times after the first killing, Rappaport unflinchingly declared that it had.

The prosecution experts acknowledged that Gacy was a textbook example of the sociopathic personality, but was sufficiently connected to reality to be considered sane. The jury agreed and convicted him of first degree murder.

The Social Meaning of Insanity

The law does not require that a defendant be psychotic in order to plead insanity, only that as a result of mental illness there was impairment of his ability to know or appreciate the wrongfulness of his conduct or to conform to the law. Significantly, none of the insanity rules defines insanity as a mental disease. Each is no more than an attempt to objectify the circumstances under which the requisite mental element of a crime is lacking. As Philip Q. Roche, Isaac Ray award winning forensic psychiatrist stated in his book, *The Criminal Mind*, "[insanity] is used as a shorthand method of summarizing the words of the test of criminal responsibility."

If mental illness is not the distinguishing element of insanity, there is no compelling reason to refer judgments on insanity exclusively to the mental health disciplines. The determination could be made by astute people irrespective of occupational background. Yet in general practice the courts require that the plea of insanity be supported by diagnosis of a mental disorder. The cognitive test of the McNaughton Rule requires the defendant to be addled to virtually a state of psychosis *when he or she committed the crime*, but not necessarily afterward. The wording of the Durham and American Law Institute versions is more flexible permitting anyone, who under the spur of severe stress or trauma commits a criminal act, to invoke the insanity defense by claiming a temporary defect of mind. There are very occasional instances where judge or jury have overruled the judgments of psychiatrists to deliver a verdict of not guilty by rason of insanity.

The renowned criminal lawyer, Clarence Darrow, was one of the first advocates to base a case for a mitigation of criminal responsibility on cultural, social, and situational factors rather than mental disorder. His celebrated defense of Richard Loeb and Nathan Leopold for the kidnap-murder of Bobby Franks in 1924 did not oppose the charge—his clients had already confessed their guilt—but rather the death penalty. Darrow attempted to show how the chain of events in the lives of the defendants led inescapably to their attempt to perform "the perfect crime." He traced the murder back to the chance meeting of the two brilliant young men of similar social background and interests. The intersection of their personalities, he contended, made the crime inevitable. They complemented one another's homosexual tendencies: Loeb the master, Leopold the self-abasing slave. Both were born to wealthy families and indulged with every material advantage. They graduated with distinction: Loeb from the University of Michigan at the age of seventeen, Leopold, from the University of Chicago at eighteen. They soaked up the intellectual ferment of their time. The inspiration of the Nietzschean ideal of the Superman, freed from conventional restraints, lifted them above the herd. Their overbearing egoism neutralized compassion for others.

The court spared the killers the death penalty, imposing sentences of life plus ninety-nine years; but not because it agreed with the kind of determinism expressed in Darrow's plea—that because something happened, it had to happen. The sentencing judge, as he later commented, was disposed not to impose the death penalty upon one as young as either of the defendants.

Insanity as a Value Judgment

More than sixty years after the "Darrow brief," there is no formal accommodation in the law for exculpation or mitigation based on a non-medical diagnosis of deviance. Nevertheless it gets sneaked into testimony by superficially disguising extreme instances of normal stress reactions using such terms as "irresistible impulse," "transient situational reaction," or "extreme emotional disturbance." The slippery language of the insanity defense has enmired criminal trials in a morass of unprovable claims and twisted logic. Its infrequent successes are rarely attributable to the factual or scientific soundness of the arguments for mental derangement. It works because it provides juries with a means to excuse the legally guilty whom they deem morally innocent or worthy of escaping punishment; it fails because juries refuse to honor the specious tales which attorneys concoct to save the authors of brutal crimes.

Psychiatrist Willard Gaylin tells an anecdote illustrative of the predicaments which develop out of the relationship between the expert mental health witness and the defense, making the courtroom conduct of the witness seem more like an exercise in the dramatic than the forensic arts. In a conversation with a psychiatrist, Dr. Gaylin was appalled by his colleague's statement that he wished to make the best possible "psychological case" for a particular client. Gaylin objected to the ethical surrender of scientific integrity. The job of an expert witness, he argued, is to swear to the facts as seen by a man of special knowledge, not to make a case. The fellow psychiatrist responded with a lesson in the machinations of trial strategy. "Let's say that you attempt to maintain such a perspective and you discover that the lawyer and his client are feeding you information that is...clearly designed to manipulate your opinion...at which point it occurs to you that you can't formulate an independent judgment very well, so you pull out of the case. At this point the prosecution becomes aware of this, and that'd be fine: 'We're going to subpoena you as our witness.' At which point you then willy-nilly become the instrument of the other side. The idea of being a neutral witness for the court is fiction under the circumstances...From a pragmatic point of view, the courtroom is a kind of theatre set up to play to either a judge or a jury and you're the witness cast in a role, depending on what side you come out on, your lines are going to be read one way or another way." (Gaylin, l982: 195-6)

In cases not involving the issue of mental stability, the standards which the court asks the jury to use in arriving at a verdict or in determining the grade of the homicide, take for granted a common denominator of experience to which jurors and defendants can introspectively refer to gauge the maliciousness and premeditat- edness of a killing. The court expects that the sharing of individual assessments among jurors will produce a pooled judgment which represents a community consensus.

Insanity, as legally defined, however, is a matter outside of the direct experience of most jurors. The juror is seldom well informed on the subject of insanity or mental health. If prospective jurors should show a familiarity with the topic during the jury selection, there is a good chance that either side, more likely the defense, would reject them. The juror must therefore rely on the conflicting opinions of expert witnesses for guidance. What the juror may not know is that there are no dependable measures for either the assessment of the *knowledge of right and wrong* called for by the McNaughton rule, or the *capacity to conform conduct to the requirements of the law* central to the American Law Institute rule. Nor are there reliable tests of the causal connection between mental disorder and criminal behavior called for by the Durham rule.

Whatever the yardstick used, judgments on mental states boil down to value judgments. The judge's instruction, to apply to the behavior under judgement a community standard of what is expected of a reasonable person in his or her "right mind," invests jurors with broad discretion. The vagueness of the definition of insanity has enabled sympathetic juries to let defendants who are manifestly lucid get away with what by legal definition is murder. But that does not necessarily mean that the jury is shirking its mandate. It is according the definition of insanity its most literal interpretation: an acute disturbance of mind or emotion that excuses the suspension of good sense or sound judgement. We all understand how events can produce passions that shatter self- possession. In mercy killings, the defense typically pleads that the accused was so overwrought by the suffering of a dear one who begged for merciful release or had declined to a vegetative state beneath human dignity, that the accused temporarily took leave of his or her senses. How then, in the face of such a piteous plight, entreats counsel, could the distraught family member act "rationally" or conform behavior to the requirements of the law?

The tale of husband-killer Francine Hughes, told in Katherine McNulty's book, *The Flaming Bed*, demonstrates the willingness of a sympathetic jury to use the insanity plea to absolve a defendant subjected to extreme provocation who willfully kills. From the beginning of the marriage, Francine suffered severe abuse at the hands of a husband who beat her and their children when he was drunk, an almost daily occurrence. Her endurance snapped after a particularly brutal episode. In a drunken rampage, the husband tore up a notebook for a course she was taking in community college, threw the meal she had prepared for him on the floor and rubbed her face in it, and savagely beat her. His rage spent, stupefied with liquor, he fell into bed. She sent the children into the family station wagon, poured gasoline over her husband soaking the bed, set it afire, drove to the police station, confessed, and was charged with first degree murder.

The killing, perhaps fortunately for Mrs. Hughes, occurred in Michigan which follows the American Law Institute rule on insanity and its corollary provision of irresistible impulse. The jury concluded that an intense emotion mingling anger and fear incapacitated the defendant's ability to conform her behavior to the requirements of the law. They found her not guilty by reason of insanity.

A less sympathetic, but not uncaring, jury had a more difficult time in arriving at a verdict, and later fixing the sentence of Houston, Texas socialite Kay Sandiford for shooting to death her husband, the renowned heart surgeon, Dr. Frank Sandiford. Although Mrs. Sandiford's upper class background placed her, socially, a world removed from Francine Hughes, her case as set forth in *Shattered Night,* a book which she coauthored with Allen Burgess, recites a similar tale of mistreatment at the hands of her husband. The defense claimed that he had physically and psychologically abused her from the beginning of their marriage. Indeed he had attempted to rape her before their marriage and afterwards made voracious sexual demands or ignored her while pursuing other women. By the time of the shooting, endless bickering had deteriorated their marriage beyond repair.`

According to the defendant's account, on the evening of the murder, she had retired to the bedroom on the second floor when she heard her husband ascending the stairs. As he entered the room she saw that he carried a number of articles, including a tennis racquet which, she thought, he was going to use to beat her. In a state of panic, she reached for a gun and shot him in self-defense. To deflate the prosecution's argument that if life with him was so intolerable, the proper recourse would have been to leave him and get a divorce, she bemoaned that powerful pressures held her in bondage—fear of the appearance of failure (the marriage to Dr. Sandiford was her second) the welfare of the children, and an invisible psychological manacle that she could not shed. Divided on the verdict, the jury compromised, convicting her of manslaughter which could have placed her in prison for as long as twenty years and cost her a fine of ten thousand dollars. Instead, since Texas empowers the jury to fix the sentence in homicide cases, they imposed a term of ten years' probation and a fine of ten thousand dollars. She didn't have to go to prison, the probation was lifted within a few years, and she could well afford the fine.

Judges too may place sympathy above strict law enforcement. Ira K. Packer (1987) reports a case decided by a judge who overrode the judgment of the Michigan Forensic Center that a young man accused of murdering an extremely abusive father was without a mental disorder. The judge pronounced him insane because he did not believe that imprisonment was warranted and had no other means of freeing the defendant.

Psychoanalyzing the Intent to Kill

Expert testimony on the mental state of the accused in the typical trial runs a predictable course. The defense witnesses will argue that a severe mental disorder disabled the defendant's self-control. The prosecution expert witnesses will aver that although the defendant may suffer some degree of personality imbalance—after all, who doesn't?—he is grossly normal. To get around the issue of the normality or abnormality of some aspect of the accused's personality, the defense can plead that the killing resulted from a powerful compulsion rising from the unconscious, that vast reservoir of forgotten and suppressed thought.

Theories of the unconscious motivation of behavior have their intellectual roots in psychoanalytical theory originated by the

Viennese physician, Sigmund Freud, in the late nineteenth and early twentieth centuries. Psychoanalysis exerts a strong appeal to defense lawyers because it provides a rationale for denying causality to malevolent intentions. Prosecution lawyers like it because its wobbly scientific pretenses render it so vulnerable to attack. The theoretical diversity of psychoanalysis provides psychiatric witnesses for the defense with a rich lexicon of motivational patterns, distinguished more for their literary than scientific merit, to draw from in devising excuses for serious crimes. All of them, however, are in agreement that murder is not to be explained as the acting out of the intentions of the killer, but rather as the expression of deep internal conflicts. David Abrahamsen who has examined scores of persons accused of murder describes one of the commoner conflicts, the expression of the universal death wish, posited by Freud. "[E]very homicide," Abrahamsen says, "is unconsciously a suicide and every suicide...is a psychological homicide...The killer is unconsciously trying to rid himself of the fear of his own death." Killing is the expression of power by individuals afflicted with a sense of helplessness. (Abrahamsen,1973, 9-37)

Forensic psychiatrist Fredric Wertham (1949) gives a dramatic example of the psychoanalytic imagination in his book, *Dark Legend*, which reports on the case of Gino who killed his own mother. The impression of senselessness was accentuated by the lack of any reasonable gain to be obtained by the murder. Following the death of his father, teen-age Gino, the eldest of three children in an immigrant family from the south of Italy, manfully attempted to fill his father's shoes by working to help support the younger children. To make ends meet, his mother took a succession of lovers. Gino angrily upbraided her for dishonoring the good name of his late father. But, as Gino complained, she persisted in her immorality until one night, outraged at her perfidy, he stabbed her to death as she slept.

Wertham did not accept Gino's explanation that he killed to avenge the dishonor of his father's good name. Rather he attributed Gino's hostility to an excessive attachment to his mother which he named an Orestes complex, after the Greek tragedy in which the father dies, the mother remarries, and the son is cast out. The Orestes complex originates in instinctual impulses and includes powerful ambivalence toward the mother-image, along with a general hatred of women, homosexual and suicidal potentialities, and profound guilt feelings. This blend of thought and emotion becomes the energizing force in a disorder of thinking termed *catathymic crisis*, the idea that a violent act is the only solution to an unconscious emotional conflict. Through the performance of the violent act, the tension is lifted and the way is paved to recovery by means of treatment aimed at imbuing the patient with insight into his motive. Wertham's belief in the therapeutic effect of murder finds support in the frequent observation of the relaxed passivity, presumably from a sense of relief, evinced by killers taken into custody after venting their anger.

Another psychoanalytically oriented psychiatrist might prefer, on esthetic, if not theoretical, grounds, to explain Gino's matricide by the interpretive framework of the Oedipus complex, named by Freud after the Greek tragedy, *Oedipus Rex*, in which the young King Oedipus, unwittingly, kills his father and marries his mother. According to Freud, the oedipal phase is an instinctual development in the male child between the ages of eight and twelve expressed in rivalry with the father for the attention of the mother. The opposition is not overt, but exists in the boy's phantasy where the father is eliminated from the domestic picture, even by death. Gino's oedipal wish was fullfilled when his father died, and he took his father's position symbolically, though any notion of sex relations with the mother remained submerged in the unconscious. When his mother gave herself sexually to another man, she committed an act of betrayal against him. Her death was the price of her perfidy.

A weakness of either of these analyses of Gino's crime, or any psychoanalytic diagnosis, is the lack of an independent test of validity. The cast of forces in the psychoanalytic scenario, oresteian or oedipal, operates as fates to determine the outcome. Another weakness, which Wertham, himself, in a later essay, warns against, is the psychoanalytic logic of effecting a direct connection between events separated widely in time. "Whenever a single traumatic childhood experience is incriminated or an explanation propounded which is too pat and leaves no room for other significant details we should—like good detectives—suspect the conclusion." (Wertham, 1966: 28)

Gino's anger toward his mother reflects sociological realities more than metaphors of Greek tragedy. Psychiatric examination showed no sign that Gino was mentally deranged. The social context of the killing more parsimoniously indicates that the emotional conflict within Gino occupied a conscious level of awareness. He believed that his mother had seriously neglected her children. By the sentiments of the south Italian peasant culture which shaped the youth's ideals regarding sex and women, she was a slut. In Gino's words, "[I]t is wrong for a girl to go [have sexual intercourse] with a man for any reason except if she is married, and then only with her husband." (Wertham, 1949: 102) The mother flagrantly violated ideals of chastity and maternal duty in taking lovers and lavishing the pitifully meagre family resources on them instead of her children. When he slew her he was seventeen, a man's age, and infused with the southern Italian-Sicilian value system which justifies the infliction of death upon a woman who has brought shame to her family. In Gino's judgment she deserved to die. That he considered himself merely the instrument of retribution is reflected in his calling out as he stabbed her, "Vigliacca, traditrice." (Bum, you dishonored the family!)

The Case of John Hinckley, Jr.

To cover the confusion generated by the muddy language of psychoanalysis, practitioners retreat to the ground that their field is art as well as science. The proportional mix of art and science as ways of expressing truth in forensic testimony all too frequently turns out to be overwhelmingly art and minuscularly science. The psychiatric evidence presented in the case of John Hinckley, Jr., the nearly successful assassin of President Ronald Reagan, strikingly illustrates the arrogation of artistic license by practitioners of forensic psychiatry. The evidence of insanity submitted by the defense lawyers indicated a history of personality disorder more authentic than that offered in most notorious insanity-murder cases. Hinckley had been in psychiatric therapy for some years prior to the crime. Signs of disturbance appeared in adolescence and worsened as he emerged into young manhood. Ever since he saw the film *Taxi Driver*, he was obsessed with the character of a twelve year old prostitute, played by the film actress Jodie Foster and the character of the cab driver, Travis Bickle, a friendless lonely man struggling to break out of his isolation, with whom he identified. He decided upon the assassination of the president as a violent dramatic act which would win Jodie's attention and by its sheer enormity, constitute a token of his undying love for her.

A parade of psychiatric withesses testified for and against the insanity issue. Dr. Park Dietz for the prosecution downplayed the seriousness of the defendant's mental problems. John was spoiled, scornful of work, and thought about how much publicity he could get out of the crime. He exaggerated his feelings for Jodie Foster and his identification with Travis Bickle in order to appear crazy. A psychiatric expert for the defense, Dr. Thomas Goldman, ladled his opinion directly out of the brew of Freudian theory. The defendant's father, John Hinckley, Sr., in a book titled *Breaking Points* co-authored with Mrs. Hinckley, credulously describes Dr. Goldman's diagnosis. "I listened absorbed as pieces of the story we had heard only in fragments came together. I had known that John resented, at times even hated me. Only now did I discover that this constituted a 'classic Oedipus complex,' that when he aimed at the President he was also aiming at me. The President, according to Dr. Goldman, was the ultimate father figure, symbol of the authoritative male who was keeping John from possessing the 'idealized mother figure' whom he saw in Jodie Foster." The elder Hinckley had no difficulty in squaring the tissue of assumptions in Dr. Goldman's story with his need to support his son: "I didn't understand how this could be, since she was so young—nor how she could be both love object and mother figure—but apparently the subconscious knew no such logical barriers." (Hinckley, 263) Dr. Goldman's analysis gives pause to wonder, given the psychoanalytical presumption of the universality of the Oedipus complex, at least in western societies, why the assault rate on authority figures in public life isn't much higher.

The parent-authors express dismay at the riot of contradiction in the opinions of opposing psychiatrists. One Harvard University expert claimed John was psychotic. Another Harvard psychiatrist claimed he wasn't. A third said he was in love with himself; still another said he hated himself. One said he was delusional; another said he had never been delusional. The inability to agree on such basic matters, the parents reasonably concluded, was confusing to the jury and to the public.

John's mother provides information that more cogently explains John's behavior. She describes how the film *Taxi Driver* inspired his attempt to assassinate the president. John saw in Travis Bickle's solitary life a replication of his own problems, and in Bickle's solution, an adaptation to overcome these problems. To his mother's distress, John aped Bickle's display of bigotry toward blacks and some of his clothing styles. John sent letters home describing non-existent persons and events suggested to his imagination by the film which he saw repeatedly. He wrote about the great life he had been leading and "Lynn," the wonderful girl he had been dating. In the film the model for "Lynn" rebuffs Bickle who procures guns and stalks the handsome presidential candidate for whom "Lynn" works as a volunteer. John did the same, arming himself and following Ronald Reagan on his speaking tour itineraries before and after he became president. The young prostitute in the film, Iris, played by Jodie Foster, is held in thrall by a loathsome pimp whom she loves and depends upon. The climax comes in a violent scene in which Bickle heroically distinguishes himself by killing the girl's pimp. Iris's parents are grateful to him for rescuing their daughter, and the formerly rejecting "Lynn," moved by his courage, wants to be with him. (Hinckley, 266-268).

Although the psychiatrists could not agree on John's mental state, there is little doubt that at age twenty-five he was locked into an adolescent level of emotional development. The need to overcome his low self-esteem impelled him to act out the scenarios of his fantasy world. The stimulation of fantasy by movies is not uncommon to mature individuals of any age; a mark of maturity is the ability to keep fantasy and reality separate. Adolescents who have yet to experience the fulfillments of adult life, like John Hinckley, are more apt to merge the two realms of experience.

The combination of physical maturity and childish daydreaming passes for normal in adolescence. In a twenty-five year old man, particularly of John's upper middle class background, it does not. In an attempt to force his son's maturation, John's father, under psychiatric advice, had driven him to the airport, put him aboard a flight, and told him to get out on his own, to grow up, as it were. John was painfully aware of his inability to make an appropriate adult adjustment. So with money provided from home, he wandered about the country. From a distance, he could regale his parents with letters describing the great life was leading, and they wishfully came close to believing him.

It is not difficult to understand why John was so beguiled by the film. It imbued him with the idea that he fit the character of Travis

Bickle and like Bickle, he could solve his own problem by an act of violence. The missing piece in the jigsaw puzzle of John's motive is why he constructed a violent solution to his problem, which unlike Bickle's, could end only in tragedy for himself and his family. The answer, I believe, lies in John's insight into his ineptness, and the notion, not unique in the annals of human depravity, that by a horrendous deed, one can acquire fame and immortality, otherwise available only to doers of great deeds. Equally importantly, by getting institutionalized, whether in prison or a mental hospital, he could get the world "off his back" for good. John was right. He now lives in a sheltered environment, where he will remain for a long time to come, relieved of the necessity of having to make something of himself. He has achieved the kind of immortality that history reserves for innovators. The case of John Hinckley has become a reference point in debates over the insanity defense, gun control legislation, and the effect of the media's depiction of violence on unbalanced personalities.

Actually John is one of a distinct, though fortunately rare, type: the loser, unsuccessful in school, work, or love who seeks entrée to the company of celebrities by killing one. Arrayed with him in this exclusive fellowship are Mark Chapman, the murderer of John Lennon, and Arthur Bremer who came within a hair of killing George Wallace, the former governor of Alabama when he was running for president.

Mark Chapman, like John Hinckley, was a loser who failed at everything he did. He too had an identity problem, a strangely dual one. He had his own "Travis Bickle" in the personage of J.D. Salinger's fictional character, the disillusioned adolescent Holden Caulfield, immortalized in *Catcher in the Rye*, a copy of which he always carried with him, including the time he killed John Lennon and when he appeared in court. Chapman believed that the book held the key to a higher wisdom, and that he was the real life embodiment of the spirit of Holden Caulfield. He also had a flesh and blood hero, John Lennon, with whom he identified so closely, that he was known to have used the signature *John Lennon* in signing out from work. According to psychiatrist Daniel Katz testifying on his behalf, he killed in order keep his identity from becoming completely absorbed into that of his idol. But no one thinks of himself as killing because of identity problems; a self-serving reason is required. Chapman found his in Holden

invariably or even usually associated with psychotic disorders. In judging sexual intercourse with the dead as psychotic, the psychiatrists in the Costa trial confused sexual preference with psychological abnormality. Could they have been unfamiliar with the wealth of cross-cultural research and the voluminous scientific literature on the versatility of the human male in developing alternative sexual outlets? Survey studies of non-institutionalized and institutionalized male populations, such as the celebrated Kinsey Reports, reveal that a wide variety of orifices or surfaces in humans and animals, and innumerable fetish objects, animate and inanimate, have served the male need for sexual release. Clinical studies in the classic Krafft-Ebbing writings, with which psychiatrists are certainly conversant, demonstrate the commonness of "unnatural" practices. Revelations from research on the sexual behavior of women show that women, too, employ substitutes, dildoes and electric vibrators, for the conventional mode of sexual gratification. Anecdotal lore of the funeral parlor industry tells of custodial workers who gratify their sexual needs with cadavers. The reason for the resort to other than heterosexual genital sexual gratification need not reside in a psychotic disorder. Like other forms of anonymous or solitary sexual activity, necrophilia makes practical sense since it involves no commitment or cost, and requires no consent. The lack of response of a live partner can be compensated for by the erotic imagination of the necrophile.

Sometimes an insanity defense can be seen in retrospect as downright silly, but still good enough to convince jurors. In his first trial Fred Milo, who paid to have his brother killed, (See Chapter 6) admitted that he had thought about killing his brother, but was insane at the time and later renounced the scheme. The murder had actually been done, he said, by a business enemy. Fred's lawyer showed a videotape of Fred being interviewed by psychiatrist Dr. Emanuel Tanay. The tape revealed an apparently unstable Fred claiming that his brother was still alive, held hostage, and that conspirators had brought in a look-alike to take his place. Tanay subsequently took the stand and declared Fred insane on the ground that "Any time a thirty-six year old man who has absolutely no criminal record goes around asking dozens of people to kill his brother, there is something terribly wrong." (What was wrong was a deep rift between the brothers over the control of the family-owned barber and beauty supply business.) Tanay continued,

"Additionally, it has been my experience that in almost all homicides where the victim is a relative or friend, the killer has been insane and not accountable for his actions." (Dear et al, 223-225) Given the large proportion of homicides stemming from quarrels with family or friends, and the very small proportion of them involving pleas or verdicts of insanity, Tanay's opinion suggests that the sample of killings encompassed by his practice is highly unusual or that he has an idiosyncratic standard of insanity for the killing of intimates.

Events would bear out that Fred Milo's problem was not some malfunction of perception or cognition. In the absence of any evidence of the identity and motive of the person who did the killing, Milo won a hung jury: ten for insanity and two for guilty. By the second trial the hit man who executed the brother had been arrested. His confession clearly established Fred at the top of the chain of incrimination and assured his conviction of aggravated murder.

Some psychiatric diagnoses display an imaginative, if disingenuous, sophistry. A defendant in a recent Michigan case, a young man with a history of homosexual assault, and suspected of another murder, kidnapped a thirteen year old boy, and sexually abused and murdered him. The defense psychiatrist testified that the killing was the product of an acute cognitive disorder: suicide, not murder, was intended. He theorized that the victim, a fair-complexioned blond individual, bore a striking resemblance to the defendant as a youth, and when the killer strangled him, he deludedly thought he was killing himself. The jury was unimpressed; the defendant was convicted

Although unsubstantiated by direct proof, psychiatrists endorse the notion that victims of serial killings are substitutes for an actual person in the life of the killer. David Abrahamsen hypothesized that the young female victims of David Berkowitz, the "son of Sam," were substitutes for his mother, his sister, or himself, all of whom he hated: his birth mother, for surrendering him for adoption; his sister, who was kept by the mother, for being preferred to him; and himself, for being unloved. In essence, "the murders were an unconscious killing of self. Every suicide, in a sense, is a psychological homicide." Abrahamsen explains Berkowitz's shooting of the women in the head as a symbolic castration of himself. How the head of the victim symbolizes the testicles of the offender is unexplained.* Still another motive, proposes Abrahamsen in a touch of pathos for his patient, was to keep these young women from ever getting pregnant and giving birth to another David Berkowitz to suffer the torments of growing up as he had. (Abrahamsen, 1985, 206-7)

The Multiple Personality Syndrome

Defendants are known to attempt to deceive psychiatrists by feigning mental disability, and psychiatrists are known to be fooled, especially when the signs and symptoms fit a rare syndrome or suggest a new one. Kenneth Bianchi whose *modus operandi* for the serial murders of young women earned him the tag "hillside strangler" easily convinced two reputable psychiatrists that he harbored a split personality, that he, the good Ken, had no recollection of what the malevolent "Steve," who surfaced under hypnotism, had done. Bianchi was later exposed as a fraud by another psychiatric expert on hypnosis, Dr. Martin Orne.

The psychiatric community is by no means agreed on the validity of the multiple personality syndrome. Proponents claim that in known cases, as many as scores of truly separate personalities constructed from relationships of a conflictive nature with people whom the patient has known, coexist with the controlling personality. These other beings reside in the unconscious layers of personality waiting to be summoned to consciousness by an activating stimulus or by hypnosis. For treatment purposes the separate psychic entities are regarded as disconnected portions of the same personality which need to be integrated into the controlling personality in order to restore the patient to a normal mental life. In denying guilt and blaming the murder on one of the personalities, the defense must propitiate both science and the law. Science requires the defense to come up with a history of an emotionally searing interpersonal relationship resulting in the subject's internalization of the personality of an abusive other. The

---

* In Roman times the Latin word *testes* meaning testicles was used as a slang expression for dome, pot, or head. It drifted in modified form into the French language to become the word for head, *tête*. Perhaps the symbolism lies more in the head of the psychiatrist than of David Berkowitz. (Frankie Rubinstein, 122, under "head.")

law demands the assurance that the defendant is undergoing successful treatment for the medical exorcism of the evil personality and is no longer a danger to the community.

Skeptical psychiatrists scoff at the empirical fragility of the multiple personality syndrome, claiming that the different personalities are products of suggestion made by psychotherapists. A clinical psychologist who examined Ted Bundy also took a distrustful view of the multiple personality syndrome, as it applied to Bundy. The different entities in a true multiple personality don't know each other. The shift in roles for Bundy was more like a professional actor taking a role on stage. To do a part effectively, the actor must capture the thought, feeling, and mannerisms of the character he portrays. The same is true of the role shifts we all make in the course of everyday life. There has always been the recognition that people present different sides of themselves depending on whom they face. A repertoire of many roles may reside in one personality: the father to his children, the husband to his wife, the Mafia hit-man to his patrons and his victims. In the transition from one role to another, the basic personality structure remains intact. From a sociological perspective, the shifts represent responses to different sets of expectations rather than a dissocation between components of personality.

Reassuringly, not in all serial sex murder cases do psychiatric experts divide so oppositely on the issue of criminal responsibility. Ann Rule's account of the case of Jerry Brudos, tried for the "lust murders" of three young women, notes that seven diagnosticians who examined Brudos found him well connected to reality and fully able to participate in his defense. Their unanimity is surprising. If the bizareness of behavior can be the basis of a claim to insanity, Brudos clearly qualified. To outward appearances Brudos was quite normal—a large man, six feet tall, two hundred, ten pounds, strong, of higher than average intelligence, an accomplished electrician, a married man with two children. He carried his kinky sexual propensities into marriage, pressuring his reluctant wife to pose in the nude for pictures. Brudos had a history of fetichism for women's shoes and underwear going back to childhood. He was incarcerated for two years in a juvenile facility for the theft of women's underwear, and when discharged, was told by prison counsellors to "grow up." He subsequently committed a number of non-fatal sexual assaults in which he forced women to disrobe so that he could photograph them naked. Needing more excitement than afforded by making his sex slaves into models, he committed a succession of sexual murders in which he enacted fantasies of sexual violence. He accosted his victims, selected for their attractiveness of face and figure, and forced them to accompany him by pointing a gun at them or flashing a toy police badge. One unfortunate woman, an encyclopedia saleswoman, had the misfortune to take him for a sales lead furnished by her employer, and entered his house to make her sales talk. She never left.

After preliminaries requiring his prey to participate in his erotic tableaux, Brudos would strangle them and use their dead bodies for his sexual pleasure, afterwards removing parts—a breast, a foot— which he stored in a freezer. He projected his morbid eroticism into arts and crafts, fabricating paperweights made from molds of victims' breasts. The bodies were disposed of by weighting them with heavy automobile parts and tossing them in a nearby river. The paraphernalia for his grisly hobby—the killing equipment, photo supplies and darkroom, and freezer— were kept in the garage which was locked and strictly off-limits to his wife and children.

None of this activity impressed examining mental health experts that Brudos was anything but psychologically normal. Although he displayed faulty social judgment, his cognitive and perceptual processes were in order. One psychiatrist attributed his killing behavior to a paranoid disorder. Another testified that he could not compare Brudos to other persons he had examined because his mental disturbances were "so bizarre that a psychiatrist might just possibly expect to see one personality like his in an entire lifetime of practice." (Rule, 1988, 199) Yet none of the psychiatrists regarded his fantasies as delusional since he understood that they were unreal. All of them had no doubt that he was an exceedingly dangerous person and should be locked up for good. Brudos pleaded guilty to first degree murder and, whether in a spirit of cooperation or grandstanding to show how clever he was, provided complete information on the circumstances of all of his killings. He received three life sentences to run consecutively.

Discussion

The excesses in the use of the insanity plea need not cause alarm. The tactic seldom works and has not escaped extensive criticism. The most effectively reasoned critique of the view of crime as an effect of mental disease comes from the sociological view that much of what psychiatrists diagnose as mental illness is a form of culturally defined deviance, not an organically based disorder. Paradoxically, a psychiatrist, Thomas Szasz (1961), renders the most forceful statement of this position, belittling the law of insanity as a game for sharpers and impeaching the scientific legitimacy of forensic psychiatry.

Central to Szasz' critique is the practice of defining as disease symptoms for which there is no identifiable physical lesion or pathology, such as found in diabetes or epilepsy. The preponderance of complaints for which people seek psychiatric treatment are moral or spiritual problems for which they might more appropriately consult a clergyman. Sounding more like a sociologist than a psychiatrist, Szasz argues that the diagnosis of schizophrenia or paranoia, is unreliable. The signs and symptoms of these workhorses of forensic psychiatric diagnosis usually turn out to be an idiosyncratic form of behavior considered deviant by the values and beliefs of the community which the psychiatrist serves. The mental illnesses ascribed to criminal defendants, if not feigned, more nearly qualify, Szasz contends, as problems of social deviance rather than psychological disorder. If there were reasonable evidence of acute mental disorder, particularly of an organic kind, like brain damage, the prosecutor would very likely elect not to prosecute in favor of agreeing to the commitment of the accused to a mental institution. If non-organic mental illness is non-existent, as argued by Thomas Szasz, it can have no demonstrable consequences, and therefore cannot be the basis for determining the state of mind or self-control of criminal offenders.

Critics reply that Szazs represents a minority view among psychiatrists. They argue that just because we haven't yet discovered a physiological basis for certain cognitive and perceptual disorders, doesn't mean that there is no disease. Shouldn't the law therefore retain the insanity plea to accommodate instances of mental disturbance so severe that the accused manifestly lacks responsibility for his destructive conduct? The encouragement of dissembling by means of the insanity plea is unfortunate, but does not defeat the ends of justice. Granted that a decided majority of the defendants who plead insanity do not at the time of trial, and doubtfully at the time of the crime, sufficiently meet the diagnostic criteria of mental disorder to be declared insane, there are still instances in which the claim of insanity needs to be put to the test of a criminal trial. The fact that it seldom succeeds refutes the objection that insanity enables killers to elude punishment.

But the low success rate of the insanity plea does not altogether certify the non-partisan objectivity of forensic psychiatrists. A reading of murder trials in which the main issue is the mental state of the defendant provides clear evidence that having the money to obtain the friendly testimony of prestigious psychiatric experts reduces the odds of conviction or the gravity of the offense. Perhaps the reason that so few cases involving the insanity plea are successful is that in the vast majority of cases in which the mental state of the defendant is at issue, the assessment is left solely to examiners employed by the state who have no incentive to devise a basis for excusing the defendant of criminal responsibility. Few accused murderers have the resources to continue shopping until they find a friendly second opinion.

13

Murder Trial Tactics

That the preponderance of murder cases result in conviction does not prove that prosecuting attorneys are better lawyers than defense attorneys. Nor does it mean that the considerable body of evidence amassed in the police investigation confers an advantage on the prosecution. In going to trial, the defense does not necessarily seek an acquittal. Most usually it strives to limit the conviction to a lesser among several possible offenses charged in the indictment. In cases of criminal homicide, the jury's finding can determine whether the convicted offender spends a few years or the rest of his life in prison. The challenge to the defense is to convince the jury that the allegations of deliberateness and premeditation in the accusation are not what the prosecuion claims them to be; that the consciousness of the defendant was invaded by forces which more or less took possession of his will. How the defense rises to that challenge is the dominant theme in the murder cases I shall use as object lessons in this chapter.

The two main examples exhibit striking parallels in the characteristics of the accused and the circumstances of the killing, but have rather different outcomes. Both cases, tried in the early nineteen-eighties, involve the singularity that the young male defendants were university students of ethnic minority statuses favored by affirmative action programs who killed upper social level white students. Leo Kelly tried in Michigan is African-American; Richard Herrin tried in New York is Mexican-American. Richard's case is the subject of two true crime books, *The Killing of Bonnie Garland* by Willard Gaylin, a psychiatrist, and *The Yale Murder* by Peter Meyer, a journalist. The information on Leo's case derives from official records and interviews with the defense attorney, prosecutor, jury foreperson, and judge. Leo did not respond to a request for an interview.

The prosecution in each trial organized the facts into a solid argument for premeditated murder. Each defense knit the facts into a sorrowful tale of how the pains of adjustment to a world in which the defendants felt themselves to be outsiders created a mental imbalance which drove them to kill. Stripped of sentimentality, the facts indicate that both defendants killed their victims out of a mixture of resentment and bruised self-esteem, certainly not for material gain. Leo was convicted of first degree murder, which in Michigan carries no provision for parole. Richard was convicted of manslaughter with the prospect of parole in eight years.

The difference between the two cases in the gravity of the crime, or the mental state of the offender hardly justifies the disparity in dispositions. What counted was the sensitivity of the defense brief to the mood of the community in attempting to diminish the appearance of maliciousness in the killing.

Early in the morning of Good Friday, April 16,1981, Leo E. Kelly, Jr., a student at the University of Michigan in Ann Arbor, tossed two firebombs down the corridor of the dormitory in which he resided, allegedly to draw the other residents out of their rooms for the purpose of shooting them. In the ensuing tumult, he blasted two fellow students to their death with a sawed-off shotgun. Leo pleaded not guilty by reason of insanity to the charge of murder and claimed complete amnesia for the period in which the crime occurred. The prosecution contended that resentment, inflamed by Leo's impending dismissal from the university for academic failure, drove him to kill. Leo had been dismissed a year earlier for failure to make passing grades in the pre-medical curriculum. University policy requires a student dismissed for academic reasons to wait a year to apply for readmission, but in Leo's case an exception was made. He was readmitted after only one school term, albeit to a less demanding curriculum.

The trial posed the disquieting question: Why did a promising black student, admitted on a full scholarship to a great center of learning and scholarlship, mindlessly, as the defense contended, or wantonly, as the prosecution charged, kill two popular outstanding white students who had never given him offense? In the absence of any ostensible motive, it fell to the prosecution to make sense of, and the defense, to deny sense to, a destructive act by which the killer had everything to lose and nothing to gain, except a spiteful satisfaction.

The circumstance that the victims were white and Leo was black hinted at a racial motivation for the killings, although no special significance was attached to the racial factor in news reports. To stunned observers the most common reaction was the senselessness of the act. A student quoted in the *Ann Arbor News* echoed the puzzled horror of the community: "It was just an incident that happened. That's all. There is no story." Leo's defense favored this reaction; it fit their strategy of *no intent, no crime*. The prosecution took a less perplexed view asserting that the shooting was planned, but equivocating on whether the selection of victims was random or specific.

The issue was joined in a winner-take-all contest. The prosecution, led by Mr. Lynwood Noah, charged Leo with first degree murder and the defense, conducted by Mr. William Waterman, entered a plea not guilty by reason of insanity. Jury selection took four days. Fourteen jurors, all white, including two alternates, selected from a pool of ninety-four names randomly selected by computer from voter registration lists, were agreed upon.

The race of persons selected for jury duty is not officially recorded, though apparent to observers. The pool out of which the jury was selected contained only six black persons, all of whom were dismissed by the prosecution for cause or by means of a peremptory challenge, which requires no explanation. The lack of a black person on the jury in a county with 11 percent of the population black disturbed Leo's attorney. But having not made an effective legal challenge to the elimination of all blacks before the jury selection was completed, he was held to have waived any objection. The prosecution denied that the absence of a black person on the jury reflected a policy of racial exclusion and attributed the small percentage of blacks on the jury assembly to the small proportion of blacks who register to vote.

That Leo did the killings was not an issue during the trial. The defense relied mainly on testimony by Leo and expert witnesses to argue that his mental state at the time of the crime met the statutory criteria of insanity. The prosecution replied with its own experts who declared that Leo was faking amnesia and showed no signs of serious mental disturbance. No one actually saw him fire any of the shots, nor did he admit that he had, but the totality of circumstances set forth in evidence make it a moral certainty that no one else could have done the shooting. The defense conceded Leo's possession of the death dealing shotgun. Leo explained, not to the satisfaction of the prosecution, that the reason he sawed off a portion of the barrel and the stock was to make it easier for his mother to handle if she needed to use the gun for protection. Perhaps more damning to Leo's case, the serial number of the gun had been filed off, which Leo denied any knowledge of doing.

A search of Leo's room by the police yielded objects suggestive of violent intentions: a knife, buckshot, a gas mask, purchased only the day before the shooting and within the period of the professed memory loss, a pistol holster containing a wooden carving resembling a revolver which Leo said he had made when he was about thirteeen, and three pairs of *numchuks*, a club-like weapon of the oriental martial arts.

Other objects listed in the police inventory of Leo's possessions, in themselves inoffensive, viewed within the context of the crime, could be invested with a sinister aspect. They included textbooks for psychology and sociology courses, books on martial arts, U.S. Army pistol and rifle marksmanship guides, which Leo acquired through enrollment in the Air Force training program, a Time-Life Book, *Gunfighters of the Old West*, and books on black-white race relations, including *The Declining Significance of Race* by the black sociologist, William Julius Wilson. The prosecution attached great importance to a note pad containing the names of residents on Leo's corridor which impressed them as a "hit list." The list included Edward Siwick, one of the victims. An undecipherable notation written by Leo next to Siwick's name was construed by the prosecution as a sign that Siwick was singled out for special attention.

The prosecution took an ominous view of certain objects made by Leo which could be seen as indications of a racial motive for the killings. Police found what appeared to be a handwritten draft of the title page of a term paper titled: *Civil rights movement, 1950-1964: Brown vs. Board of Education, Topeka Kansas*. Printed diagonally across the lower left corner of the page and underlined were the foreboding words, "it's all meaningless, this is it." A sketch of a nude female, artfully drawn and acknowledged by Leo as his work, was mounted on a closet door. Leo denied a suggestion by Prosecutor Lynwood Noah that the picture represented a white woman: it could be any woman.

Police investigation established that Leo was distant, even chilly, in his relationship with his dormitory mates. Asked later in cross-examination, why, if he didn't associate with the other young men in the dorm, he had their names on a list, Leo replied, "They were all introducing themselves to me, and, you know, I figured I was going to be living here, it would be best to at least know their names."

Psychological tests suggested some degree of instability, but not more than might have lodged in any anxious university student attempting to survive academically in a competitive student body, or someone tormented by the tension of awaiting trial on a murder charge.

The defense constructed their case for insanity out of events in Leo's life which, they declared, inflicted deep psychic wounds compounded by the stress of coping in a hostile environment. They depicted Leo in a mood of depression brought on by the anticipation that he would be dismissed from the University for the second time because of failure to maintain a passing academic record. Latent fears carried over from childhood stemmed from watching the assassination of President Kennedy and the Detroit riots of 1967 on television. Leo lived close enough to where the riots occurred to have heard some of the sounds of the violence. These fears, activated later in life by threats of striking workers picketing a construction site in Texas where he worked as scab labor between periods of enrollment at the university, brought on nightmares and created a powerful delusion of being marked for destruction, much like the "post traumatic stress syndrome" invoked to explain violent crimes of Viet Nam War veterans.

Leo's lawyer attempted to show how these psychic disturbances came to a head as Leo moved closer to the brink of academic collapse. His failure to meet the deadline for completing the work of a sociology course assured a second dismissal from the university. The threat to the self-esteem of this star performer at Detroit's premier academic high school and the impending humiliation overwhelmed his inner defenses so completely that Leo dissociated, regressing so deeply to a stage of childish ego development, that he was legally insane. Shocked into a return to reality by the killings, the horror of what he had done was so unbearable that, being an essentially good person, he blocked out all memory of the shootings and events for a period of seventeen hours spanning the time before, during, and after the crime.

The prosecution, in their turn, totally rejected the claims of insanity and loss of memory. They told a tale of Leo, frustrated by his failures and burning with resentment toward his victims' academic brilliance and popularity, carrying out a plan directed toward the diabolical end which he succeeded in achieving. They fortified the element of premeditation by stretching the time Leo spent in contemplating the crime at least as far back as the procurement of the ammunition for his shotgun, a week before the shootings.

The jury found Leo guilty of first degree murder. On each of the two counts of murder, the court pronounced sentences of life imprisonment, from which, under Michigan law, there is no release except by a commutation from the governor. Defense attorney William Waterman responded, more in sad reproach than denunciation. He condemned the system of jury selection from voter registration lists, in which a disproportionately large number of blacks do not enroll, for having the effect of slighting the feelings and raising the anxieties of minorities and, worse, denying their rights. Thinking ahead to the possibility of a new trial, he suggested locating it in adjacent Wayne County, which contains Detroit's large black population, a fairer place to contest issues loaded with a potential for racial bias. Waterman blamed the recent trial of would be president-assassin John Hinckley for casting a shadow over Leo's trial, implying that Hinckley's unpopular success with his insanity plea could have prejudiced Leo's insanity plea.

Leo spoke at the conclusion of the proceedings. In a rambling, but not pointless critique, he expressed disappointment with the trial, denying its fairness or impartiality. He complained that the largely circumstantial evidence presented by the prosecution did not prove guilt beyond a reasonable doubt. He noted that there were no eyewitnesses to the homicides who could positively identify the killer, and that prosecution witnesses gave conflicting testimony. The prosecution's only evidence to support premeditation, he protested, were "some meaningless notations." The names in the pad were not a hit list, he explained, merely a way to remember the names of dormitory mates. Edward Siwick's name was marked, Leo explained, because he was the resident advisor, the one to whom complaints about dorm matters should be referred; also because Leo "...wasn't sure about his first name, whether it was Edward or Ward." (Edward Siwick was called Ward by other dormitory residents). The receipts for the gas mask and other items found in his car, Leo argued, shouldn't have been admitted into evidence because there was a lapse of five days between the occurrence of the incident and the finding of the car by the police. The clerk in the Army-Navy store and the "alleged" eyewitnesses, didn't remember a gas mask.

Leo censured the jury and the manner for its selection. A change of venue, he believed, should have been granted, not only because of the selection procedure which excludes minorities from the jury, but "because in a small rural area like such as this, I feel it is impossible to pick a jury which has not been exposed to some sort of biased information about a case such as mine." That Leo perceived Ann Arbor, a great university center, with a metropolitan population of over 200,000, and high scores of cosmopolitanism by whatever index one might apply—level of education, income, research and high technology enterprises, and patronage of the arts—as a "small rural area" suggests that Leo's standard of urbanism was grounded in the experience of growing up in the more heavily populated, predominantly black, environment of Detroit. But more crucially, it conveys a sense of alienation from the white world of Ann Arbor and the university community.

Leo's recital of the injustice he endured charged the prosecution with requiring him, against his will, to take a polygraph test (which was not introduced into evidence), pressuring his parents into an interview with "extremely biased psychoanalysts," wanting to deny him the insanity defense if he needed it, and the unsuccessful attempt by the prosecution to make him submit to a brain scan. Leo denounced the legal strategy and much of the argument set forth by his own counsel. The insanity defense was character assassination. he had no mental disorder resembling Viet Nam post-traumatic stress syndrome incurred from watching President Kennedy's assassination or the Detroit riots. Leo disparaged the psychological testing procedures, ridiculing the conclusion, drawn by the prosecution's clinical psychologist, that because he drew a female figure first in the *Draw-a-person* test, he had homosexual tendencies. He accused the court of denying him and his parents their rights and pointed to a parallel between his own case and the *Dred Scott* case in which the United States Supreme Court declared, prior to the Civil War, that persons of African extraction could never become citizens and have the rights of white men.

In contrast to Leo's case, the defense in the trial of Richard Herrin for the murder of his lover Bonnie Garland blurred the outward appearance of a terrible crime by a strategy designed to infuse the jurors with sympathy for the offender. The prosecutor's case contained all of the ingredients for a conviction of murder: premeditation, deliberateness, and malice. But the jury found Richard guilty only of aggravated manslaughter, thereby reducing the minimum sentence to one-third of the time Richard would have to serve had he been convicted of murder. The unexpected twists by which an open and shut case of murder was diminished to manslaughter are rivetingly told in *The Killing of Bonnie Garland* by Willard Gaylin and *The Yale Murder* by Peter Meyer.

Richard Herrin grew up in the economically depressed Chicano barrio of Los Angeles. He managed to overcome the disadvantage of his background by becoming the valedictorian in a class of 415 at Abraham Lincoln High School. His academic achievement won him a scholarship at Yale University where, in his second year, he met Bonnie Garland, then a freshman. Their acquaintance ripened into an intense love affair. Bonnie enjoyed the advantages of growing up in a wealthy family residing in the affluent suburb of Scarsdale, New York. Her father was a distinguished international lawyer.

Richard was the more dependent of the two lovers. He envied in Bonnie an easy self-confidence and joy in living that he lacked. Burdened by feelings of inferiority, he imagined that if Bonnie were to try another lover, she would find Richard wanting sexually. The distraction of his passion for Bonnie adversely affected his school work, although he was not in any immediate danger of failing. Despite the mediocrity of his undergraduate record, Richard managed to get a graduate assistantship at Texas Christian University, an award for which his Hispanic minority status was not a disadvantage. The move to Texas placed Richard at some distance from Bonnie. Although they managed to see each other occasionally, the long periods of separation aroused Richard's anxiety that Bonnie might find another lover. His fears were realized when Bonnie left on an extended European tour with the Yale Glee Club, and weeks passed without word from her.

The fuse of the tragedy was ignited when, at last, Richard received a letter from Bonnie stating that although she still loved Richard, she had an interest in another man who was her constant companion on the tour, and she was "terribly confused" by it all. Richard sought to relieve his anguish by making a trip from Texas to Scarsdale in the belief that if he could see Bonnie and talk to her, the relationship would be restored. He admitted to having suicidal thoughts on the way and bringing a rope which he considered using to kill himself. When they met, Bonnie further eroded Richard's self-regard and inflamed his jealousy by telling him about his rival and informing him that she would be seeing other boys and that their relationship would be reduced to "just friends." For Richard, it was the collapse of his world.

The discussion of the end of the romance did not interfere with the physical side of their relationship, each act of love rekindling Richard's torment at the thought of Bonnie in someone else's arms. Their last meeting took place in her bedroom in her parents' residence, where Richard had been an occasional, but barely welcome, visitor and occupant of the guest room. Bonnie told Richard that her mother wanted him out of the house and out of Bonnie's life by morning. They hugged and kissed for the last time. Bonnie was drowsy from medication she had been taking and went to bed. Then Richard, by his own account, resolved to kill her. He found a hammer on the basement landing, returned to Bonnie's room and, as she lay sleeping, bludgeoned her head so severely that she died within hours.

Richard's attorney hedged a plea of not guilty by reason of insanity with the defense that because of *extreme emotional disturbance* Richard was less than fully responsible for his conduct. Under New York law, extreme emotional disturbance is a mitigating circumstance which reduces murder, subject to a minimum sentence of fifteen years to life, to manslaughter in the first degree, with a maximum sentence of eight and one-third to twenty-five years. In support of the defense's insanity plea, an expert witness, Dr. John Train, offered a diagnosis that allowed Richard to appear normal, yet be mentally ill. He testified that Richard was suffering from a severe mental disease termed *transient situational reaction* which he characterized as "an adult adjustment problem." Train explained: "We apply this term to individuals who appear to be relatively normal, in that they have no history of being in mental hospitals, they have no history of attending psychiatrists. And they seem to be getting along quite well except that they are relatively unstable." The standard by which Richard was found unstable by Train, is that with an IQ of 130, indicating a superior mental capacity, Richard made barely passing grades. People such as this, Train explained, lack psychological flexibility and when faced with great stress, collapse under the strain. (Gaylin, 159)

If scholastic underachievement, accompanied by higher than average mental capacity, be a predictor of violent proclivities, as Dr. Train seemed to think, our institutions of higher learning may contain armies of deranged students or, worse, murderers. But educators and parents of underachievers need not fear this alarming prognosis. For as Gaylin explains, "Train had set up a theoretical discussion to serve the needs of his client. He had to convince the jury that Richard was crazy enough to be excused from responsibility for the dreadful acts that were done. But he could not frighten the jury. Richard could not now be crazy because a jury need not be logically accountable, and culpable or not, Richard might be convicted simply because these twelve ladies and gentlemen might rest more comfortably in their beds at night with a potentially 'crazy' Richard locked up. So Train allowed for a 'slow' return to normal." (Gaylin, 159-160) In his zeal to obviate any criminal liabilty, Train may have overstated the severity of Richard's "transient situational disturbance." Quite correctly, he identified it as a form of personality disorder, but according to the *Diagnostic and Statistical Manual III*, it ranks below psychosis and neurosis in severity. It is a kind of emotional storm commonly experienced under stress.

As jerry-built and vulnerable as Richard's psychiatric defense was, the prosecutor, whether from high confidence in the strength of his own case, contempt for, or lack of familiarity with, psychiatric diagnosis, let much of the defense testimony pass unchallenged. Unlike Leo's case, there was no need to grope for a motive. Richard's confession made it glaringly apparent that he had willfully killed Bonnie, and why. The intent of the act was explicit in Richard's narration of events leading up to and including the killing. He searched about the house for a weapon. He admitted that he had considered slashing Bonnie's veins and then lying down beside her and doing the same to himself, but on second thought, Bonnie would resist and it might not work. Finding the hammer crystallized his intent, which in turn clarified his motive. He was impelled by a mixture of self-pity and jealous rage; if he couldn't have her, no one else could. Bonnie's inconstancy cost her the wrath of Richard's retribution.

The sociological implications of Richard's homicidal behavior were unexamined by either side, understandably, because the law makes no allowance for them. A confusion of mind sufficient to excuse or mitigate the crime must result from a diagnosable mental disorder. The defense of necessity fell back upon stock psychiatric clichés, uninformed by insights concerning the ethnic sentiments and values which nourished the cognitive and emotional base of their client's inner life.

Richard Herrin came from a Mexican-American background with powerful traditions of female chastity and the obedience and subordination of women to men. He judged Bonnie's insistence on consorting with other men as a violation of the monogamous ideal he had sacrificially accepted for himself since his Hispanic heritage imposed no such obligation on him as a man. Understood in this light, the unbearableness of the image of Bonnie lying with another man, although in part stemming from Richard's lingering adolescent sense of inadequacy, could be dignified by attribution to a moral code. To explain Richard's motive for the crime in terms of Richard's cultural background, however valid the insight, would be strategically unwise for either side: the prosecution, because it could arouse the accusation of racism; the defense, because it would clearly attest to the rationality of Richard's mental state.

The verdict was a trade-off. The jury rejected the defense's insanity plea, but also denied the prosecution its murder conviction. They arrived at a compromise of first degree manslaughter which the sentencing judge, to compensate for the jury's softness, toughened with the maximum sentence allowed: eight and one-third to twenty five years.

Gaylin believes that the prosecution lost the murder conviction because it directed its argument only to the murder charge and did not contest the manslaughter issue. Another possible factor in Richard's conviction of the lesser degree of homicide was an outpouring of sympathy from various segments of the community, particularly the Catholic chaplaincy at Yale University which supported him with bail bond, a place to live while awaiting trial, and, most significantly, heavy funding for his legal defense. One life was already destroyed, they lamented; why not help him to dispel guilt feelings, to mend and make whole his own life? Although it is difficult to estimate the effect of such support on the jurors' attitudes, the highly visible presence of Richard's partisans in the courtroom and the clear sign that they deeply cared and were concerned for him, cannot be dismissed from the equation for the verdict that was delivered. Gaylin believes that the prosecution's failure to create equally a presence of the victim in the proceedings resulted in her loss being overshadowed by concern for the offender.

There was no comparable show of community support for Leo Kelly from civil rights or religious groups or associations devoted to minority causes, not even his fraternity brothers. Other than a few complaints of racism in the conduct of the trial and the verdict and some murmurings that institutional racism at the University of Michigan drove Leo to a state of murderous desperation, there was no move to use Leo's case as a rallying point to attack campus racism or university indifference to the needs of minority students. The funding for his defense was supplied out of the modest means of his parents.

The black student community adopted a low profile. In the weeks after the shootings, while the university community was still recovering form the shock of the tragedy, one black student, taking a bolder posture, wrote to the *Michigan Daily*, the student newspaper: "Having gone through the University of Michigan as an undergraduate and subjected to racist acts by professors, Caucasian students, and [College of Literature, Science and the Arts] counsellors, I can understand why Leo Kelly, Jr. allegedly reacted the way he did."

In the next issue of the *Michigan Daily*, prominently positioned above a letter from a student denouncing the rationalization of the murder in the letter of the black student, there appeared a syndicated column by a black intellectual, Professor Manning Marable of Purdue University, commenting on the then still unsolved Atlanta murders of twenty-six or more black children. Marable set forth a militant black perspective on black violence in terms remarkably concordant with the view of the black student letter-writer and what many black students were saying among themselves: "The killings are a direct product of white racism. It does not matter who is actually murdering the Black youth of Atlanta, Georgia. The climate of white racism and political repression has nurtured the social pathology of the killer or killers." (The cases were later closed by the conviction of Wayne Williams, a black man, who, though tried for only two of the killings, was believed responsible for all of them.)

Whether Leo's apparent legal guilt inhibited the emergence of activist support efforts is doubtful since commonly they are draped in the rhetoric that social injustice rather than a moral deficiency of the offender is the cause of the crime. Persons convicted of the most heinous crimes have attracted the sympathy and support of celebrities, civil libertarian associations, fan groups, or lawyers who specialize in defending underdogs. Literary figures and social critics of such diverse ideological stance as William Buckley and Norman Mailer, have been in the forefront of movements to obtain clemency for brutal killers.

The lack of support for Leo can be traced, in part, to a changing ideological climate. By 1982, the year of Leo's trial, a political and social conservatism had displaced the raucous campus activism of the nineteen-seventies. There was less disposition to convert criminal cases into *causes célèbres* for liberal objectives. The circumstances of the crime, not to mention Leo's uningratiating demeanor, cooled any inclination of liberal activist elements in the University and civic communities to mobilize support for him. The apprehension surfaced that Leo had transported the murderous violence of inner city Detroit into Ann Arbor's peaceful haven of learning and culture.

However problematic the factual foundation for that anxiety, the defense in dealing with an all white jury needed to come to grips with the pervasive association of young black males with violent crime and the fear it generates in white people, as well as the predominantly black victim population. The defense needed to check the rub-off of harmful racial stereotypes on Leo by confronting the racial issue head-on, and in their own terms. The defense could have laid a plausible foundation for an expert opinion on how the pains of minority status prodded Leo's drift to violence. Other than complaints directed at the exclusion of blacks from the jury, however, there was an avoidance of the subject by the defense.

Leo Kelly, like Richard Herrin, was the beneficiary of a university affirmative action program which awarded him the honor of a full scholarship and then thrust him into a role for which he was handicapped by acculturation in the ghetto. Both young men experienced academic difficulties from the beginning. To be sure, many black and Hispanic students have difficulty in coping with college level work, but don't deal with their frustrations by violent behavior, let alone murder. Leo and Richard, however, were special. Although most black or Hispanic students who enter top drawer universities like Yale or Michigan receive some form of financial aid, few have as good high school records or as generous scholarship aid as these two, and therefore do not bear the pressure of as high expectations. For a decided majority of minority students in "white" universities there is the presumption that they will need special help and counselling if they are to complete the four-year program and graduate. Most full scholarship awards to black male students are for athletic prowess and require maintaining only a passing average, which at some universities can be managed for students with scant academic preparation or interest by designing special curriculums for them or pressuring faculty to award them passing grades.

The University of Michigan takes pride in its reputation as one of the finest universities in America, and to insure its continued excellence, maintains high standards of admission. Preference is accorded applicants who have achieved excellent academic records in high school. In the interest of recruiting students from a diversity of backgrounds, promising minority students are frequently exempted from strict admission requirements. The high level of expected academic performance and the encouragement of individual initiative in learning promote a competitiveness that works to the disadvantage of minority students since they are not, on the average, as well prepared as the other students.

The mass production model of undergraduate education adopted in large publicly supported (and many private) universities in the United States, including the University of Michigan, adds to the disadvantage of students who are handicapped by deficiencies in preparation or incentive. The fact that much of the instruction is given in large lecture sessions with enrollments running into the hundreds, discourages students from going directly to their professors with questions or for needed assistance. Some senior faculty do not encourage visitation by undergraduate students since it takes time from their "real work"—the writing of grant applications, the supervision of graduate students in research funded by the awarded grants, and turning out research publications by which they enhance their scholarly reputations and value on the job market. Likewise junior faculty know that their application for the treasured status of academic tenure will be judged more by their output of scholarly writing than by teaching effectiveness.

To compensate for the impersonalness of the lecture hall, the system provides for students to meet weekly in small sections devoted to discussion. Offsetting the advantage of a gain in intimacy, a large share of the instruction is delivered by teaching assistants, themselves graduate students, much of whose time is taken up with the demands of their own goals—coursework, studying for qualifying examinations, or writing the doctoral dissertation—and whose understanding of their subject and teaching effectiveness not uncommonly lack professional maturity.

Given the unevenness of the quality of instruction and the indifference to the plight of the individual built into the system, many white middle class students, as well as minorities, encounter academic difficulties. In the panic of "sink or swim," many drop courses in which they are doing poorly by a specified deadline in order to avoid a poor or failing grade on their record.

When originally admitted, Leo undertook a difficult program of study in the natural sciences and mathematics, areas which very few black students and progressively fewer white students elect, often for want of an adequate secondary school preparation. The demands of the academic program did not loom as a hindrance to Leo since he had attended a high school noted for the high quality of its educational program and specialization in the sciences. But the course load turned out to be more than he could handle. He managed a low passing average in his first year. He blamed his lackluster performance on having joined a fraternity whose initiation rites made excessive demands on his time. In his second year, he sampled courses like physics and calculus for engineers and found he couldn't handle them. The complaint, rendered in testimony, that he had no business taking courses in classes with people preparing for engineering careers when he was just trying them out, should not be taken as a lame excuse. An alert concerned academic advisor would have taken note of Leo's difficulties in the first year and counselled him away from so heavy a concentration in difficult courses which were not essential to his program. There is no indication that Leo sought special help with his studies. Like many other black (and white) male students who conceal anxiety over their work by exhibiting an air of self-sufficient composure, the impression that others perceived him as in less than full control would be an embarrassment.

The source of Leo's academic difficulties after his readmission is less apparent. There is no reason to doubt that he was up to the intellectual demands of the courses, which were not as difficult as those of his previous enrollment. If he had any deep worries or concerns, emotional or financial, he kept them to himself. What is certain is that his work flagged and he succumbed to the apathy of discouragement which afflicts so many black male students in "white universities." They withdraw psychologically, frequently cutting class and neglecting to keep up with reading assignments long before the official pronouncement that they are dismissed.

Both sides awkwardly sidestepped the injection of the racial factor into the trial. Except for the defense's complaint concerning racial discrimination in jury selection and the reference to the Detroit riot of1967 as a factor in the paranoia imputed to Leo, Leo's lawyer did not inject the black experience into his defense. He hardly touched the subject of how growing up black may have influenced Leo's attitudes and behavior and the behavior and attitudes of whites toward him. Nothing was made by either side of Leo's avoidance of whites, expressed in his coolness to overtures by the residents of his corridor and his preference for exclusively black social companionship.

The theme of a racially grounded resentment as a factor in the killings obliquely entered the prosecution's case in the form of the note found in Leo's room containing the cryptic epitaphic statement: "Civil rights
　　　Brown v. Board of Education,
　　　Topeka, Kansas
　　　It's all meaningless
　　　This is it"

These words may have served the purposes of the prosecution insofar as they connoted the coiling of the spring of premeditation out of a sense of racial injustice.

The prosecution avoided the direct injection of the racial factor, except in a dispute with the defense over the admissibility in evidence of the picture sketched by Leo and hung on the door of a closet in his room. Since the jury was dismissed from the courtroom while the issue was argued before the bench, the matter did not enter into their deliberations. Nevertheless the episode shows that behind the polite facade of avoidance, the implication of a racially-toned motive for the killings lurked within the prosecution's thinking. The prosecutor hinted, over the defense's strenuous objection, at a connection between Leo's sketch of a nude woman, perceived by the prosecutor as a white woman—she was drawn on white paper and unshaded—and Leo's possession of William Julius Wilson's book, *The Declining Significance of Race*. Although the explicit nature of such a connection was unstated, and it is unknown what use the prosecution might have made of the drawing in the examination of witnesses had it been admitted into testimony, the jurors could project onto it whatever sexual imagery their racial attitudes might evoke. The judge recognized the possible prejudicial effect of such testimony and ruled in favor of the defense.

Leo's denial that the woman had any racial identification drew credence from the fact that no features were drawn on the face. The thesis of Wilson's book, which was not stated in the trial, is innocuous enough relative to the theme of racial conflict: simply that social class is replacing race as a criterion of social standing. It is ironic that education, the engine of social mobility that would lift Leo out of the bind of racial disadvantage, was delivered in a social context that enhanced his feelings of racial apartness and furnished him with a justification to apply the rhetoric of black rage to himself in his declamation after sentencing.

Leo's counsel might have been well advised not to oppose the prosecution's introduction of the picture. An attempt to attach a sinister significance to it, in the absence of any evidence of a malign symbolism, could have provided the defense with "just another instance" of the sort of insensitivity which, it could claim, aroused in Leo a sense of racial injustice, sufficient to neutralize his self control and give vent to a gnawing rage. Instead the defense drew out of one of its expert witnesses, a clinical psychologist, the testimony that Leo said he had no feelings of hate for white folks; he didn't hate anybody. To the contrary Leo's statement after sentencing, expressing indignation as a black man at the violation of his rights, reeks resentment against whites.

The omission by either side to bring up the variance between blacks and whites in the distribution and average of scores for the MMPI personality test may have added tarnish to Leo's already sullied character. To apply MMPI norms based on predominantly white populations to a black person could be misleading. A prosecution clinical psychologist testified that Leo had an elevated score on the scale for *psychopathic deviant* which, he explained, measures criminal tendencies. Given that Leo received his cultural orientation in Detroit, a community distinguished by high rates of violent crime, some departure from the general population in attitudes affecting test performance on this scale, but not necessarily overt behavior, is understandable.

Unless it appears in a blatant form, the effect of racial prejudice on the handling and disposition of criminal cases is difficult to assess directly. Charges of discrimination get their scientific gloss from studies showing disparities between minority and majority offenders in the legal disposition of cases. Appellate courts have not been sufficiently impressed by the results of such studies to use their findings as a basis for imputing prejudice to trial court proceedings in specific cases, especially when the merits of the case justify the outcome. An appeal to the United States Supreme Court in the case of *Maxwell vs. Bishop* relied heavily on a statistical study which showed a disproportionately high number of blacks among those sentenced to death for rape in a sample of counties in southern states. In rejecting the appeal and the evidence of the study, without disputing its scientific value, the court dealt the disappointed researchers a costly lesson on the difference between law and social science in the meaning of evidence. It held that proof of the kind derived from a survey study is no proof of discrimination in specific cases. The court also faulted the study because the sample of dispositions lacked cases from the county in which the appellant, Maxwell, was tried.

The statistical studies which supply evidence of racial discrimination at the trial level are not without methodological flaws. Although they show that blacks are convicted of more serious

crimes and receive stricter sentences than whites, they fail to take
into account sufficiently, or at all, social class linked racial
differences in criminal behavior patterns: blacks commit a higher
proportion of the more serious crimes of violence, over half of all
murders and non-negligent manslaughters and robberies, and have
worse records of serious prior criminality.

The charge of racial discrimination in the disposition of
homicide cases derives its authority from data which show that the
killing of blacks, which seldom involves white offenders, results in
lesser sentences than the killing of whites, regardless of the race of
the offender. The interpretation that the courts put a cheaper
evaluation on black lives is contradicted by the facts: black *vs.*
black homicides are predominantly crimes of passion which lack the
degree of malice or premeditation required for first degree murder
and frequently qualify as no more than manslaughter. Homicides
involving white victims, whether committed by blacks or whites, are
more likely to be first degree murders since proportionately more of
them are committed in the course of a felony, usually a robbery.

There could be no basis for a complaint that racial discrimination
entered into the strict sentence imposed on Leo since Michigan law
mandates a life sentence with no eligibility for parole for first degree
murder. Leo's only hope for eventual release, other than a possible
retrial resulting in a verdict of less than first degree murder, would
be a commutation of the sentence at some time in the distant future.
The jury selection procedure, on the other hand, may have put Leo,
as a black person, at a disadvantage. There was little that counsellor
Waterman could do about the prosecution's peremptory challenge
to all of the black potential jurors since the procedure is legal. The
dismissal of blacks does not in itself prove prejudice since there are
many reasons unrelated to race for excluding individual blacks.
Nevertheless we cannot dispel the misgiving that an all white jury in
a community with a decidedly middle-class ambience would not
favor Leo with as much benefit of doubt or willingness to mitigate
the charge as a jury with black representation in a trial held in a
county with a large black population.

In order for the jury selection issue to have had legal effect it
would have been necessary to raise it before the trial in the form of
a claim that local prejudice would prevent Leo from getting a fair
trial. One way to have strengthened that claim would be to compare
potential jurors in the county in which Leo committed the crime

with those in other Michigan counties with respect to attitudes toward the issues involved in the case. Surveys to obtain this kind of information are expensive and available only to wealthy defendants or those aided by sympathizers who raise defense funds. They have proven beneficial to defendants in politically toned crimes. A notable example is the case of Joan Little, a black woman acquitted of stabbing to death her white jailer who, she charged, repeatedly raped her. James Reston, Jr.'s account of the trial in his book *The Innocence of Joan Little* tells of a well organized effort to assess the effect of the location of the trial, and by implication, the racial composition of the jury, on attitudes toward the issues in the case. Face-to-face interviews of a biracial sample of residents of Beaufort County, North Carolina, where the crime occurred, revealed important differences between blacks and whites in attitudes toward the poor, capital punishment, rape victims, authority generally, and the Joan Little case in particular. The widely publicized findings showing a pronounced "prosecution orientation" among Beaufort whites resulted in a judicial decision to move the trial to another county. The judge in the case was inclined to move the trial to adjoining Pitt County, unless it could be shown that attitudes there militated against a fair trial. The defense retained a survey research organization to field a telephone survey comparing attitudes in Pitt County with those in relatively more liberal Orange County. The results showed that respondents in Pitt County expressed a much greater pre-judgment of guilt than those in Orange County, to a degree that justified doubt that Joan Little could get a fair trial there. To strengthen the claim that Pitt County would be an inappropriate choice, the defense commissioned a speech expert to do a content analysis of press coverage of the crime in selected North Carolina newspapers. The method consisted of identifying word clusters favorable and unfavorable to the defendant and counting their frequency. An unfavorable cluster was "the ice-pick stabbing" and a favorable cluster, referring to the condition of the jailer's body, was "nude from the waste down." The investigator, lacking the time to do a statistical analysis, estimated that unfavorable coverage exceeded neutral or favorable coverage. To have selected or rejected any of the counties surveyed would put the judge in the position of making the politically imprudent ruling that the people of one county are more bigoted than another. So he moved the trial to Raleigh in Wake County which had not been surveyed. Thus we can't be sure to what extent the subsequent acquittal of Joan Little was favored by holding the trial in Wake County or by the strength of the case made on her behalf.

The desirability of surveying the attitudes of potential jurors derives from the assumption that personal prejudice will bias jurors' judgments. Celebrated cases in which scientific jury selection procedures have been successfully employed by the defense have been mainly political, involving trials of activist celebrities in the nineteen-seventies. Critics claim that the the outcomes in these trials resulted less from the selection of sympathetic jurors, than from the weakness of the cases against the defendants.

There is considerable anecdotal evidence of the inattention, incomprehension, or prejudice of jurors in murder trials. Systematic evidence does not deny that individual jurors may have failings, but finds that they are corrected by the diligence of the more capable jurors. Findings from the landmark study by Harry Kalven and Hans Zeisel, *The American Jury*, show that jurors in criminal cases tend to go with the weight of the evidence, and if there is a bias, it is a pro-defendant bias.

But even if evidence of prejudice in a community is found, it is not a compelling reason for a change of venue; all communities exhibit some degree of prejudice. Even in a liberal community, there are persons with illiberal attitudes. The law accommodates this eventuality by allowing attorneys the means to eliminate jurors suspected of prejudice.

Could Leo's defense have been disadvantaged by a tendency of white jurors to be less inclined to concede insanity or personality imbalance to blacks than to whites, and more inclined to attribute black criminality to an inexcusable lack of ordinary self-control? Although there is no direct answer to the question, Kalven and Zeisel's jury study found that blacks are held to the same standard of responsibility as whites. In a comparison of 134 cases of black *vs.* black with 385 cases of white *vs.* white crimes of violence, they observed a closely similar distribution of acquittals and convictions and about the same pattern of agreement-disagreement between judge and jury on the verdict. (Kalven et al, 342).

The high visibility of court procedures may be an effective inhibitor of racial discrimination, but does the race of the accused affect judgments made at more covert levels? An analysis of the effect of race on the likelihood of referral for psychiatric evaluation of criminal responsibility and on the outcome of the evaluation was conducted at the Forensic Center that evaluated Leo, coincidentally for the period in which Leo's evaluation took place. The results showed that blacks are less likely than whites to be referred for evaluation, but once evaluated, blacks have the same probability of being diagnosed insane. The author conjectures that the lower rate of referral may reflect either a disadvantage of blacks in the legal system or a racial difference in homicidal behavior patterns. (Packer)

Even if the Ann Arbor jury dealt more strictly with Leo than a hypothetical Detroit jury might have, such a disparity would likely reflect a regional rather than a racial bias. had Leo been white, there is no reason to think that he would have been treated more leniently. Dispositions are less severe in heavily urbanized high crime rate areas of Michigan than in less densely populated lower crime rate areas of the state. Not only are sentences less severe in the more urbanized areas, but plea negotiation is more frequently and openly practiced, resulting in a wholesale reduction of the gravity of the offenses originally charged. In the Recorder's Court of Detroit, where it is likely that counselor Waterman, as a black man, would have felt more comfortable and confident in arguing Leo's case, plea bargaining is a standard practice. Bureaucratic exigency unites judge, prosecutor, and defense lawyer into a smoothly functioning team to facilitate the flow of cases through the docket. A comparison of Detroit with Baltimore and Chicago by political scientists James Eisenstein and Herbert Jacob, based on court records of the nineteen-seventies, shows that Detroit far exceeded the other cities in the amount and standardization of plea bargaining. (Eisenstein et al)

Generalizations on the racial factor in the administration of justice however, may not hold in particular cases. Contingencies affecting the selection of the presiding judge or the jurisdiction in which the crime is committed can have an unpredictable effect. Compare Leo's case, for example, with a more recent inter-racial killing, the disposition of which became a *cause célèbre* for racial justice in ethnically pluralistic southeastern Michigan. Vincent Chin, a young Chinese-American, got into an argument in a bar with two white Americans who took him for a Japanese and berated him for the loss of jobs in the American automobile industry to Japanese imports. Heated words led to an exchange of blows; no one was badly hurt. The two whites left the bar, went to their pickup truck, and got a baseball bat. They lay in wait and when Chin left the bar, they attacked him; the one holding the baseball bat clubbed him to death. The crime included the use of a deadly weapon and premeditation, but whether it amounted to first or second degree murder did not become an issue. Presumably the use of a baseball bat to bash a person's head did not suffice to hold the defendants to a presumption of an intent to kill. The defendants were allowed to plead guilty to felonious manslaughter and were awarded probation because the judge believed that they had no prior record of violent crime (actually, one did), were regularly employed, and had a history of social stability suggesting that they were unlikely to offend again.

The leniency of the disposition enraged the victim's survivors and their supporters, including the Asian-American community nationally. The intensity of the protest led to the rearrest of the killers on charges of depriving the victim of his civil rights. This time one was acquitted and the assailant who wielded the bat was convicted and sentenced to prison for nineteen to twenty-five years. His conviction was later overturned on appeal. In a retrial ordered by the United States Justice Department, held in a different federal district, the defendant was acquitted.

Sociological Slants

Despite the lack of explicit testimony or judicial instructions of a sociological nature in the general run of criminal cases, the facts of killings provide a rich store of data for the generation of sociological insights which, if artfully presented, could, much more directly than oblique psychiatric analysis, promote insight into the intents, purposes, and motives of killers. The cases of Francine Hughes, who incinerated her abusive husband, and Richard Herrin are illustrative. Both cases neatly fit standard categories of sociological analysis. Richard's situation epitomized the state of *culture conflict*. He was a *marginal man*, a product of two cultural worlds, Hispanic and Anglo-American, and not fully at home in either. The sense of inferiority generated by the inability to bridge the social gap between his barrio upbringing and the privileged atmosphere of Yale came to a head in his relationship with Bonnie and exploded with her rejection of him. His solution for his problem was not the gentlemanly renunciation that Bonnie would have expected of a boy friend from her social set. Rather it emanated from the barrio tradition of taking extreme measures to deal with female infidelity.

Husband-killer Francine Hughes was steeped in a lower class Appalachian culture in which the corporal punishment of errant wives was customary, though doubtfully of the degree of brutality which she suffered. The liberal humanistic value system to which Francine was exposed by her education and contacts in the community college aroused a spirit of rebellion, but she lacked the resources or the help to free herself from the menace of an abusive husband. Killing him was clearly a defensive act. The prosecutor failed to anticipate the impact of the hidden sociological agenda in the defense strategy. The unvarnished facts of the killing so clearly supported a conviction of first degree murder that he was disinclined to consider a plea of guilty to a lesser offense, which he could have gotten.

Leo's defense, on the other hand, did not evoke sufficient sympathy from the jury to moderate the first degree murder charge; nor, as in the cases of Francine Hughes and Richard Herrin, was the jury given reason to be sympathetic. Their compassion went to the bereft parents of the victims who were a visible presence in the courtroom. Leo's counsel failed to engage the jury's empathy in language that would enable them to find grounds to mitigate the maliciousness of the killing. Where Francine Hughes was shown to have justifiably killed her harshly abusive husband, and Richard Herrin was seen to have been so deeply hurt by Bonnie that his self-control was impaired, Leo's crime had no such mitigation. He killed two young men who had given him no offense to vent his despair at failing out of the university and satisfy an ill-conceived grievance. To add to the outrage, he expressed no contrition or regret for the loss and grief he brought about.

The failure, if any, of Leo's defense to obtain a mitigation of the charge against him was not due to any denial of legal rights or a failure of the defense to exploit any obvious hole in the prosecution's case. Hindsight, the great teacher, suggests that the defense should have exposed the minds of the jurors to alternative theories of motivation by which to put the crime in a less malevolent light. An adaptive defense should recognize that the formal instructions to the jury for determining insanity or diminished responsibility are vague and tend to oversimplify the complexities of human thought, feeling, and action. Skillful attorneys take advantage of the obscurities by subtly bending their interpretations of events to conform to the judge's instructions and at the same time convince the jury that anguish from soured social relationships unhinged the mind of the defendant at the time of the crime. The defense in effect has to blend sociological criteria of social disorganization with psychiatric criteria of mental disorder.

To show, in Leo's case, how situational and background factors created an emotional derangement sufficient to justify a mitigation of the charge would require his attorney to enter directly into an area of racially sensitive themes. First, he would need to impart to the jury an awareness of the gap between the all-white jury's world of middle class values, by which Leo sought, unsuccessfully, to prove himself academically, and the somewhat different subset of those values characteristic of the cultural world whence Leo came. Second, the jury needed to be informed of the socially ingrained source of the hardships of blacks in bridging the gap through education, a matter on which white, and even most black, jurors are ill-informed, and how Leo was affected by these adversities.

Research on the complaints of black students in predominantly white universities confirms that a principal dissatisfaction is the perceived unfriendliness, if not hostility, of the university environment. Jacqueline Fleming's research on the adjustment problems of black university students, reported in *Blacks in College*, observes that the feeling of being lost on large mainly white campuses is the commonest complaint of black students, and that black students more often and more keenly than white students experience social estrangement and alienation.

A survey of black undergraduate students at "white" universities, conducted by the Center for Afroamerican and African Studies at the University of Michigan, revealed that two-thirds of 695 respondents reported little or no integration into student activities on campus; three-fourths reported little or no contact with black faculty or staff; a large majority mentioned that white faculty and students avoided them outside of class; and more than half claimed to have experienced an act of discrimination. The students judged relations between black students and white faculty and staff to be poor, but when the probe shifted from the evaluation of black-white contacts generally to personal contacts, 80 percent said that their own experience in that regard had been good. Those who felt rejection most keenly coped by avoiding sociability with whites, confining their associations to blacks, and cultivating a black perspective. Blacks view their disproportionate drop-out rate, higher in white than in Negro colleges, as proof of institutional indifference to their educational needs.

With the exception of the best qualified who gain admission to elite schools, black students find themselves inadequately prepared for university level study. Not only do many lack the vocabulary to comprehend source materials, they have difficulty in reading textbooks which over the years have been increasingly simplified to serve the declining reading skills of the university student born in the television era. Although many white students are similarly handicapped, the problem is more pervasive among blacks, and falls with particular strain upon black males, who, failing to see the relevance of the subject matter of their courses to the success they hope to attain with the help of a college degree, discourage easily and give up.

University student affairs personnel have recognized that they can't effectively help black students by only the remediation of academic weaknesses; they must also deal with the molds in which black students cast the thoughts about their plight. Blacks feel that the existing course content does not deal fairly with the black experience. They want dormitory and social space set aside where they can be together. They express distrust of the "white establishment." They would like an increase in the number of black faculty, a vain wish for the present, in view of the fact that so few blacks who take post-graduate education are willing to undertake the years of uncertainty—the extensive coursework, written and oral examinations, foreign language exams, and the writing and defense of a dissertation—required to qualify for the license to be a university professor: the doctor of philosophy degree. Most black high achievers enter professional schools—law, medicine, or business—which offer more definite time schedules of completion, and the prospect of more substantial income.

The third, and most crucial theme in a plea for mitigation in Leo's trial would have required explaining in poignant terms the resentment born of the crushing humiliation of failure. Momentary glimpses of the pains of adjustment of black students to the white campus flashed subliminally during the trial. The evidence showed that Leo dealt with his "white problem" at the University of Michigan by sharply restricting his contacts with the white world. During his first three years at the university, he managed to avoid intimate contacts with whites by living in private housing and confining his sociability to the black fraternity with which he had affiliated. Financial difficulties on reentering the university, however, necessitated taking a room in a university dormitory with a nearly all white population. His aloofness and avoidance in response to the overtures of his white dormitory mates attest to his discomfort with their company.

The defense's only hope for less than a conviction of first degree murder was the forging of an empathic bond between the members of the all-white jury and the self-absorbed inner city black youth. To accomplish this Leo's attorney needed to show that morally Leo was one of them; that his downfall resulted, paradoxically, from sharing their middle American values. Leo's failure in the pre-medical curriculum and dismissal from school had staggered the self-confidence of this young man who had graduated with honors from the best secondary school in Detroit. While in this vulnerable state, the recurrence of academic deficiencies and the threat of a second dismissal added to his anxiety. The defense attempted, but ineffectually, due in part to Leo's uncooperativeness, to show the progressive devaluation of his self-esteem. Displacing the disappointment in himself onto bitterness against the system further estranged him from the university community. The chilling awareness after he was readmitted that he was doing poorly and might fail again deepened his hostility. He attempted to palliate his depression by large doses of vodka and the companionship of fraternity brothers. The realization that his neglect to get his sociology term paper in on time would ensure his dismissal from the University of Michigan a second time brought Leo to a state of desperation.

The case for Leo required showing how setbacks which most people experience in one form or another and yet manage to cope, convulse people like Leo, and Richard, with rage. To do this would require putting the jury into touch with the attitudes, values, sentiments, and beliefs which comprise the defendant's world of meanings. These motivational forces, it can be argued, take command of will just as completely as the exculpating paranoia-schizophrenia syndromes invoked by forensic psychiatrists. Insurmountable obstacles to the individual's ability to move toward valued life goals can break down self-control as certainly as severe mental disorder.

In short, the insanity plea or any other claims of mental distraughtness that might be set forth in mitigation of Leo's crime, to have credibility, should have been coupled with a sociologically grounded explanation. The defense attorney would need to show how pressures of the social system, impinging on the kind of awareness instilled in him by his life experience in a demeaned subculture of that system, drove him to destroy the lives of his victims, as well as his own, for no gain other than the momentary gratification of resentment.

Leo's defense might have gained strategically by committing only one of its expert witnesses to an insanity defense based on psychotic derangement complicated by amnesia. The other witness should have concentrated on the mitigation of responsibility based on the defendant's rage traceable to the cultural contradictions stifling the lives of minorities. To convince the jury of the anguish actuated by these forces, yet stay within the bounds of the legal provisions for any reduction of criminal liability, the defense could invoke the *catathymic crisis, transient situational reaction*, or any other of the psychiatric syndromes pertaining to the loss of control under attenuated emotional states. The two strategic objectives, insanity and reduced responsibility, are difficult to mesh: one claims mental illness and the other psychological normalcy. Keeping them separate would have enabled the defense to do a cleaner job of advancing its case for a mitigation of the verdict by moving on two different salients. One caution, however: although the sociological slant makes more common sense than psychiatric theories in explaining the *temporary* insanity of normal people, in applying it the defense should arm itself for a prosecutorial onslaught against the common but incorrect image of sociology as an apologizer for deviants, perverts, and criminals.

Leo's attorney should not be faulted for failing to impart a sociological spin to Leo's defense. Few lawyers evince a grasp, let alone appreciation, of the conceptual scope of sociology and its application to criminal behavior, criminal law, and law enforcement. Such insights are uncommon in contemporary legal education or inadequately treated in books on practical advocacy. Whether a sociologically informed strategy could make a difference in Leo's case is a moot question, unless an appeals court should grant Leo a new trial. It could have certainly accorded Leo a broader line of defense and provided a more complete truth for explaining the tragedy. It is unlikely that an amplified defense would have prompted a jury to find Leo insane, but it would have strengthened a case for a verdict of guilty of less than first degree murder.

14

Killing And Forgetting

What better defense to an accusation of murder than "I don't remember"? If there is no recollection, if the slaying is performed in a zombie-like fugue, there is no intent, and without intent there is no responsibility. The trick is to convince a jury that while in a non-recallable mental state, the defendant could mobilize and concentrate the energy needed to seek out and kill the victim.

Amnesia comprises several types of memory loss differentiated according to the source. The more deeply imbedded kinds are organic, rooted in lesions of the brain; chronic memory losses stemming from complex psychological disorders; and multiple personality disease in which each of the patient's personalities have no direct awareness of the others. Then there is limited amnesia, defined by psychologist Daniel Schacter as "...a pathological inability to remember a specific episode, or small number of episodes from the recent past...produced by emotional shock, alcoholic intoxication, head injury, or epileptic seizure." (Schacter, 48)

Issues related to the more serious forms of amnesia seldom arise in criminal trials, because their manifestly disabling effects would render the accused incompetent to stand trial. The plea of limited amnesia, however, is not unusual: Schacter's review of the literature finds that this disability is claimed by as many as 30 to 65 percent of individuals convicted of homicide. (Schacter, 49)

When successful, the amnesia defense depends less on clear evidence of loss of memory than on circumstances which arouse the jury's sympathy or antipathy. A college student accused of drowning her newborn baby in a dormitory toilet said she didn't remember being pregnant or giving birth. The jury found her not guilty by reason of insanity. The prosecution's argument that the killing was the willful act of a selfish immature young woman faltered under the testimony of nine mental health experts who agreed that the defendant did not know the difference between right and wrong because she was smitten with a "dissociative disorder" which detached her from the pregnancy as well as reality. (*Sarasota Herald-Tribune*, Sunday April 8, 1990) The diagnosis of mental disorder provided the jury with the leverage to forgive this appealing young woman with no history of wrongdoing other than a moment of folly in a state of despair.

Sleep-walking as a special case of amnesia was the sharper side of the double-edged defense of Steven Steinberg, found not guilty by reason of insanity for stabbing to death his wife, Elana, in their bedroom. Steinberg declared that a couple of bushy-bearded burglars broke into the house, stole his wife's jewels, and held him down while they stabbed her. The authorities didn't believe his story and charged him with murder. The defense scuttled the intruder story and pleaded insanity. One defense psychiatrist expounded that Steinberg had killed his wife in a dissociative state while sleep-walking. His conscious will had departed and his mind was taken over by untamed forces. Another defense psychiatrist, Dr. Martin Blinder, of "twinkie" defense fame in the trial of Dan White for the murders of San Francisco mayor George Moscone and city supervisor Harvey Milk, led another sortie. He conducted a psychiatric autopsy of the victim based on traits and actions, recounted to him by, of all disinterested persons, the killer. The results conveyed a distasteful impression of the victim and insinuated that she provoked her spouse to the breaking point. Shirley Frondorf's book, *Death of a "Jewish-American Princess:" The True Story of a Victim on Trial*, contends that Blinder caricatured the cultural role of the traditional Jewish wife to present her in a bad light to a Jewishly unknowledgeable jury of gentiles. She speculates on whether the jury swallowed the sleep-walking diagnosis or were moved to acquit Steinberg by the defense's depiction of the victim as a nagging, materialistic, sexually frigid "Jewish-American princess."

Ms. Frondorf deplores the flimsiness of the medical evidence set forth in support of Steinberg's claim of somnambulism. During the trial a defense psychiatrist testified to a "wealth of scholarly articles" about homicidal sleepwalkers which, he said in the course of Ms. Frondorf's interview with him four years after the trial, he had located by computer on the American Medical Association data base. Later she was able to retrieve those "scholarly articles" and was shocked to find that they were no more than anecdotal accounts, mainly from foreign journals, worded sensationally, much in the style of articles in the tabloid press. For example: "French detective missing one toe walks in his sleep and then solves the case himself: 'It was I who killed André Monet, I can see it by the missing one toe [which presumably left a distinctive foot track]— but I have no motive, I was walking in my sleep,' says the detective." Ms. Frondorf reports that in the ten cases on record, the conclusion that the killers were in a somnambulistic state seems to be based on the fact that they were all acquitted and the killings seemed to make no sense otherwise. She found no clinical evidence to substantiate these reports nor any other attempt at confirmation.

Dr. Blinder's own account of the case, in which he disguises the names of the principals, radiates self-satisfaction over having convinced the jury of the mindlessness of the killer, despite the evidence of a very practical motive for the murder. "Solly" (Steven Steinberg) was a big stakes gambler who lost more than he won, and at the time of his wife's death was in debt to bookmakers for over one hundred thousand dollars. He felt himself trapped in a hopeless relationship with a nagging, unaffectionate, shrewish, wife who accommodated him sexually but in a jaded manner. One night after falling asleep he arose, went to the kitchen, got a knife, and returned to his wife's side of the bed, none of which he remembered. He claimed to recall only that there were two intruders in the room and one plunged a knife into his wife fifteen times—by coincidence, once for each year of their marriage. Three days later Solly realized that there had been no intruders and that he had done the killing. Blinder's diagnosis put Solly in a mental state of discovering "...that his survival depends upon reconciling the irreconcilable. Overwhelmed, his mind leaves the scene, taking with it judgment and restraint, placing the actor in a state of insanity. Primordial instincts can then direct behavior, briefly free of any awareness of the need to conform to social mores or obey the law." (Blinder, 16-28)

Now whether Solly really "left the scene" can be neither confirmed or disconfirmed. The "diagnosis" obtains its authority only from Blinder's assertion. An awareness of all of the circumstances of Solly's uxoricide—his money problems, abraded marital relations, and the renounced "intruder" account—suggest that the jury may have been as much moved by sympathy for the henpecked husband as by a belief in his dissociation.

The circumstances of Solly's case, overall, are quite like those of the general run of spousal homicides, except that most are committed by people of lower socioeconomic status who lack the means for private counsel and the steep fees of friendly psychiatric witnesses like Dr. Blinder. They must rely on an attorney from the public defender's office who has limited time and resources to devote to one client. Their cases are commonly resolved by negotiated pleas of guilty to second degree murder or, if they are lucky, manslaughter.

In order to escape conviction on grounds of amnesia, the defense must show that the memory loss disabled their client from knowing the criminal nature of his conduct or conforming his conduct to the requirements of the law. The manifestly self-serving function of the plea of amnesia invites malingering and arouses the skepticism of courts and mental health workers, many of whom claim that their clinical expertise enables them to distinguish real from simulated amnesia. Perhaps some therapists do have this acumen, but many lack it. Dr. Schacter's summary report of studies comparing the ability of experts and non-experts in detecting deception found that the accuracy of the experts in distinguishing between genuine amnesiacs and simulators does not differ appreciably from the chance expectation of 50 percent. (Schacter, 56-7)

The experimental research literature supplies indirect evidence of the reality of amnesia as a factor in some homicidal attacks. Dr. S.D. Parwatikar and associates compared the test results of a group of accused killers who claimed amnesia with those of a group who confessed to their crimes. They found that seventeen out of the total of twenty-four in the amnestic group displayed characteristics which broadly differentiate them from the confessed offenders. The self-ascribed amnesiacs scored higher on measures of depression, hysteria, and hypochondriasis, but not to a degree to justify the inference that the amnesiacs who score lower than the majority of their group are faking amnesia. (Parwatikar, et al, cited in Schacter, 50) The study touches upon a fundamental problem in amnesia research: the reliable assignment of subjects to the amnestic group.

If a person shamming amnesia is successful in deceiving those who make the assignment, the data contributed by his participation will contaminate the results.

Leo Kelly's plea of memory loss, reported in the preceding chapter, did not exploit all of the angles offered by that defense. Amnesia by itself is not an exculpating factor. In pleading insanity Leo's defense needed to prove that the amnesia disabled him from appreciating the wrongfulness of his act or conforming his behavior to the requirement of the law. The claim that an act committed in a state of amnesia is involuntary invokes the *automatism* defense, a plea recognized in law, but unappealing to juries. Leo's counsel attempted to overcome juror resistance by explaining the mindlessness of his attack as a case of *post-traumatic stress disorder* (PTSD), the Viet Nam War version of the World War I shell-shock and the World War II combat fatigue. The maneuver required fuller development. The defense needed to make a closer fit between Leo's conduct and the signs and symptoms of PTSD, recognized as a valid clinical entity in the *Diagnostic and Statistical Manual III*. Researchers and consultants on PTSD, John P. Wilson and Sheldon D. Zigelbaum, describe the disorder in essentially the terms that Leo's attorney vainly sought to apply to his client: "The survivor [of life threatening events] experiences elements of the trauma in dreams, uncontrollable and emotionally distressing intrusive images, dissociative states of consciousness, and in unconscious behavioral reenactments of the traumatic situation." (Wilson et al, 70)

A number of considerations oppose the applicability of the PTSD defense to Leo's case. First, the nature and duration of his exposure to the stressful events reported in his testimony were trivial by any measure of the stress of military combat. He spent only a few hours in front of the television set during the broadcast of the urban riots and endured briefly the taunts of the workers in whose eyes he was a strike-breaker.

Second, and more critically, there is no proof that the strains generated by war experience account for the criminal violence of Viet Nam war veterans. The accused persons on whose behalf the PTSD defense is entered are predominantly persons of lower socioeconomic background who, with or without war records, have high rates of violent crime. A large proportion of young men of middle or upper socioeconomic background, with much lower crime rates, sought a haven from Viet Nam service in draft-deferred student status, conscientious objection, or flight to Canada. Those above the lower class who did enter the military had the benefit of better education and higher than average scores on aptitude tests. Except for those picked to be combat officers, they received training as specialists of a sort that allowed them a greater distance from combat with its recurrent threat of imminent death or injury. Those with poorer education or no specific skills or aptitudes were more likely to get training which fitted them for combat roles. The unresolved issue is whether the crime of these veterans is an effect of the stress of their combat exerience, or whether criminal tendencies and the assignment to combat duty are both effects of the disadvantages of affiliation in the underclass. To answer the question calls for research comparing Viet Nam combat veterans with control groups of non-veterans, equated for age and socio-economic status, with respect to the frequency of violent crime.

To illustrate the use of PTSD as a criminal defense, Wilson and Zigelbaum (1983, 74) refer to the case of *State of Louisiana vs. Charles Head*, (1981). The defendant, an ex-marine with combat experience in Viet Nam, was accused of killing his brother-in-law. The authors state that he used infantry assault tactics in committing the killing while "in a dissociative state and without much conscious recollection of what happened." Then they supply information which suggests, contrary to their evaluation of the killer's mental state, that the killing, like other garden variety domestic homicides, was not without an apparent motive. The accused, they explain, "was under stress because his wife took their children and fled to the victim's home." More direct and commonsensical than PTSD is the explanation that the victim had provoked his demise by taking sides in a family quarrel and, worse, challenging the killer's status as family head. The victim's action was ill advised in a subculture of the deep south with a heritage rich in gun lore and a rhetoric of violence concerning the redress of slights to manly self-esteem.

Returning to the case of Leo Kelly, his claim of amnesia could have been made more convincing by developing in greater detail the testimony that he had been drinking a few hours prior to the early morning shootings. A supply of Librax capsules, used for stomach problems associated with stress, and which contain the tranquillizer Librium, were found in Leo's room following the shootings. Librium and alcohol are both depressants; each may intensify the effect of the other. The issue is problematical, but raising it could widen the region of "reasonable doubt." The prescription for the drug had been issued a few years before, and the dosage had long since been discontinued; but a recurrence of the symptom from anxiety over academic problems could have prompted taking some of the pills. One of the prosecution's psychiatric examiners testified that Leo had been out drinking until three oclock of the morning his term paper was due for the course whose failure meant dismissal. Leo later denied, however, that the paper had been turned in late. He said that he went to the class to turn in the paper only to discover that the class had been dismissed early. There is reason to suppose that Leo had been drinking between the time he returned to his room after learning that class had been dismissed and "crashing," as he put it, into a period of non-recall. Leo testified that he had vodka, bourbon, and gin in his room; rum was also found when his room was searched.

The amnestic effects of alcohol on heavy drinkers are well known. But neither drunkenness nor amnesia voids the general intent to commit a crime since the defendant is presumed to know that intoxication may lower inhibition or produce memory loss. Nevertheless evidence of such a state may nullify *specific* intent, or make it harder to prove the premeditatation required to sustain a charge of first degree murder. (Rubinsky et al) Both sides, however, preferred to portray Leo as moderate in the use of liquor or marijuana. This tactic was advantageous to the prosecution in building its case for first degree murder by conveying the clear-headedness of Leo's mental state; but it was injurious to the defense, which offered no convincing explanation for Leo's amnesia or, indeed, proof that he had amnesia.

A creative use of memory loss in the design of a criminal defense appeared in the California trial of Norma Winters charged with conspiracy to commit murder. The story of the case, told by her attorney, Milton J. Silverman, and writer Ron Winslow in their book, *Open and Shut*, qualifies as uniquely bizarre in the annals of criminal advocacy. The defendant learns from her teen-age daughter that her husband, the girl's natural father, has been sexually abusing the child over a period of years. The mother, outraged, goes to a local businessman rumored to be an underworld figure and inquires if he can help her to hire someone to kill her husband. He curtly dismisses her and reports the incident to the police. Soon she is contacted by a person who purports to be a hit-man. They discuss arrangements and negotiate a fee. He turns out to be an undercover police officer, who arrests her for conspiring to commit murder. She gives a full confession which imposes on her attorney the burden of defeating a seemingly "open and shut" case. Meanwhile Norma's husband has admitted to indiscretions with his daughter and conveniently commits suicide.

Attempting to construct a defense, Silverman determines that Norma has been regularly taking diet pills with a content of amphetamine and thyroid. Within a few months she had lost seventy pounds. A consulting psychiatrist agreeably concludes from his examination that the pills have made Norma nervous and irritable producing an overlay of aggressiveness on her basic passive dependent personality. But an expert in psycho-pharmacology gives the opinion that the dosage was not great enough to have that effect, dampening Silverman's hope of arguing for diminished responsibility based on the excitative effects of the drug.

Casting about for other leads, Silverman repeatedly takes Norma over her recollection of events. While reviewing her activity in attempting to recruit a hit man, Silverman becomes puzzled by gaps in Norma's memory of events which he thinks should be very clear. She does not remember how she got to the office of her would-be hit man procurer, nor how she got his name. "It just popped into [her] head." She doesn't remember calling him for an appointment or how she got his telephone number. Thinking she is lying he throws up his hands and derisively exclaims, "Amnesia? Hyp-nosis?" Whereupon the defendant's daughter, who is present, interjects, "He was always doing that to us too." Electrified by the possibility that Norma shopped for a hit man while in a hypnotic trance, Silverman ascertains that the alleged "hypnotist" is a business consultant and adviser to Norma who became her brother-in-law by virtue of having recently married the sister of Norma's late husband. The hypnoses were performed as a parlor recreation on Norma, her sister-in-law, and daughter, ostensibly for the purpose of inducing relaxation. The sisters-in-law remained close friends despite the fact that Norma attemped to have her sister-in-law's brother killed.

Silverman retained an expert on hypnotism, Dr. Barry Unger, who put Norma in a hypnotic trance in which she recalled that her visit to the businessman, reputed to have underworld connections, and her subsequent dealings with the supposed hit-man were in response to a post-hypnotic suggestion delivered indirectly by her brother-in-law. It was the sister-in-law who, under a post-hypnotic suggestion from her husband, directed Norma to contract for the husband's murder. The defense did not deny that Norma had formed a criminal intent; rather that the intent was not the product of her own will, having been implanted by the hypnotist brother-in-law.

Why the brother-in-law should want Norma to pay someone to kill her husband in a way that was doomed to failure and bound to get her into serious trouble raises unanswered questions about his motives. According to Norma, he had long shown an amorous interest in her, notwithstanding his intimate relationship with Norma's sister-in-law, but not in a way to suggest that he wanted her husband out of the way or that he wanted to "set her up." The authors cast him in a villainous role for having taken advantage of Norma's passivity and exploiting his business relationship with her in legally and ethically dubious ways. A suspicious mind could speculate that with Norma out of the way, in prison for attempted murder, the brother-in-law as business adviser, might obtain control of her assets. Whatever his intention may have been in instigating the alleged post-hypnotic suggestion, if indeed he did, neither side took the chance of summoning him to testify. Norma was found not guilty by reason of insanity.

Silverman's strategy cheekily defies the axiom that a post-hypnotic suggestion will not work if it bids the subject to violate personal moral standards. It required the pivotal witness, Dr. Unger, to insert a plug of credibility into any hole that the prosecution might poke. Unger, though never before an expert witness in a trial, played his role admirably, unshakeable in the conviction that his clinical analysis was correct.

The instructions given to the jury were helpful to the defense by excusing from criminal liability "persons of sound mind who suffer from some force that leaves their acts totally without volition." Unger, under cross-examination, however, had admitted that Norma had some volition. Silverman thinks that this admission may not have hurt Norma if the jury also recalled that Unger believed that Norma was powerless to resist the post-hypnotic suggestion, and that if the volition was working against the suggestion, it did so at an unconscious level.

Perhaps the true genius of Silverman's advocacy was not the scientific truth of his case for non-responsibility, but persuading the jury that the victim deserved the fate that Norma had planned for him. Since there is no independent test of the validity of the hypnosis defense, the real issue for the jury boiled down to the question: was Norma worthy of acquittal? Was Dr. Unger's abiding commitment to his diagnosis based on a sufficiency of evidence or the love of his own creation? The prosecution effectively attacked the credibility of the defense's tale and may have even planted serious doubts in the minds of jurors; but they lost the verdict. For Silverman had provided the jury with a reason for moving with the tide of their feelings, to forgive the lady for entertaining murderous thoughts against the self-admitted incestuous violator of her daughter, a man whose personal characteristics, as they were portrayed to the jury, evoked little sympathy if not revulsion. After all he was dead, so much the better by his own hand. The best interests of the community would be served by dropping the matter.

15

THE EVIL MIND

The evil-doer who strikes the common sensibility as rotten to the core but doesn't display any psychotic or neurotic disorder vexes legal and scientific classification. The notion of unbounded maliciousness dates back to the beginning of cultural memory in the personages of wicked gods and fates who intervene in human affairs and the moral lessons of good and evil in religious testaments. Medieval European faith personified evil in Satan and his minions. The evildoer, in exchange for earthly delights, consigns his soul to eternal damnation. In those days reliance was placed on the clergy to ascertain the possession by evil spirits. The state of unregenerate wickedness was later reconceptualized as *moral insanity* to suit the spirit of modernity. The use of moral as a modifier of insanity did not, however, sit well with the emergent behavioral sciences since insanity refers to a "natural" condition over which the individual has no control, and moral signifies a willful viciousness of spirit.

By virtue of the historical accident that the the law assigns the assessment of the mental states of deviant people to psychiatry, it is not puzzling that repetitive callous offenders who are clearly attuned to reality and fully comprehend the consequences of their behavior are pronounced mentally unbalanced. Mental hygienists label this human enigma by the term *psychopath*, *sociopath*, or *antisocial personality*. The blame-removing connotation of disease in these terms is more compatible with the scientific norm of objectivity. I will use *sociopath* in preference to either of the others since that is the preferred term in the *Diagnostic and Statistical Manual III* and because it signifies a   social rather than a biopsychological state.

The Sociopathic Personality

Critics maintain that the diagnosis of sociopathy is a disguise of ignorance. The term itself is a tautology; it merely applies a scientifically flavored term to people who have no scruples. It explains nothing to say that the amorality of the sociopath explains his evil. It is equally inane to conclude that anyone who does such awful things must be deranged. A more logical, but scientifically wobbly, explanation links sociopathy to inherent psychoneurological defects which hinder learning from experience. The proof consists of studies showing that the sociopath is insensitive to moral education or to punishment inflicted to change him.

Every imaginable malicious tendency is imputed to the sociopath—cruelty, treachery, indifference to the feelings of others, and a willingness to lie, cheat, steal, or kill to gratify egoistic desires. Remorselessness looms as his most repellent trait; the indifference and, at times facetious attitude, of the apprehended sociopathic murderer toward the suffering he has inflicted evokes even in opponents of the death penalty the conviction that he is a deserving exception. The term sociopath has become a mainstay of the vocabulary of behavioral science. Scientific and literary crime writers, puzzled by the apparent psychological normality of a subject who strikes them as a fiend incarnate, take refuge in the characterization of him as a sociopath.

Hervey Cleckley's exposition of the nature of the sociopath in *The Mask of Sanity* (1955) contains an extensive inventory of the traits of the sociopath, among them, unreliability, mendacity, insincerity, shamelessness, bad judgment, and overbearing egocentrism. William and Joan McCord, in their book *Psychopath* (1964) regard the sociopath as a highly impulsive, aggressive, unsocialized misfit, driven by uncontrolled desires. The McCords' inventory of sociopathic traits includes every form of anti-social behavior, and many forms that are not inherently harmful to others—glibness, exaggerated self-esteem, need for stimulation to ward off boredom, sexual promiscuity, and lack of realism in planning for the future.

None of the sociopathic traits relates to any disorder of perception or conception; they are all character failings which, in moderate amounts, are deeply imbedded in the human condition. After all, as the saying goes, no one is perfect. In all of the treatments of sociopathy, there is no guide to how much of any undesirable trait, or how many in combination, it takes to qualify as a sociopath. Like the problem of pornography which resists formal definition, those who use the term define it by what people diagnosed sociopathic do; or, as the aphorism regarding pornography goes: I can't define it, but I know it when I see it.

Explanations of how people become sociopathic run the gamut, from *inborn* to *product of learning*. The claim that sociopathy is innate progresses through cyclical phases of acceptability. The revisionistic criminology textbook of Wilson and Herrnstein, *Crime & Human Nature*, exemplifies the resurgence of biologically oriented theories in espousing the view that sociopaths are congenitally different from the rest of the human species.

Wilson and Herrnstein cite research which finds that the nervous systems of sociopaths and normal people differ in arousal level. Sociopaths compensate for a low level of internal stimulation by looking for external stimulation in the form of excitement. They are less conditionable, in the Pavlovian sense, than others. Their lesser susceptibility to aversive conditioning is shown by lower levels of skin conductance to painful stimulation such as electrical shock or hypodermic injection administered in a laboratory setting. Simply put, the threat of punishment does not operate upon them the same as upon non-sociopaths to inhibit criminal tendencies. They are more impulsive and less anxious than persons deemed non-sociopathic.

Some, but not all, of the studies involving electroencephalographic tests reviewed by Wilson and Herrnstein show differences between subjects diagnosed sociopathic and non-sociopaths in abnormal brain-waves: the sociopaths exhibit a tendency toward drowsiness or unalertness. (Wilson and Herrnstein, 198-207) Brain damage and neural defects are found to a greater extent among sociopaths than control groups, but most sociopaths are not ascertainably brain damaged or neurally defective.

The differences in test response between sociopathic and non-sociopathic subjects arguably result more from research procedures and unexamined social background differences than from some hypothesized neurological defect. A study of inmates in a Canadian prison cited by Wilson and Herrnstein (202-203) as proof of the neurological hypothesis illustrates the point. The professional staff were asked by the researchers to identify "clearly" psychopathic, marginally psychopathic, and nonpsychopathic inmates. The label psychopath was applied presumably to the more troublesome inmates, and the label non-psychopath, to those who gave no trouble. Pavlovian tests employing moderately painful shocks were administered to ascertain differences among the groups in conditionability. The resulting differences were consistent with the criteria of selection. The non-psychopaths showed a greater response to the experimental stimuli. They were more apt to change their behavior to avoid punishment. Could it be otherwise? If the criterion for assignment to psychopath and non-psychopath groups was some measure of conformity to rules of conduct, it stands to reason that the higher level of conditionability exhibited by the non-sociopaths is an expression of their greater willingness to conform.

The recurrent research finding of the relationship between moral callousness and organic states of the individual, though not statistically significant, may actually capture some reality. Does the association mean, as advocates of congenital theories of violent crime propose, that seemingly purposive behavior is an effect of factors with a reflexive rather than meaningful connection to the individual's intentions in acting? Doubtfully. It seems reasonable that people who have repeatedly engaged in anti-social behavior would test differently from more self-controlled people. The sociopath's lower degree of aversity to pain, his lower level of conditionability, and his greater impulsiveness suggest a greater defiance of conventional requirements. They imply no more than that he is the kind of person who is willing to endure hardship and risks in attaining his objectives. In short, by the standards he values, he is proving that he is tough. The crucial question is how did he get that way. An explanation based on social stimulation is more consistent with the totality of facts than any theory of neuro-psychiatric aberration. Put in its simplest form: growing up in settings where violence and predatoriness are commonplace, he is perceptually and cognitively adjusted to a greater tolerance for danger and risk.

Not all of the traits or tendencies imputed too sociopaths are inherently base, or distinctive of sociopaths. There is no binding connection between looking for excitement, one of the outstanding traits imputed to sociopaths, and criminality. Young men and boys have adventurous spirits. The individual's capabilities, how he learns to satisfy the need for excitement, and the available outlets are primary factors in determining whether the need is served in scouting or street crime. The characteristics of sociopaths revealed by tests, therefore, are more consistent with socialization in a subculture that values duplicity, violence, and self-aggrandizement, or one that carries the competitive ethic to the extreme, than with congenital factors.

The presumption that sociopathy is caused by innate factors is contradicted by the observation that populations in which callous brutality is relatively common do not differ in organic makeup from more orderly populations. The flagrant violation of rules of civility or the form of the violation is a social not organic fact. By the standard of repetitive criminality, the majority of inner-city male youth could qualify as sociopathic by the time they are in their teens. By the standard of duplicity and evasion, many middle and upper class male youth could meet the test. The most significant antecedent of the propensity for wanton violence is the experience of brutality, emotional deprivation, or inattention in the early years of development. If we accept the premise of bonding theory—that common decency is not innate, but needs to be implanted and cultivated—the origin of ruthless amorality loses its mystery. A considerable body of research indicates the paramount importance of childhood neglect, rejection, or abuse in producing adults who lack both self-esteem and the capacity to love others. Nevertheless, many children subjected to these deprivations, even when combined with neural defects, do not become remorseless violent offenders. Perhaps more importantly, *the personal histories of many murderers labelled sociopathic do not reveal any greater hardships of growing up than the majority of people of their generation and background.*

The Ordinariness of Evil

A close look at the behavior patterns of individuals who have qualified, by some "expert" judgment for the label sociopath reveals that the rotten streak in them seldom pervades all relationships. Rather it is situational, depending on the role of the persons against whom the violence or deceit is directed. Studies of military mass-killers of defenceless civilians or prisoners of war show how decent people can easily turn into pitiless murderers. A former Japanese soldier recalls boastfully of having beheaded more than forty prisoners and torturing many others. The first was the hardest. Ordered by his comander to decapitate a Chinese captive, he was appalled by the prospect, but more fearful of disgracing himself. The rest came progressively easier. (Karnow, *New York Times Book Review*, 11/22/92, 13) The same metamorphosis appears in the numerous accounts of concentration camp guards in World War II, noted earlier in this book.

If the unscrupulous pursuit of self-interest regardless of the consequences for others be the criterion of sociopathy, the syndrome is more prevalent than supposed. Many people with sociopathic traits do not commit serious crimes, and many have no criminal records. Criminal sociopaths are often identified in a process of circular reasoning by no more than lengthy prior criminal records. Persons of elevated social status—physicians, lawyers, businessmen, and politicians—have resources and power that may obviate the need to resort to crime, but, in notorious instances, they have displayed a callous indifference to ethical, moral, or legal requirements. The personality traits of sociopathic murderers appear in the character of great political and military leaders of history. Many culture heroes are irreligious or hypocritically religious. Consequently the punishments or rewards of the hereafter have no power over them. Like Nietzsche's superman they take pride in the courage to make their own rules and run free of the herd. Because they are socially detached, their attitude toward the fate of the victim does not differ appreciably from that of soldiers at war toward the enemy. A rich vocabulary of self-justification can be invoked to remove any twinges of remorse: the victim deserved to die, the gains from the death outweigh any losses, the victim is dead and knows no suffering, remorse leading to the discomfort of guilt, or confession solves no problem for anyone and only disturbs the life of the offender.

A muted form of these sentiments is expressed by executive level personnel in the private and public sectors of work, people of outwardly impeccable character who are indifferent to the harmful conseqences of organizational policies. Their form of sociopathy is most evident in practices with an eye on the profits from the manufacture and distribution of products known or strongly suspected to affect individuals or the environment in ways that produce serious harm, even death. Responsible parties in monitoring governmental agencies add to the danger by permissive oversight or deliberate indifference. Moral crassness among the business élite is revealed in the looting of financial organizations by their own officers and the resultant losses to depositors and investors of lifetime savings. The plunder is abetted by the inattention of agencies entrusted with regulation.

The rampant egoism that defines sociopathy is not as alien to normal sensibilities as it is represented to be. In every generation social critics remind us of the insatiable appetites which drive people to put aside morality in the quest for material or sensual gain. No one fails to comprehend the hypocrisy of proclaiming adherence to conventional morality while secretly breaking the rules. The cynical aphorism that everyone has a price for exceeding moral limits existed long before the concept of anti-social personality was formulated.

Social critic Christopher Lasch identifies the syndrome of egoism as a generator of sociopathy in his book, *The Culture of Narcissism*. He observes that the patients who presented themselves for psychiatric treatment in the 1940's and 1950's had symptoms different from those in classical psychoanalytic practice—no fixations, phobias, or the conversion of repressed sexual energy into nervous ailments. Rather they complained of vague dissatisfaction with life, feelings of the futility and purposelessness of existence. They act out rather than sublimate or repress their conflicts. Lasch explains the change in complaints as an expression of the social and cultural transformations affecting Freudian processes that have occurred since the early days of psychoanalytic practice. The new cohort of patients have shallow emotional lives; they avoid close involvments. Their personalities are constructed of defenses against rage "...and against feelings of oral deprivation that originate in the pre-Oedipal stage of psychic development." Studies of disorders on the border between neurosis and psychosis describe personalities that put on a false front, demand admiration, yet are contemptuous of those who give admiration. They crave emotional experience to fill an emotional void and are terrified of growing old and dying. (Lasch, 71-85)

Since poor people do not present themselves for psychoanalytic therapy, Lasch's narcissistic syndrome is presumably based on the analysis of persons above the working and chronically unemployed classes. It problematically applies to the population from which the vast bulk of killers are drawn and would hardly apply to robbers who makes no bones about their anti-social intentions and motives. The syndrome may, however, aptly characterize the hidden amorality of the rare middle or upper class murderer. Joe McGinniss, the author of *Fatal Vision*, for example, finds in his subject, convicted wife and children-murderer Dr. Jeffrey MacDonald, the epitome of Lasch's conception of the narcissistic personality. But while narcissism may explain the gentler immoralities, it does not suffice for murder. There must be, by Lasch's standard, millions of middle and upper class narcissistic personalities in social circulation who do not engage in violent crime. So to connect MacDonald's narcissistic personality with the killings, McGinniss resorts to the theory that excessive dosages of a diet drug taken by MacDonald produced a temporary psychosis. (McGinniss, 1983, 600)

The muddled definition of *sociopathy*, the unreliable effort to link it to neuropsychological defects, and its uncritical application have not prevented the concept from becoming a catch-all for bad actors who do not fit any of the established diagnostic categories of mental abnormality. It provides law enforcement, mental health examiners, and the literati with a convenient, albeit simplistic, solution to the problem of awful things done by normal-looking people: The wrongdoers have a mental disease, affecting the moral rather than the perceptual or cognitive faculty, a disease for which there is no cure.

The Evil Mind as a Sociological Fact

A. Youthful Members of the Underclass

A consideration of the social factors which define the setting for callous amoral conduct exposes the fallacy of considering "sociopathy" in isolation from the individual's social experience. Psychiatrist Samuel Yochelson and clinical psychologist Stanton Samenow, authors of *The Criminal Personality* incline toward this error. They convert virtually all criminals into sociopaths. Their conception of "the criminal," derives from observations of persons committed to St. Elizabeth's Hospital in Washington, D.C. for psychiatric evaluation under the loosely defined Durham Rule of the District of Columbia, hardly a representative cross-section of people arrested for crimes. Dr. Samenow in a later publication, *Inside The Criminal Mind*, carries forward the earlier work. Eschewing conventional clinical psychological theories of crime, he propounds that the cause of crime is "thinking like a criminal," a mind-set whereby the sociopath entitles himself to do whatever he wishes regardless of the consequences for others. He converts the legal term *criminal*, an abstraction which refers to one convicted of an act forbidden by the criminal law, into a concrete form of degraded humanity.

Dr. Samenow's attribution of criminality to "thinking like a criminal" is a gem of redundancy. It skips the question of how criminal thoughts get into the mind of the offender. For Samenow criminal thoughts are self-generated in quirky minds and occur without respect to the social background or experience of the offender. While he concedes some worth to the hypothesis of their origin in some genetic disturbance, sociological explanations which, as he understands them, deal with the pains of poverty and deprivation, are not the answer. After all, Samenow observes, most deprived youngsters do not commit crime.

To the contrary, most deprived youths do commit crime. Marvin E. Wolfgang and R. M. Figlio found that of ten thousand boys born in Philadelphia in 1945, a depressingly high 35 percent, the vast majority of lower class origins, had been arrested by their eighteenth birthday. This proportion does not include that percentage of miscreants who were not caught or were dealt with informally by the police. In a study of the the effects of migration on the crime of inner-city youth in Philadelphia, Leonard Savitz compared the arrest rates of youths born in the city of Philadelphia with those who had migrated from other parts of the country, preponderantly from southern states. He demonstrated that although the native born tended to have higher arrest rates at earlier ages, by the time the boys reach the age of 18, virtually all of them, migrant and non-migrant, will have acquired a police record.

For law enforcement personnel and diagnostic specialists, like Yochelson and Samenow, who confront the chronic violent offender in their role of agents of public safety, the judgment of the criminal as a ruthless egoist is reasonably founded. But there are other beholders who relate quite differently to the same kinds of offenders and arrive at benign judgments. An interview in *Time* magazine (March 16,1992, 16) with Ms. Léon Bing who has written a book about black youth gang members displays a rather different impression of their character. Where investigators like Samenow and Yochelson find nothing redemptive in their sociopaths, Ms. Bing regards hers sympathetically and even affectionately. Although the setting of her work in Los Angeles is physically removed from the Washington, D.C. locale of the Yochelson and Samenow investigations, the social and cultural backgrounds of the two sets of subjects are quite the same. Both studies focus upon young people reared under conditions of family and community disorganization in crime ridden inner cities.

In a mixture of anthropological field research and investigative reporting, Ms. Bing went to their haunts, won their confidence, and secured their cooperation as informants. But where Yochelson and Samenow perceive their subjects as incorrigible dregs, she endows hers with an aura of romantic outlawry. She observes in them a tenderness toward fellow gang members and loved ones and judges them for what they are rather than for what they might have done.

Ms. Bing sentimentally interprets their feelings about themselves with a touch of pride that they opened up to her to the extent of incriminating themselves in murder. Readers may feel that she goes beyond a scholarly or journalistic role to condone their conduct and to invest them with good heartedness. The following items are illustrative.

—To be seen as threatening to the white people the gang boys encounter on the streets is insulting to them. So they fulfill the prophecy by mugging or some predatory act.

—She was invited to see their collections of Uzis and Kalashnikovs, and was even told about the murders they did.

—As to their being armed and dangerous, "[they]...are among the quietest people you'll meet...when a little kid drifts into a gang he just doesn't get a gun thrust into his hands. He's gonna get homeboy love."

—Paraplegic gang members, disabled in gang wars are "lovingly attended."

—One gang member spotted an enemy on the street and machine gunned him along with his wife and baby. Ms. Bing, in writing about it, thoughtfully attributed the killing to another gang member because she knew his mother would read the book, and the revelation would "kill" her.

The statistical record of the concentration of violent crime in the underclass powerfully indicates that *sociopathy*, as interpreted in the psychological literature, is a coverup for an unpalatable sociological truth: That the failure to inculcate compassion and civility into children is disproportionately a lower class condition and a problem we prefer not to see. Virtually all of the clinical signs of sociopathy reflect faults of character structure that emerge from the monotony and impediments of lower class existence. These include moral ignorance, the reckless quest for thrills as a compensation for a poverty of mind, the resort to property crime to get the stuff of the good life, the lack of self-discipline accompanied by an aversion to external discipline, and the irrelevance in the lower class experience of the deferral of immediate gratification for future gain. The lower class boys' brazenness, lack of anxiety, emotional shallowness, and predilection for engaging in dangerous activities reflect less any organic or psychological trait than an experientially created indifference to the stigma or inconvenience of falling into the hands of the law.

B. The White Suburban Sociopath

Whites of ambiguous social class background produce a share of sociopaths. Writer Ann Rule tops off her absorbing account of the case of convicted murderer David Brown with the judgment of him as a classic case of the complete sociopath. Ms. Rule joins other true crime writers in employing *sociopath* as an explanation for perverse conduct rather than a symptom. Her tale of Brown's depravity, in a book titled *If You Really Loved Me*, reveals complexities of character unaccommodated by the simplistic notion of sociopath. Serendipitously, however, it contains the ingredients to construct a sociological context that makes more sense in explaining the killing. I offer such an alternative analysis with thanks to Ms. Rule for the collection and organization of the considerable detail to facilitate the job.

The book describes the emergence of an arrant egoism in a man of working class background and eighth grade education whose suddenly acquired ability to make a lot of money plunged him into the heady confluence of insatiable demands for material wants and the atrophy of the social control of personal conduct, a state that sociologists term *anomie*.

To collect insurance worth over $800,000 and get rid of a wife who allegedly no longer suited his fancy, he duped his daughter by a previous marriage and his sister-in-law into conspiring with him to murder her. That David Brown killed, as well as lied, cheated, and stole to advance his fortunes reflects a distinctive turn of events in his life.

The thirty-two year old Brown's household domain comprised his wife, Linda, age twenty-three whom he had married when she was fifteen, their infant daughter, a daughter from Brown's first marriage, Cinnamon, age fourteen at the time of the killing, and his wife's sister, Patti, age seventeen, with whom he had begun an affair when she was eleven. He enmeshed them in bonds of obedience and emotional commitment to him by lavishing expensive gifts upon them, working on their sympathies by feigning illness, and prefacing his outlandish demands with, "If you really loved me." Also included in his patriarchal hegemony were his parents who moved in with him after Linda's death, and relatives whom he employed in his business.

He enlisted Cinnamon and Patti as accomplices in the plot to kill his wife, Linda, by fabricating the tale that she was conspiring with agents of organized crime to kill him. He couldn't, or wouldn't, kill her himself; they had to help him by doing the job for him, and if they didn't do it now, it would be too late to prevent her from killing him. He egged Cinnamon into shooting Linda as she lay asleep and established an alibi for himself by leaving the house before the killing took place. He had given Cinnamon a quantity of pills—which he later described as sufficient only to give her a bellyache, to make it look as if she was trying to commit suicide— and ordered her to take the pills and hide in the doghouse after the shooting. Actually the pills were a potentially lethal dose, which, if they worked, would have eliminated her as a witness. They made her quite ill; she might have died if she had not soon vomited them. She was held in the hospital after the shooting to get over their effects. The fake suicide attempt by pill-taking was a compromise with David's original plan He had tried to induce her to "knick" herself in the head with a gunshot, but, naive as she was in other regards, she refused.

Cinnamon was a reluctant participant. She went along with the plot in the mistaken belief that she was saving her father's life; also she wanted to please him. Patti was lured by the promise of replacing her sister Linda as David's wife. David assured Cinnamon that because she was so young her punishment would be slight, a few years in prison at the most, and that he would pull strings to get her out as soon as possible. Cinnamon believed him and took full blame for the killing, saying nothing of the role of David and Patti. Later she clammed up entirely stating that she had no memory at all of what happened. Her memory was jogged when, after some years of imprisonment, with few of the promised visits from her father or Patti and the knowledge that Patti had replaced Linda as her father's wife, it dawned on her that she had been used. She asked to see a detective who had worked on the case. Throughout the investigation he was not convinced that Cinnamon had acted entirely alone in the killings, but had been unable to pry any additional information from her. This time she related the whole story. The case was reopened and eventually enough evidence was obtained to arrest David and Patti on charges of first degree murder.

The relationship between David and Patti had soured. Although they had married while on a trip to Las Vegas, he did not recognize her as his wife nor acknowledge Patti's child as his own. He disavowed paternity by accusing Patti of having had an affair. Just before the two were arrested he had turned to his child's baby-sitter for sexual solace. Moved by guilt, anger, and humiliation, Patti confessed her role in the killing and implicated David.

While awaiting trial in prison David, undaunted by the threat of trial and conviction, laid plans to extricate himself from his predicament. He befriended a fellow inmate being held as a material witness in another case, a man accomplished in the martial arts who had built up a legend as a fearless hit-man, and engaged him to kill the detective who had nailed him, the prosecuting attorney seeking to convict him, and Patti whose testimony he feared. The hit-man snitched to the authorities who attached a hidden recording device to him which enabled them to get enough information to thoroughly incriminate David in a conspiracy to commit murder.

In her book of almost five hundred pages, Ms. Rule depicts David as a manipulative, cowardly, exploitative, deceitful wretch with no saving grace. Yet his personal history revealed none of the usual events or circumstances that presumably cause sociopathy. Unlike the general run of killers labeled sociopathic, David Brown was a law abiding citizen. He had no criminal record (after the killing, investigators unearthed evidence that he had engaged in some insurance frauds). Hardly qualifying as handome, he had no dearth of female companionship. He had been married five times and had many entanglements with women between marriages. His womanizing was confined to teen-age girls of low income and poor educational background. He selected women whom he regarded as beneath him in age, experience, brains, and ability; he wanted them to look up to him as a man of great substance. To offset feelings of inferiority in his relations with men, he affected a super-macho manner which did not jibe with his short stout build and acne-pocked complexion. He had no close male friends.

David grew up in a lower class social setting. He was the sixth of eight children. His father was an unskilled worker; his mother never worked ouside the home. David went to work at an early age. By the time he was eleven, he claimed, he ran a gas station all by himself. His formal education ended with the completion of the eighth grade. He told rather different accounts, depending on whom he was talking to, of his relations with his parents, from very warm to so abusive that he ran away from home when he was fourteen. By the time he was fifteen he had a steady girl friend. When he was sixteen and she fifteen, they struck out on their own, working at a series of menial jobs. They married and shortly thereafter became the parents of Cinnamon. They were poor, living on food stamps and a modest stipend from Aid to Dependent Children. David was ambitious, and worked hard on the job. He took the General Education Diploma test to qualify for a high school equivalency certification, scoring somewhat above the national average of high school seniors.

His fortunes soared when he stumbled onto a skill that would lead to wealth beyond his expectations. He went to work for a company that specialized in computer data retrieval and learned techniques of recovering data from failed computer disks. He added a few technical improvements and started his own business. His income tax returns showed that his annual earnings prior to going into business for himself were $11,255. In his first year of self-employment they increased to $98,143, and in subsequent years his declared income ranged from $114,000 to $171,000. Boastfully, he claimed to have millions stashed away. In a quantum leap this poorly educated young man went literally from rags to riches.

David furnishes a prime example of what sociologists call *status inconsistency*: he suddenly had earnings near the top of the national income pyramid with a prospect for becoming a millionaire, but had only a lower class value system to direct him in using it. He splurged on material possessions—several autos and trucks which he traded in when he tired of them, a mansion with a large swimming pool for which he paid cash from the proceeds of the insurance on his late wife, and expensive presents by which he sustained the fawning adoration and loyalty of his close associates.

The prospect of unlimited fulfillment of material wants and the private repudiation of any restrictive morality powerfully drive the gratification of wishes, no matter what the cost to others. David's wife Linda was an obstruction to his demand for dominance. Her growing maturity and the needs of her child, diverted her from making him the hub of her life. In the past, he had resolved his differences with wives by divorce. Since his accession to material fortune he could meet the requirements for the purchase of large amount of insurance on his wife's life, which he thoughtfully spread out among a number of insurance companies. Divorce would not have accrued any insurance benefits, moreover it might cost him an expensive settlement and support payments.

C. The Corporate Sociopath

Persons in the upper social tier, who are caught in the same anomic currents as the lower classes, but have the polish of a more culturally enriched upbringing, are clever enough to use less direct, but equally egregious means of self-aggrandizement. The social and physical distance between them and their victims eases the formulation of guilt relieving excuses. The crimes of corporations in polluting the environment or in marketing products—pharmaceuticals, insulation, autos, tires—for which there is powerful evidence of life threatening danger are well documented in official records of the proceedings of governmental oversight agencies. These include exposing workers and residents of adjacent areas to poisonous substances from manufacturing and mining processes which produce lung disease and shorten lives, polluting the environment by chemicals and radiation to raise the levels of cancerous disease, fudging statistical data from the testing of products to give the appearance of harmlessness, and denying or covering up known extensive damage or injury. (Mokhiber) The fact that the law treats the consequences of these corporate decisions made in the boardroom as civil violations should not conceal their deadly nature. The willingness to sacrifice the lives of a statistically predictable aggregate of unsuspecting people to the "bottom line" of the profit and loss statement is as unconscionable as any deadly assault by a sociopath who seeks his goals more directly.

The frequent blowout of steel belt radial tires manufactured in the 1970's by a leading American manufacturer, the Firestone Tire and Rubber Company, resulted in "[T]housands of accidents, hundreds of injuries and at least 34 fatalities..." (Mokhiber, 198). Firestone's reaction is one of many well-documented accounts showing how business executives who may be decent people in their private lives can accord profits a higher priority over the lives of those at risk. In the face of a record of known product failures compiled by the National Highway Traffic Safety Administration (NHTSA), including thousands of returns by dissatisfied customers, and complaints from dealerships, the manufacturer argued in court that the report should not be released. The survey was released to the press amidst demands that the defective tires should be recalled and taken out of use. Instead, as Mokhiber notes, Firestone put the remainder of its stock on sale at bargain process. Firestone's intransigence resulted in the NHTSA having to resort to lengthy legal action to force the company to recall some eighteen million tires. In the meantime most owners were unaware of the danger and continued at high risk.

More reprehensible was General Motors' attempted coverup of design deficiencies in the ill-fated Corvair motor car which were known before the Corvair went into mass production. There was evidence of numerous deaths in accidents due to malfunction of the suspension system of the million Corvairs on the road. The length to which General Motors executives went to suppress that information became a national scandal. Ralph Nader, whose book *Unsafe At Any Speed* exposed General Motors' cover-up of the safety hazards of the Corvair and their willingness to gamble with the lives of their customers, found himself the target of a conspiracy allegedly launched by General Motors to defame his character by hiring a private investigations firm to dig up scandalous material about him.

Stuart Speiser, in his book *Lawsuit*, provides a detailed account of how General Motors mobilized its enormous resources to discredit Nader, but failed to reckon with his determination to stand fast and counterattack. Speiser's account begins with an investigation into the matter by the United States Senate which climaxed in an apology and admission by James M. Roche, the president of General Motors, that an investigation of Mr. Nader had been initiated, but only for the purpose of obtaining information on his possible connection with impending Corvair litigation, whether as an attorney, witness, or consultant. Roche said that if any investigation more intrusive than admitted had happened, it was without General Motors' knowledge and the work of an overzealous detective agency.

This minimal admission satisfied the Senate and did not seriously compromise General Motors, but it did not mollify Nader. Evidence that General Motor's intentions had been much less innocent prompted Nader, supported by a prestigious law firm who took his case on a contingency fee basis, to institute a lawsuit against General Motors. The complaint charged that General Motors, having learned of the impending publication of *Unsafe At Any Speed*, embarked upon a campaign to smear Nader which they carried out by interviewing, under false pretenses, people who knew him. The interviews were used as a cover for impugning

Nader's beliefs, integrity, sexual proclivities, and personal habits that might involve the use of liquor and narcotics. To find evidence of any possible indiscretion, detectives put Nader under intense surveillance over an "unreasonable" period of time with a view to catching him in sexual compromising activities. Depositions taken by Nader's attorney from a member of the private investigative firm that had been retained by General Motors established the credibility of the charges. Additional charges which were less proveable alleged the attempt to entrap Nader into illicit sexual relationhips, making threatening telephone calls, and installing improper wiretaps.

The main issue before the court was whether the specific items of the complaint added up to an intrusion of privacy sufficient to accord Nader grounds for suing General Motors. It took a procedure extending over four years, beginning with a referee's hearing and moving through a series of appeals up to the highest court of New York to determine that Nader had a cause of action for invasion of the right of privacy. At that point, rather than submit to a public display of dirty linen sure to unfold in such a trial, General Motors settled with Nader for $425,000, a record settlement at that time for a lawsuit of that nature.

The behavior of General Motors in producing and marketing the Corvair is analogous to that of common killers deemed sociopathic. First by engaging in an activity that fully qualified as predatory by concealing information that would have surely reduced the sales of the Corvair to an unacceptably low figure. Second by denying and suppressing knowledge of any connection between the alleged design defect and the road casualties. To persist in this deception while people were being killed was morally, if not legally, murder. Like the armed robber who kills to avoid detection, or David Brown who sought to terminate the detective, prosecutor and chief witness in the case against him, General Motors attempted to assassinate the character of the crusader who seriously threatened their corporate image.

A similar scandal developed around the production of The Ford Motor Company's Pinto, a small car marketed in the 1970's to compete with fuel-efficient Japanese imports. A poorly designed and badly positioned fuel tank tended to burst into flames when hit from the rear. A number of Pinto occupants were incinerated in rear-end collisions. Ford undoubtedly knew of the defect long before the car was put into production since repeated tests involving rear end collisions produced ruptured fuel tanks. Ford estimated that the cost of redesigning the Pinto to eliminate the defect would cost more than the company's estimate of the cost of the loss due to the defect. (The cost of a human death was set at $200,000) So Ford did nothing. A series of civil lawsuits resulted in large judgments rendered against the manufacturer. A criminal case against Ford was not successful. Evidence that had been conclusive in the success of the claimants against Ford in the civil cases was ruled inadmissible and hence not available to the jury. (Mokhiber, 381-382)

The concern of a corporate executive with "the bottom line" in deciding that a certain number of deaths was an acceptable price to pay for not remedying the design defect reflects an acute moral detachment, which if exhibited by an individual engaged in predatory crime, would certainly qualify as sociopathic. The Corvair episode occurred in the 1960s just before the challenge of foreign-made automobiles began to cut into American automobile sales. The Pinto, introduced in 1972, was Ford's answer to the challenge from imported cars. Ironically, competition from imported automobiles has done more than the courts or legislation to bring about the moral rehabilitation of the American automobile industry.

Summary

The wanton obliteration of human lives in the pursuit of self-interest expresses less a biological or psychological state than a profound sociological fact. The slaughter based on tribal, ethnic, religious, national or political differences has its counterpart in consumeristic mass society bombarded by the daily media fare of wish fulfillment through violence. Conflicts of interest between groups and unfulfilled wishes and grievances in close relationships within groups conduce to moral isolation, which in turn begets the arrant egoism that typifies the "sociopath." If there is a lesson in all of this for understanding the impersonal infliction of death, whether by the poor and ignorant in a holdup or by the rich and smart in a decision made in the boardroom, it is the ease with which morality can be put aside in the service of self-interest. The big difference between the upper and lower social tiers is less one of a degree of immorality than of available opportunities.

16

Killing Without A Cause

The doctrine that every event must have a cause is axiomatic to cultivated scientific, legal, and religious thought. The converse, that killing, like any other occurrence, is a happenstance in a universe without meaning can be unsettling to those who need a world of order and design. The French existentialist writer, Albert Camus, takes this rare stance in his celebrated novel, *The Stranger*. Camus brings the act of murder into the orbit of *absurdity*, a term signifying the meaninglessness of life. He treats murder, like all other happenings in the flow of human existence, as one in a series of discontinuous events, accorded design only in the awareness of those unawakened to the reality of the absurd. An admiring critic notes that the composition of the novel is itself the epitome of the absurd: "Each sentence, like each instant, forms a whole, a small enclosed universe, attached by nothing to what precedes, and drawing nothing in its wake...*The Stranger* puts us in contact with 'pure' reality in the crude state, where lurks the absurd, to contaminate us." (Maquet, 59)

Camus delivers his preachment in the depressing tale of a young Frenchman surnamed Meursault, living in colonial Algiers, who while strolling on the beach, fortuitously in possession of a gun, shoots and kills a young Algerian lolling in the sun. He is convicted and sentenced to die. The narration is by Meursault. To call him the protagonist stretches the meaning of that term. His passivity, indeed helplessness, almost to the end, in the face of the events leading to his doom, hammers home the author's message of the inherent pointlessness of existence.

Meursault is a man of thirty, a minor office functionary employed by the Algerian branch of a French firm. Ordinary events preceding the crime take on as great an importance in the trial as the killing. The story begins with the death of Meursault's mother in a nursing home. His conduct at the funeral is marked by a perfunctoriness that typifies all of his relationships, in this instance, an indifference to the prescribed appearances of mourning. The day after the funeral he goes to a public beach where he renews an acquaintance with Marie, a stenographer. The relationship quickly ripens into intimacy. Raymond, a friend and neighbor in the apartment house in which Meursault resides, creates a tumult in the building by beating his mistress, an Arab woman, for her infidelity. The police are summoned and issue a complaint against him. Meursault, at Raymond's request, later accompanies him to the police station and gives evidence on Raymond's behalf which prompts the police to let Raymond off with a warning.

Meursault is set on the path to both his destruction and salvation when Raymond, in gratitude, invites Meursault and Marie to spend a Sunday with friends at a seaside bungalow. Raymond confides his uneasiness at being followed by some Arabs, one of whom is the brother of the woman he had beaten. After a morning on the beach and a mid-day meal, Meursault, Raymond, and their host go for a walk on the beach where they encounter two Arabs, including the brother of Raymond's ex-mistress. Raymond and the host engage them in a brawl, broken off when Raymond receives superficial knife slashes across the arm and the mouth. After his wounds are treated, Raymond angrily insists on returning to the beach by himself to look for the Arabs. Meursault, worried about his friend's mood and wishing to restrain him, follows. They find the Arabs. Raymond reaches for a revolver with the question, "Shall I plug him?" Meursault, fearful that Raymond means what he says, replies that it would be wrong since the Arabs have not given offense anew. Recognizing his friend's determination to provoke the Arabs into a fight, Meursault suggests that Raymond give him the revolver and take on one of the Arabs and if the other interferes, he will shoot. Before the plan can be carried out, the Arabs vanish behind nearby rocks. After the two companions arrive back at the bungalow, Meursault returns to the beach and finds one of

Raymond's Arabs lying on the sand. Mutual recognition is almost instantaneous. The burning sun of the Mediterranean beach piercingly fixes Meursault's consciousness. He moves forward; the Arab appears to draw a knife. The reflection of the blade against a film of briny tears blinds him. Meursault's reactions are described as sensations from without: "a fiery gust...from the sea, while the sky cracked in two from end to end, and a great sheet of flame poured from the rift." (Camus, 76) His nerves tautened like "steel springs," Meursault's grip closes on the revolver; a shot explodes, followed by four more tearing the life out of the Arab.

Camus ventures no explanation for the shooting nor even a presumption that it was caused. Whatever Meursault did could just as easily have been done another way or not at all. Nothing in the routine of the absurd existence has the least importance. Nothing matters, since we are all destined for death.

On trial, Meursault is berated not only for the killing, but for refusing to show any commitment to the the popular sentiments that affirm the meaning of existence. For Meursault life is a bore, barely relieved by the gratifications of sex, sport, and food. He is a spectator, rooted in the present, objective, too detached for his own good. He innocently fails to meet conventional standards of appropriateness. He doesn't exhibit the grief of a loving son at his mother's wake, declines to look at his dead mother before the coffin is permanently closed, disrespectfully drinks coffee, smokes a cigarette at her coffin, and nods off to sleep during the vigil. He is obliging to his associates, but asks nothing of them. Marie on a number of occasions asks Meursault if he loves her. He tells her quite frankly that he thinks not, but that doesn't stop her from asking if he would marry her. He tells her he would if it would please her. His response to his employer's offer of the prospect of a transfer to Paris is agreeable, but unenthusiastic. Meursault's natural honesty, his refusal to dispense the conventional pieties and platitudes, is his undoing.

In making his philosophical point, Camus leaves out of consideration two important facts that would rule out the death sentence in a real court of law. The flashing knife blade was provocation for the shooting, and, there was no demonstrable premeditation. What elevated the court's view of the killing to a capital crime was prejudice against Meursault incited by testimony of his disrespectful conduct at his mother's funeral and, to compound the insult, going the following day on a recreational outing and taking a mistress.

Camus personifies in Meursault's unself-conscious directness— his indifference to the past and to the future and his alienation from the ties that give life meaning—the absurdity of human existence. He is anybody, the unvarnished essence of everybody. Camus' existential humanism eschews the volitionalism of a God-driven universe and the causality of scientific determinism to locate the individual in the disorder of an absurd universe. The realization of the absurd frees people from dependency on conventional beliefs and enables them self-consciously to take charge of their own lives.

Conceived as an absurdity any killing can be deemed a chance emission in a chaotic universe. The events leading to the killing of Richard Adan by Jack Henry Abbott, beginning with the meeting of the glances of the two men, and ending with Abbot's death-dealing blow, have that quality of disconnectedness that characterizes the absurd. Bill, the nurse-killer was on a course leading to progressively heavier delinquency, but it is doubtful that he intended to do more than stun his victim in order to get her purse, and possibly facilitate a rape. His friends, Max and Dave had the rotten luck of being with Bill, their ties of peer loyalty dooming them to share his fate. The killings by ex-convict Gary Gilmore were anticlimaxes, each taking a few minutes in a series of events extending over months. They occupied only a few of the more than one thousand pages in Norman Mailer's book.

Any judgment as to whether the events leading up to these killings were existentially continuous or discontinuous with the killings would reflect a philosophical preference. Nothing in the course of events described in these tales of murder compelled the killings; they could just as well have not happened. The same can be said of the killings by Dale Pierre and William Andrews. The tortures inflicted by Pierre on the victims, if we wish to find a cause for them, make sense only as spice to the main course, the diversion of malicious spirits unleashed.

The response of an accused killer to his trial and conviction can be seen by the behavioral analyst as a means to restore self-esteem, and by the existentialist, as an effort to triumph over the absurdity of human existence. Leo Kelly's personal history and his demeanor during his trial resemble in many ways Camus' portrayal of

Meursault. Both exhibited a bland passivity in the face of events which befell them. Like Meursault who seems disconnected from his crime, Leo also took a remote view of his crime—so remote, he claimed not even to remember it. He seemed overtly detached during the trial; "indifferent" is the term used by some observers. He spent much of the time during the examination of witnesses in doodling, at which he displayed a fair hand, drawing abstract designs, concrete representations in a flat bas-relief style (a stylized prancing horse was one of his best), and writing notes to himself. He returned his attention to the ritual of his debasement with grimaces of distaste when things he found offensive were being said about him. His own counsel found him a difficult—if not, at times, uncooperative—client. Like Meursault, Leo was upbraided by the prosecution for not professing contrition, although Leo did not admit that he remembered doing anything to be contrite about. The disbelief in his claim of amnesia only intensified the indignation at his apparent remorselessness.

The experience of being an accused—bearing the stigma of evil-doer and undergoing the ritual degradation by the criminal justice system including, in Leo's case, having to submit to the demeaning definitions and evaluations of psychiatric examiners—drains personal dignity. The elimination of individuality in Meursault's trial goes so far that his lawyer, who by Camus' portrayal might just as well have been an agent of the prosecution, speaks for him in the first person. In Leo's trial it took the form of the attorney deciding upon the the insanity plea as the only means to succour his client. But Leo, like Camus' existential protagonist, remained true to himself and in the end denounced the insanity plea as his attorney's idea and distasteful to his integrity.

The dénouement of Leo Kelly's case was less uplifting than Meursault's. Before going to the guillotine, Meursault in a leap of insight, finds a new freedom from the bind of absurdity by recognizing that the moral vacuum accords him the power to take charge of his own destiny, and in the closing lines of the narrative, to open his heart "to the benign indifference of the universe." The path of Leo's life, on the other hand, led him from an optimistic commitment to conventionality to an embitterment without the revelation of freedom provided in an absurd existence. Evidence of Leo's excursion into the void of moral nihilism, the note the police found in his room with the inscription "This is all meaningless, this is it," lent credibility to the belief by an examining clinical psychologist, that Leo sought to leave the world "in a blaze of glory." If life is meaningless, as Camus believes, cutting life short can make sense, as witness the high suicide rate of young people anticipating the intolerable weight of the impending burdens of life.

But Leo may have realized, in his own terms, as do many who reject the solace of religion, that self-destruction is also a denial of the capacity to confront the absurd and to create meaning. His "valedictory" to the court attempts such an affirmation by attacking the hypocrisy of the world of his accusers. Leo, however, did not have a Camus to speak for him. Lacking the facility with words to capture and portray the sense of alienation of a young black man on trial twice—first to prove his worth to the white gatekeepers of academe, and then for his life before an all-white jury—he delivered himself of a harangue heavily seasoned with the hackneyed rhetoric of racial suppression.

But at the very end, in a triumphant last word that a Camus would have applauded, Leo did have his moment. By denouncing the sham and pretense of the insanity defense devised by his attorney and the learned experts who testified on his behalf, he regained the control of his destiny. When Leo complained, as a black person, of the unfairness of the trial, his charge of the denial of due process missed the mark, namely the failure of his defenders to address his true grievance: the indifference of a system that launched him on a perilous journey into an unfriendly environment without the social moorings or the inner resources for coping.

A belief in an amoral universe can have pernicious consequences. Those who inhabit a moral universe may seek some form of atonement for the evil they do. The person who doesn't believe in anything is unbound. He can conform when it is expedient, and when inexpedient, he can create his own hierarchy of values. Thus the labelling of a "ruthless" killer as a sociopath may rest on the misapprehension that he lacks the ordinary moral sensibilities. To the contrary, he may have very strong concerns for the welfare of persons who are important to him, concerns which do not extend to persons outside of that circle. Like many seemingly upright people whose crimes shock those who know them, the killer nurtures a secret indifference toward those conventional values he finds unacceptable and justifies his violation by an appeal to some nihilistic philosophy that proclaims that the individual is the creator of value.

Robert Lindsey's account of bomb-killings by Mark Hoffman exemplifies this turn of mind. The killer was a young man with all of the outward signs of respectability required in the strait-laced Mormon community of Salt Lake City. As much as most men, he seemingly gave and received the love and loyalty of his wife and parents. He had earned a reputation as an expert on rare documents pertaining to Mormon history. Secretly he was a master forger who managed to fool the experts. His fabrication of hundreds of documents so skilfully forged that they were adjudged genuine by the most skilled evaluators earned him millions of dollars. He was also a self-taught explosives journeyman, able to make simple pipe bombs which detonated by a mercury switch.

With no direct evidence of any motive for the bomb-killings, the prosecutors and detectives working on the case sifted through the available facts and gradually narrowed their suspicions to Hoffman. The papers which brought Hoffman to the brink of murder were "discoveries" of the highest significance which, he claimed, would shed new light on the foundations of Mormonism. Naturally the Mormon hierarchy was interested in securing these papers, to suppress them if unfavorable, to publish them if favorable. Actually, the papers did not exist, but Hoffman fraudulently held out the prospect of huge profits from their sale as collateral for the loan of large sums of money from investors.

Hoffman's creditors grew impatient and pressured him to produce the papers. A detective on the case testifying at the preliminary hearing proposed that a motive for one of the killings was to ease that pressure. He had information that one of his creditors warned Hoffman that if he did not deliver the papers, the creditor would subject him to a civil suit, criminal prosecution, the ruination of his reputation as a dealer in rare documents, and excommunication from the Mormon Church. That creditor became the first victim of the bombings.

To divert police investigation away from connecting the killing to the documents, Hoffman marked the central figure in a widely publicized financial scandal as the second victim. As chance would have it, the intended victim's wife opened a package containing a bomb left at her front door and was killed by the explosion. A third bombing attempt, which also misfired, was aimed, detectives surmised, at relieving Hoffman of the obligation to deliver the non-existent papers to his creditors. They believed that Hoffman intended to plant a bomb in an associate's car along with a package of valueless old documents. The débris from those documents, he could claim after the explosion, was the collection of papers which were in delivery. The bomb exploded prematurely in Hoffman's car seriously injuring him and, for a brief time, directed suspicion away from him.

After his conviction, an attorney from the Salt Lake County attorney's office attempting to tie up some loose ends of the case, interviewed Hoffman in prison. Hoffman, candid in his recital of events, set forth, in terms remarkably similar to to those of Meursault on the eve of his execution, a nihilistic view of life, shared by a many, not only those who kill without compunction: "I don't feel anything for them [the victims]. My philosophy is that they're *dead..* They're not suffering. I think that life is basically worthless. They could have died just as easily in a car accident...I don't believe in God. I don't believe in an afterlife. *They don't know they're dead.*" (Lindsey, 378)

Lust killer Jerry Brudos, neither a dull-witted nor a delusional person, expressed the same credo. Ann Rule reports that a former law enforcement official on the case visited Brudos in prison after his conviction and asked him if he felt any remorse, or sorrow for his victims. "There was a half piece of white paper on the table between us, and [Brudos] picked it up, crumpled it in his fist, and threw the ball of paper on the floor. 'That much,' he said. 'I care about those girls as much as I care about that piece of wadded-up paper'"(Rule, 1988)

Summary

The existential perspective, taken as a cautionary restraint on theorizing rather than a cosmological doctrine, has the value of tempering a strict determinism with a sensibility for the mixture of helplessness and control by which people handle the contingencies of life. A theme running through all types of killings is the tension between happenings disordering the life of the individual and the attempt to regain control. The craftily conceived murders of spouses and children represent the attempt to wipe the slate of unhappy lives clean and to make a fresh start. Robber killers wish to obviate uncertainties that go with pulling off or getting away with the holdup. Killing restores the emotional balance of people upset by the inability to control the responses of others. Killers in the name of morality for a brief moment are recreating the world as they would like it to be. Recreational killers find their playing fields in the order based on the mutual expectations by which people govern their everyday affairs.

An appreciation for the absurd restores a respect, indeed a sense of awe, for the freedom of the human actor and reminds us of the ephemeralness of any reputedly *definitive* explanation of homicide.

17

Nostrums And Cures

No advanced nation spends more on crime control and gets less in return than the United States. Existing policies and agencies of law enforcement have little effect on violent crime in areas of high crime rates and deserve little credit for maintaining the peace in areas of low crime rates. The fact that the murder rate in the United States is as constant as the seasons, notwithstanding the steady increase in the number of violent offenders taken out of circulation by imprisonment, disability, or death should tell us that something beyond the reach of law enforcement keeps the engines of murder running at open throttle.

In a more optimistic vein, the enormous variation in murder rates among social groupings within the United States holds out the attainability of environments in which murder is a rarity. In 1990 the rate of murder and non-negligent manslaughter in the capitol city of Washington, D.C. was 77.8 per hundred thousand of population, higher than the known rate of any nation of the world, and 97.25 times as great as the rate of 0.8 of the state of North Dakota, as low as any nation of the world.

The core of large and small American cities replicates the Hobbesian state of nature. Metropolitan newspapers daily inform readers of last night's slaughter of intended victims and those innocents caught in the crossfire. An investigation by the National Center on Institutions and Alternatives found that on any given day of 1991 in the District of Columbia, the nation's capitol, with a black population comprising 66 percent of the total population, 42 percent of black men age 18 through 35 were under some form of restraint imposed by law enforcement agencies: 15 percent were in prisons, 21 percent were on probation or parole, and 6 percent were on bond or fugitives from the law. If they survive the perils of youth, black men are likely to have acquired a criminal record: by age 35, 70 percent have been arrested; 85 percent of all black men have been arrested at some time in life. (*New York Times*, April 18, 1992, 1) Neighboring Baltimore, not to be outdone, reported that 56 percent of its 60,715 black men between 18 and 35 were under supervision by some branch of the criminal justice system on a given day in 1991. All American cities with large inner city black populations record the same arithmetic of moral disintegration.

The American law enforcement system fails to curb this massive disorder because it is based on the faulty premise, formulated by gentlemen philosophers of the eighteenth century Age of Enlightenment, that the threat of swift and certain punishment would suffice to inhibit crime. The threat was no doubt real for people of substance and good reputation who had a great deal to lose from merely the exposure of dishonorable conduct. Its effect on the poorer classes was doubtful then, as it is now. Crime flourished notwithstanding the severity of penalties, their imposition undelayed by the lengthy appeal processes that today reduce the certainty of punishment. Today, as then, the deterrent power of punishment applies more to people reared in stable family and community environments than in the disorganized urban or rural slum.

The fear of punishment, however, is not the main reason that people refrain from killing one another. The orderly society rests less on coercion than on obedience to the rule: *Do not do to others what you would not have others do to you.* Manifestly there are social groupings in which that sentiment is not effectively transmitted to many individuals. We have essentially three ways of coping with that omission.

(1) *Incapacitate the offenders.* Law enforcement—the police, the courts, and the correctional facilities—upon which society principally relies when moral control fails, deal with the consequences, not the sources of violent tendencies. The dependability of arrest, prosecution and punishment is necessary, but not sufficient, to maintain an acceptable level of civic tranquillity.

(2) *Uproot the causes.* The ultimate source of orderliness resides in the self-control of anti-social impulses. To implant that restraint in individuals identifiably at risk of growing up without it requires the

mobilization and reinforcement of community resources on an unprecedented scale.

(3) *Restrict the availability of the weapons which make it easy to kill.* Laws that would effectively reduce the large number of guns in circulation could warrantably moderate the lethality of criminal assaults. But when proposed they confront powerful political opposition, and if enacted are so diluted that they encounter knotty problems of enforcement.

Catching and Punishing Killers

The public and policy-makers expect too much of the coercive and punitive goals of law enforcement. The ill-fated *Violent Crime Control Act* (S 1241) passed by the United States Senate in 1991, and aborted by the threat of a presidential veto has some provisions aimed at promoting pro-social attitudes among juveniles, but relies primarily on beefed up law enforcement: more police and stricter penalties. The enactment of such legislation would likely influence some reduction in the general run of street crime. The notion, however, that the presence of more police on patrol will inhibit murder is delusional; few killings, or other forms of violent crime, are done in the presence of the police.

The threat of conviction and punishment doubtfully suppresses homicide. Of all industrial democracies, the United States imposes the severest penalties for violent crime, yet endures the highest rates of murder. There is no way of knowing the extent to which people who harbor homicidal wishes are restrained by the fear of apprehension. In personal accounts and confessions killers declare that the prospect of punishment did not enter their thoughts, entangled in the passions of the moment. The covertness of the more carefully planned slayings belies the presumption that the killers are intimidated by the penalty that might befall them. Most killers, their passions spent, do not effectively elude apprehension or try to conceal their identity. Of all serious crimes murder has the highest rate of clearance by arrest, about 70 percent of known cases. For killers from lower class backgrounds, the effect of incarceration in inhibiting future crime is counterbalanced by the benefits of institutional life—regular meals, medical care, recreation, and the indulgence of illicit appetites appetites by smuggled narcotics and unconventional sex. A case can be made that inner city youths are safer in prison than on the streets. Granted that gang vendettas may carry over from the outside into prison, the homicide rates of gang members are lower in prison than on the outside. The rapid replacement of criminals sent to prison by fresh cohorts of criminal aspirants should tell us that legal repression does not accomplish its deterrent goal.

No agency of law enforcement has ultimate responsibility for guaranteeing the peace. The job is divided among the police, the courts, and the correctional system. Each agency blames the other for the failure to suppress violent crime. The police complain that their dedication is crippled by laws soft on crime, persnickety prosecutors and judges who hold police to excessive standards of Constitutional requirements in making arrests, and wrist-slapping leniency in sentencing. Prosecutors and judges reply that the police fail to exercise the knowledge and skill required to make "good arrests" consistent with *due process* and complain of the shortage of personnel needed to accommodate billowing case loads clogging the dockets of metropolitan courts. The public complains of the overcrowding of prisons which forces the release of offenders long before the expiration of their terms of imprisonment. At the same time they oppose the levy of new taxes or the transfer of funds to build more prisons.

Public officials seem wedded to the naive belief that severe punishment is the best way to scare people out of committing violent crime. The death penalty in force in most of the United States, and paradoxically in states with the highest homicide rates, has a robust appeal, notwithstanding its demonstrated ineffectiveness. The most important aim officially ascribed to the death penalty is *deterrence*, the notion that the fear of execution will inhibit homicide by serving notice of the supreme price to be paid. *Retribution*, paying back the offender for the harm he has caused, though not an avowed aim of public policy, is the more popular function of the death penalty.

Retribution bears an odium in the minds of people for whom it negatively connotes vengeance. Defenders of retribution specify a clear distinction between retribution and vengeance. Retribution is punishment measured out by recognized authority in accordance with a politically enacted standard of what fits the crime. Vengeance is inflicted by self-appointed judges who decide for themselves how much punishment it takes to even the score. Societies that lack a sovereign law to administer retribution are plagued with debilitating blood-feuds. The evil of vengeance, as the historical record of lynch mobs shows, is that the punishment may be all out of proportion to the pain or loss it seeks to redress. The judge who, in denouncing a convicted offender from the bench, tells him that a portion of his sentence is merited by the atrociousness of his crime, is sharing and propitiating, but at the same time limiting, the vengeful mood of the community. The pious tone of the belief that retribution is nothing more than legalized vengeance and unworthy of a civilized society, ignores the community's need for the reaffirmation of the violated norm and the need of the victims' survivors for satisfaction. For a large segment of the public, death is the only punishment that matches the enormity of cold-blooded murder. The American man of letters, Jacques Barzun regards life imprisonment as a drearier prospect, and hence more retributive, than execution—a judgment in which most people, particularly those sentenced to die, would not concur.

The staunchest supporters, and opponents, of retribution appear among the survivors of murder victims. Unlike the rest of us who muster the fortitude to bear other peoples' bereavement from murder, so long as it is kept at the distance of the television evening news broadcast, survivors may require some kind of balancing of accounts to get on with their lives. The equalization may fall between the extreme of granting forgiveness, based on religious teachings or humanistic values, sometimes disguised as insights from behavioral science, and the opposite extreme of obtaining the emotional release that only harsh punishment can bring.

In granting forgiveness the mourner seeks consolation in some cosmic scheme of things. Believing the killing to be in some way an expression of the will of God or the operation of natural forces outside of personal control enables the survivor to grant moral absolution to the killer and find peace of mind. The father of a small girl, sexually molested and killed by a fifteen year old youth almost fifty years ago in Philadelphia, dealt with his grief by writing a letter to the editor of a local newspaper. In a tone of charity he chided those who clamored for retribution. Putting the blame on society, he transformed the killer from a moral pariah into a psychiatric case study. As magnanimous as the grieving father's response may have been, it confidently reposed the solution of "senseless' killing in some as yet unaccomplished restructuring of society or undiscovered medical advance. Today, with the benefit of untold hours of research invested in the problem, we are no closer to a resolution.

Another appeal of forgiveness is the hope that the example will kindle a spark of decency in the offender. The news photo of Pope John Paul II visiting and receiving the apology of his would-be assassin satisfies both sentiments: the victim pardons the offender and the state exacts retribution.

For survivors who crave the release of seeing the killer get his just deserts, hitches in the law enforcement process—the failure to apprehend the killer or, if he is caught, breakdowns or delays in the grinding out of justice, the conviction of a lesser offense, or the award of a lenient penalty—feed the torment of unrequited retribution. The common perception that the system devotes more concern to the killer's welfare than to the irreparable loss of the victim adds to the sense of outrage. Alice R. Kaminsky mustered her considerable rhetorical skills in the book, *Victim's Song,* to cry out her grief over the murder of a son. Eric Kaminsky was standing on the platform of a New York subway station where he was robbed, fatally stabbed, and thrown on to the subway tracks by two young men. At the time of the fatal assault he was returning from a practice session in preparation for a career as a concert pianist. Mrs. Kaminsky sought to purge her sorrow by writing of her abhorrence for murderers and their crimes. Her lamentation, at once pathetic and strident, denounces the permissiveness of social science, psychiatry, and religion, which seem to her to play down the enormity of murder in deference to some higher enlightenment. She is the voice of bereaved parents who have been emotionally savaged by the support thrown to killers of their children by celebrity figures and by the willingness of the courts to accept a plea bargain that will occasion the killer minor inconvenience while their children will never know the life that lay before them.

The issue of the moral legitimacy of the death penalty has been a perennial mainstay of debate in state legislatures and high school debating societies. Questions such as the right of the state to kill or the inability to correct the mistake of executing an innocent person, cannot be addressed by data on the administration of capital punishment laws, only by value judgments. Accordingly the debate on capital punishment has centered on the researchable issue of whether or not the death penalty has a chilling effect on homicidal intents and purposes. A survey of pertinent research by the distinguished criminologist Thorsten Sellin (1959) summarizes studies which compare homicide rates between states with and without the death penalty for the period 1920 to 1955. He uses the results to assess the effect of the abolition or introduction of the death penalty on homicide death rates in American states and the effect of the death penalty or its absence on police safety. By and large, Sellin finds no warrant for confidence in the deterrent effect of the death penalty.

A sophisticated regression analysis performed by Isaac Ehrich holds, to the contrary, that the death penalty works: that in the period 1930 to 1969, for every execution eight killings were prevented. Ehrlich's research method has generated considerable controversy. Critics contend that the deterrent effect of the death penalty does not register for most of the years covered by the study, from 1930 to 1961; that the deterrent effect for the total study is a statistical artifact produced by the upturn in rates of violent crime beginning in the years 1962-1963 and the suspension of executions nationwide in 1967 pending a judgment from the Supreme Court on the constitutionality of the death penalty. (Walker, 77-78; Blumstein et al)

The bulk of research on the deterrent effect of capital punishment has favored abolishment, but the statistical evidence has become almost irrelevant since, in recent decades, the death penalty has so seldom been carried out. California, the most populous state in the Union and a capital punishment state, between 1967 and 1991 had not executed anyone, not however, for a lack of persons sentenced to death. In 1992 California resumed execution, sending one person to the gas chamber. The vast majority of doomed killers reside on death row for years, often exceeding a decade, until they are removed by commutation of the death sentence to life imprisonment, death from causes other than execution, or occasionally the award of a new trial followed by a lesser sentence or acquittal. Therein lies the strongest argument against execution: the luckless few who do go to the gallows, electric chair, gas chamber, lethal injection couch, or firing squad are not necessarily worse than others of their lot. They are more like the winners in a lottery with the odds loaded against hitting the lucky number. Even the worst among them may be able to evade or delay their executions for years. Boston Strangler Albert DeSalvo, who killed or violated many victims was one of the successful. Dale Pierre who carried out the music store robbery, killing and torturing the victims, and his accomplice William Andrews, staved off execution by the state of Utah for, respectively, thirteen and eighteen years. Andrews had the benefit of a lengthier appeal process because he did not directly participate in the torture or the killing of the victims. John Wayne Gacy, sentenced to death in 1980 for the murder of thirty-three young men, remains alive in 1993. A meticulous 144 page decision delivered by a United States District Court Judge rejected Gacy's claim that he did not get a fair trial, and removes any impediment to his execution. The newspaper report states that the way is now clear to execute Gacy within two years. How long it will take remains to be seen.

The capriciousness in carrying out the death penalty—the uncertainty over who among those sentenced to die actually get executed and how long it takes to carry out the punishment— argues for a life sentence for capital crimes. The number of death row residents subjected to the death penalty has already been vastly reduced by delaying tactics. Legal abolishment would permit a speedy resolution of litigation in capital offense cases. Contrary to the belief that execution saves the state the cost of maintaining the prisoner for the rest of his life, lawyer's fees and court costs in death penalty appeals are far more expensive. The answer to the complaint that a life sentence, usually with some provision for eventual parole or the possibility of commutation, does not match the enormity of the crime, could be the exclusion of eligibility for parole, a stricture that some states allow. Some restriction on the normal movement or activity permitted prison inmates could even further assuage retributive demands.

Nevertheless, for advocates of the death penalty, there is the galling fact that inmates make adjustments, viewed by opponents of capital punishment as rehabilitation, that enable them to find satisfaction in living. Robert Stroud, the "Birdman of Alcatraz," while serving a twelve year sentence for manslaughter, killed a prison guard and was sentenced to death. His sentence was commuted to life in solitary confinement. He began to raise birds as a hobby and eventually became famous as an expert on the diseases of birds. Richard Loeb and Nathan Leopold while in the Illinois State Penitentiary established a correspondence school for inmates and enjoyed a great deal of autonomy in the management of the enterprise. They had their own cell quarters which they converted into a business office where they were able to remove themselves from the normal prison routines to the extent of preparing and dining on delicacies supplied by their parents.

Preventive Incapacitation

Much criminal violence does not result in homicide, but not for lack of trying by the offender. The only demonstrable means of protecting the public from the legion of violence-prone persons undeterred by previous conviction or punishment is to remove them from circulation by long terms of imprisonment. Most research studies with policy implications for incapacitation focus on the prevention of the general run of serious crimes, but seldom include homicides. One that does, a study by an Ohio State University research team shows that a number of the lives lost to homicide in 1973 could have been saved by sentencing all adult offenders convicted in an Ohio county of a felony during the five-year period before 1973 to a term of five years. Almost 28 percent of arrests and 13.8 percent of convictions on counts of homicides would not have occurred, and 7 of the 36 persons indicted for homicide would have still been in prison. Less encouraging results were obtained for the prevention of robbery, violent sex offenses, and assault, none of these offenses exceeding an incapacitation rate of 1.9 percent. (van Dine et al)

Opponents of incapacitation by imprisonment appeal to practicality and morality, arguing that sentencing all violent offenders to long prison terms would swell prison populations and impose an impossible fiscal burden. No matter how successful the warehousing of large numbers of offenders might be in quelling violent crime, it infringes upon human rights to keep inmates in prison after they may no longer be a threat.

The argument that a policy of preventive incapacitation punishes offenders for the evil they might do rather than what they have done can be rebutted by noting that most repeaters in violent crime are legally subject to far longer terms of imprisonment than the hypothetical five years of the Ohio State study. Many states have seldom used statutes which permit adding to the maximum penalty if the offender has prior convictions of serious crime. The possible unfairness of such a policy could be minimized by taking into account the record of each offender's career in violence given in the typical pre-sentence investigation. Prisoners with records of violent behavior could be kept in prison closer to the maximum permissible term and those who meet rigorous standards of rehabilitation could be granted an earlier release.

Obviously a policy of preventive incapacitation based on a prediction of what individuals might do in the future can have only limited effect. If it cuts down materially on the number of killings, as the Ohio State study forecasts, the amount of error in retaining prisoners who score high on some index of dangerousness, but may no longer be dangerous, is an unfortunate though necessary cost. Any reductions in other forms of serious crime would add to the credit side of the ledger. The risk of confining prisoners who meet the standard for preventive incapacitation, but who may actually be no longer dangerous, could be reduced by due, but not exclusive, regard for what is perhaps the most practical single indicator of the petering out of violent tendencies: *aging*. Only 11 percent of homicides are committed by people who have passed their fortieth birthday.

The objection to incapacitation by detention, that it is costly, makes a practical appeal to the voter. New prison construction is expensive, reputedly running as high as $50,000 per inmate space. Economies could be effected by removing non-violent inmates, many narcotics or property offenders for example, from maximum and intermediate security prisons to less expensive facilities, even halfway houses, to create more room for violent offenders. Estimates of how much it costs to provide for the total welfare and security of a prisoner range, depending on the secureness of the facility, from $7,500 to $25,000 a year. As high as the expense may be, it would substantially offset the material cost of all murders, mayhems, and permanent disabilities that a policy of incapacitation would likely prevent. The moral return from the savings in human life is beyond calculation.

Cures for Homicide

The exhortation to attack the *root causes* of violent crime rolls easily off the tongue. Unfortunately, the causes are not as self-evident as advocates of various theories of causation presume. The individual treatment of prisoners, probationers, or parolees directed at some physical, mental, or spiritual flaw has not produced results directly traceable to the tenets of the therapeutic prescription applied. The stakes in the relationship between the therapist and the patient, or between the prison chaplain and the convert prompt a positive response, sincere or contrived, by the inmate, and a willingness to believe on the part of his healer. By professing to be "cured," the inmate improves his chances for early release, and the "cure" gains the therapist proof of his effectiveness.

Skepticism toward therapeutic programs hardens from the recurrent news story of the prison inmate convicted of robbery, rape, or murder, who after a long period of incarceration is declared rehabilitated and returned to the community, only to commit another gruesome crime. Statistical studies of repeat offenders show that imprisonment is often an all too brief interruption of careers in violent crime. (Petersilia et al)

Controversy within the therapeutic community arouses uncertainty over the efficacy of individual treatment programs. Robert Martinson stirred up a hornet's nest with his negative assessment of programs to rehabilitate offenders. His survey includes the evaluation of prison inmate training programs, individual and group counseling, the improvement of institutional environments and medical treatment, psychotherapy, and intensive supervision of parolees and probationers. His answer to the question, "What works?", is: practically nothing. Critics of Martinson complain of the immoderateness of his critique. They counter that many segments of the programs he consigns to uselessness have demonstrated value.

Programs aimed at the modification of social conditions most prominently associated with violence make more theoretical sense than those aimed at changing personal traits. As noted in Chapter 3, the preponderance of killers come from the lower class. Now while it is true that the vast majority of lower class people do not kill, the more important policy implication is the extreme rarity of killing at middle or upper class levels. It is not clear, however, what dimensions of social class difference account for the vast differential between the two levels in killing behavior. An intrenched sociological view blames the pains of poverty—educational deficiency, lack of job skills, and degraded social or ethnic status—for the crimes of the poor. A more refined version, noting that many impoverished people are law-abiding, contends that material deprivation, in itself, is not the goad to crime, for there is no fixed standard of poverty. What may be material inadequacy in one social grouping could be material well-being in another. Accordingly, the true incentive to crime is a feeling of deprivation *relative* to some standard developed out of the individual's experience in a particular social setting. The revision accounts not only for the crimes of the poor, but for the crimes of the rich, whose sense of deprivation consists in not being rich enough.

The pains of material deprivation may somehow provoke homicidal outbursts in the poor, but, if the statistics of upper class homicide are an indication, do not incite homicide in the well-off. Neither version, however, absolute or relative deprivation, explains why, no matter how deprived they may be, the vast majority of the underclass do not kill and many do not have serious criminal records. The critical difference between the law abiding and the lawbreaking lies not in material inequality but in the attitudes, values, and sentiments which adjust the balance between egoistic gratification and respect for the needs and requirements of others. Cross-cultural studies suggest that people who grow up in a morally integrated social environment are more likely to accord others the civility that is indispensable to orderly interpersonal relationships. Accordingly, the foremost goal of public policy should be to infuse the underclass with the sentiments and values commonly associated with, but not exclusive to the middle class—the virtues of self-esteem, sobriety, planning for the future, diligence, a stake in the community, and most important, an abhorrence for violence. These sensibilities do not thrive in a state of material insecurity, particularly in wealthy nations; hence the importance of strengthening the capabilities of the lower classes for making a living. Until the poor can be trained in marketable skills, government will need to encourage capital investment in enterprises that can employ the capabilities of the underclass. Most urgently government could create employment by assisting in funding the repair of the crumbling infrastructure of cities and in the cleansing of pollution from the land and the water. The reply to the objection of the costliness of such a program is that the quality of the environment and infra-structure are indispensable to the economic health of communities. The absorption of the unemployed, particularly the youthful unemployed, into the workforce will reduce the bill for crime and inculcate patterns of industriousness and civic responsibility into a large segment of a generation at risk of growing up redundant.

The job of instilling the right sentiments is educational and must start with the very young. If by the time children are of age to start school, they have fallen considerably below a minimum standard of readiness, it is difficult to catch up. The blame for the failure falls on the manifestly ineffective parenting received by large numbers of children in the underclass. To break the cycle of moral ignorance requires intervention by an expanded educational institution. The task calls for no structural changes in American society. It merely requires that we make better use of existing institutions. Head Start programs for pre-school age children of deprived backgrounds have been effective in implanting attitudes and skills needed for success in school. But the record shows that if the effect is to endure, it must be followed up with continued support beyond the pre-school period. Activities in which successful adults associate with poor youth to give example, encouragement, and companionship compensate for the lack of grownup men in the lives of inner city boys. Instruction in peaceful conflict resolution is a promising step toward getting youngsters to deal with their differences in dialogue rather than fights—in some inner-city schools, gunfights. A master lesson plan in public and private education should convey in plain language an understanding of the bases of self-esteem and of the ego-protective functions and cultural roots of violence. There is no reason why the inculcation of social-behavioral understandings of this sort has to wait until the student gets to higher levels of education where they are normally delivered, and then only on an elective basis. Correctional agencies—prisons, and probation and parole authorities—have the power to enforce attendance in programs to learn how to handle aggressive impulses constructively and to isolate and retain those who resist or show no aptitude for learning these lessons while in prison. The press and watch-dog organizations can turn the spotlight on laxness in the enforcement of gun control laws and leniency in the handling of repetitive violent offenders. Commercial television should appeal to constructive rather than destructive tendencies by supplying other than the steady fare of gunplay, reckless driving, murder, and mayhem served up in the numerous action series.

The fulfillment of the promise of a "kinder gentler society" requires recognition that the social matrix in which homicide flourishes produces many of the other social disorders bedeviling American society. Thus the violence-prone require more than "role-models" or "rap sessions" to change. They need insight into how destructive forces from the culture get into their private world of meanings. They should know how the alienation endemic to mass society generates these forces, particularly in the lives of poorly educated people locked into monotonous unrewarding routines; and how in states of emotional distraction, intoxicated by liquor or drugs, easy access to lethal weapons leads to violent self-destructive solutions to problems of interpersonal relations.

Popular thought on how to deflect vulnerable children and youths from violent tendencies betrays an oversimplified conception of the formation of constructive aspirations. There is the fatuous notion that media exposure to celebrity "role models" will inspire the appropriate ambitions and the "work ethic" in inner-city black youths. The mass media parade a procession of exemplars consisting of very high-paid athletes, rock stars, sit-com performers, and fictional physicians and judges in soap-operas and violence-centered TV dramas. They omit to say that there are limited openings in the work force for celebrities and top of the line professionals, that the vast majority of the targeted audience, or any general audience, lack the aptitude, ability, motivation, or good fortune to be a star performer, brain surgeon, or judge and will have to settle for more modest, but nonetheless fulfilling, positions in life.

Neglectfully, the purveyors of popular culture fail to inform consumers that infinitely more important than the living image of success depicted by a "role model" with an annual income in the seven figures is the development of the self-discipline required to master any field of technical or professional competence. The entertainment media's casting of minority types in prestigious occupational roles requires supplementation by the depiction of the years of unwavering application for the learning of these roles. This point needs to be impressed on minds at a very early age. Waiting until adolescence is too late in the majority of cases; by then the mold has been set.

In addition to the presentation of practically attainable models for emulation, everyone should be exposed to a variety of role patterns which span the range of relationships in which the individual is likely to engage. For boys and youths to regard women as other than instruments of sexual and emotional exploitation, they must be instilled with a sympathetic under-standing of the role expectations of women. Young people of both sexes need to be indoctrinated with the insights to provide stable family relationships for themselves and their own offspring.

The alarming ignorance revealed in educational test scores of school age children has touched off a lather of concern with the public educational system, particularly since there are progressively fewer menial jobs that can be filled by the unskilled or people unable to absorb on-the-job training requiring basic verbal and math skills. Proposals to remedy the deficiencies by revolutionizing educational methodologies, teaching black or brown children about their heritage, paying for private education out of public funds, or drastically increasing the funding of education reflect a naiveté about the learning process: that somehow these background changes will set the stage for teachers to push the correct psycho-logical buttons to instill knowledge into children.

Policies based on the belief that the remediation of the problem of learning requires changing the environment for learning—the expensive unvalidated practice of busing to achieve racial balance, for example—or the presumption, endorsed by educational experts, that learning can be effortless if the teaching is artfully done, flies in the face of the time-honored knowledge that learning is *work*. A favorable environment for teaching and learning requires firm discipline. The degree of decorum in the classroom needed for teaching and learning must be strictly enforced. Learning, like teaching, is a job that requires a focused effort to absorb information from classroom teaching and schoolbooks into the mind. Depending on the kind of subject matter, learning demands study in the form of drills, exercises, and some degree of memorization. Parental coop-eration is necessary to overcome the child's almost natural inclination to avoid the discipline of homework and go out to play or watch television. If the parents themselves are poorly educated, the educational outlook for the child is dim, unless there is effective intervention.

The responsibilty for teaching children the requirements of civility during the most crucial period of development has lain with the family. This function is handicapped in the single parent, predominantly mother-headed, family that has become the norm in the American lower class. It is even less well served to the increasing number of children who are abandoned by either parent and shifted around among relatives, unequipped or unmotivated to do a diligent job of parenting. Until the lower class family structure can be strengthened, the socialization function must be assisted by extra-familial organizations—school, church, day-care and social work agencies.

In order for the agencies to do the remedial work with culturally, emotionally, or physically neglected children, fiscal necessity requires that the target population be kept within the capacity of the community to provide the needed material resources and social skills enhancement. This entails a revaluation of apparently benign public policies which indirectly perpetuate the violent propensity. Most pertinent are welfare programs which enable and encourage unwed immature teen-age girls and young women—themselves largely the offspring of women, like themselves, with incomplete or inferior education, and no job skills, steeped in substance abuse problems, and raised in communities with high rates of every measure of social disorganization—to have children whom they are unable to nurture physically or morally. Apologists argue that the paltry amounts given to welfare recipients can hardly be considered an incentive to remain on welfare. But relative to the standard of living to which most beneficiaries became accustomed prior to going on welfare, the monthly payments, supplemented by food stamps, offer a more attractive prospect than employment at low wage levels.

The rationalization on behalf of these adolescent mothers, that they have children in order to have something to love or to fulfill their womanhood, hardly justifies the the harvest of neglected children. Many of these children are at serious risk as early as the prenatal stage from their umbilical connection with drug or alcohol using mothers. Unwanted for their own sake, they languish in neglect. Their cries for attention, as inner-city hospital records abundantly attest, result in abusive punishment from mother or mother's boy-friend, driven to distraction by the inability to silence the child or pained by the inconvenience of having to tend to it. Often abandoned, these children are consigned to foster home placement of uncertain merit. Street associates, older children and peers, like themselves neglected in childhood, become their mentors in life adjustment and criminality. By the time the male children arrive at their teens, they are at alarming risk to become chronic offenders or victims in violent transactions; the female children pepetuate the pattern by following their mothers' example.

Curtailing the trend of having of children by people not ready for responsible parenthood is politically difficult since it involves divisive conflict over issues like abortion, birth control, sex education, and an intervention in the lives of people deemed sinful by religious standards and intrusive by civil libertarian standards. The advocacy of measures to curb the reproduction of underclass women has been condemned as genocidal toward African-American or Hispanic people. But however the problem is faced, whether by action programs or left to the tolling of Malthusian processes— which in our time take the form of homicide, drug overdose, alcoholism, HIV infection, or inferior personal hygiene—it must be resolved if we are to put a stop to violence at the source.

Taking Guns Away from Killers

The undisciplined passions and stunted self-esteem that incline vulnerable individuals to engage in violence are not in themselves sufficient to account for the high homicide rates of the United States. Other countries with low homicide rates have large under-classes addicted to violence, but of a sort that leaves the victims with bruises, contusions, broken bones, or, knife slash wounds— bad enough, but seldom fatal. A prime factor in the equation of homicide in America is the ready availability of firearms, mainly handguns, to a large segment of the population deficient in self-control and regard for self or others Once the sentiments of civility are broadly diffused in the population, the presence of guns (as in countries where all able bodied males of military age are army reservists and keep their guns at home) will no longer be an invitation to use them on slight provocation. In the meantime the widespread possession of guns in the underclass, more than any personal proclivity for violence, sustains the American homicide rate.

The opposition to the enactment of laws to control guns is led by the National Rifle Association on specious grounds. Their solution to the problem of violent crime, the imposition of strict sentences on offenders who use guns, deals with the problem after the damage is done. Nor would the long term imprisonment of gun using criminals stop their replacement by fresh cohorts of gun using criminals. The National Rifle Association's call to gun owners to resist any form of gun control has an overreactive tone since none of the national organizations devoted to gun control has seriously advanced a scheme that would deprive people of their guns for sports purposes or self-protection. The pro-gun forces have reacted to modest proposals to keep guns out of the hands of the irresponsible as if any concession to gun-control is a step toward tyranny and a loss of fundamental rights. They have refused to balance the possible inconvenience of gun controls against the savings in life that such restrictions would bring. They have opposed attempts to outlaw military assault weapons or plastic handguns that elude metal sensing security devices at airports.They express horror at improved procedures for the registration and the screening of applications to purchase handguns on the ground that they violate the Second Amendment to the Constitution which protects the right of citizens to bear arms in order to maintain a well regulated militia. Given the nature of modern warfare, it is difficult to imagine a call-up of citizen-soldiers with orders to bring their handguns, shotguns, and hunting rifles.

Official statistics show an unmistakable connection between guns and homicide rates. Guns are the instrumentality in 60 percent of the more than 20,000 criminal homicides committed annually in the United States; handguns are the weapon of choice in 77 percent of killings by gun. Thousands of persons annually die or incur serious injuries in instances where a weapon stored for protection is used at some later time to resolve a personal quarrel or to commit suicide. In addition there is the toll of accidental killings, the children playing games with guns which their parents have left within easy reach, instances of shooting a "prowler" who turns out to be a person lawfully on the premises, and the thousands of suicides which are less likely to occur in the absence of guns. But that's not the total accounting of the damage from firearms. Guns were used in 33 percent of the 543,000 robberies and in 21 percent of the 910,000 aggravated assaults committed in 1988, among which are many failed homicidal attempts resulting in the infliction of serious injury. (*Uniform Crime Reports*, 1988: 21,24)

Whether, and to what extent, in the absence of guns, homicidally intent individuals would resort to some other method of killing is a crucial question in the controversy over gun control. Research inquiries lack the conclusiveness that would prompt either side to concede the issue. Marvin E. Wolfgang concluded that few homicides due to shootings in his Philadelphia study could have been avoided if a firearm were not immediately present; the offender would select some other weapon. He based this judgment on a comparison of homicide rates between the state of Pennsylvania and the city of Philadelphia. He found that with practically the same homicide rates, guns were used in 68 percent of the statewide homicides and in only 33 percent of the city homicides. (Wolfgang, 1958, pp. 81-83). The remainder of the killings were accomplished by fists, feet, blunt instruments, and a miscellany of other means. There is reason to suppose that the difference between state and city in the means of killing reflects a socioeconomic difference between the two populations. The city residents of the period studied, 1948 to 1952, disproportionately poor black people, were less able to afford guns. Wolfgang's data reflect the condition of black people prior to the social upheaval of the civil rights movement of the 1960's and its insurrectionary climax in large cities. One of the consequences of the racial strife was an increasing reliance on guns for self-protection as shown by gun registration applications. Competition in the firearms business and a glut of guns on the illegal market lowered the price of guns and broadened their distribution. By the mid 1980s the homicide rate of Philadelphia far exceeded that of the state. With 14 percent of Pennsylvania's population, the City of Brotherly Love accounted for 53 percent of the state's known felonious homicides.

Studies completed since Wolfgang's show that firearms are pervasively owned by black and white persons, and that they are the principal weapon in homicide. Research inquiries shed some light on whether the expanded availability of guns has increased the number of killings or merely replaced killing by other means. A direct measure of the effect of firearms on fluctuations in American homicide rates is given by Richard Block in his statistical study of homicide in Chicago extending over the period of 1965 to 1973. During this time the homicide rate more than doubled, from 11.4 to 25.3 per hundred thousand. Block concluded that "...the entire increase...can be statistically accounted for by homicides where a gun was the weapon." Philip Cook, in a study of robbery-murder in fifty American cities for the period 1976 and 1977, found a victim rate of 9.0 in gun robberies compared to only 1.7 in robberies effected by other weapons.

The risks attending the legal sale and distribution of automatic weapons designed for military combat are recurrently dramatized by mass killings motivated for no other reason than that the victims are available scapegoats for a grievance of the killer. The unsuspecting victims have recently included the Hispanic patrons of a fast food restaurant slaughtered by a "quiet" man who didn't like Hispanics, children playing in a schoolyard mowed down by a young woman with a history of mental disorder, the employees in a workplace shot by a disgruntled former employee as he methodically moved from department to department, and a graduate student whose doctoral dissertation was rejected by the faculty calculatedly going from office to office, killing as many of his dissertation committee as he found before killing himself. Without the massive firepower provided by these weapons, the killers could not so efficiently lay down a deadly fusillade nor hold off the police while continuing to maintain their threat. Nevertheless opponents of gun control in a rampant show of indifference to the public safety rant that legislation to register or impose reasonable restrictions on automatic weapon ownership is an inconvenience tantamount to a denial of constitutional rights and a trick of centralized government to prevent insurrection against a totalitarian regime that might take over the United States, not to mention a denial to hunters of their recreational pleasure.

Prospects for the resolution of the gun control controversy remain slim. There is no tenable middle ground between the obdurateness of the opponents of gun control and the lack of a politically viable solution offered by proponents. The political will to stake out a middle ground is lacking. Public opinion polls, which include input from gun-owners, have consistently shown a strong support for stricter gun controls, which a minority in the Congress and unsympathetic presidents have managed to foil. (A ray of hope was provided recently when former President Ronald Reagan, long a supporter of the NRA, opposed the NRA to favor a waiting period to investigate the backgrounds of applicants to buy guns.) Organizations opposed to gun control legislation play on the myth of a criminal class, blaming ineffective law enforcement for not keeping criminal gun users locked up, and by warning that if gun ownership is restricted, only criminals will possess guns. They are on solid ground in demanding that gun-using predators get strict punishment, but they are wrong in the presumption that most homicides are committed by this class of offenders. The notion that gun owners divide into good people and bad people, and only the bad people do bad things with guns, collapses under a mass of research data showing that most killings are not for predatory gain and the perpetrators are not career criminals. They are troubled, poorly educated individuals, unadjusted to work roles or familial roles, who, in the throes of anger or grievance, their minds numbed by alcohol or narcotics, use the guns, which the social order has legitimized and the entertainment media have glamorized, to redress grievances.

Undoubtedly, gun owners have killed some criminals in self-protection, but the known instances are rare, and on occasion, the lawful gun user gets killed in the exchange of fire. The evidence set forth by the National Rifle Association on the efficiency of handguns in stopping crime is largely anecdotal. The statistical evidence is meager. Federal Bureau of Justice Statistics for 1987 show that firearms were available to victims or potential victims in only one-half of one percent of incidents of actual or intended violent crime. Information on whether the gun was used to stop the crime is not available, (Sugarmann, 145)

Increasingly the gun owner class includes negligently parented children and teen-agers, who ape the techniques they see in films and television to steal fashionable shoes and jackets from other children, or even to "waste" a policeman. Some of the killings are not imitative of anything, except the casualness of killing in the TV and movie crime shows. Some seek only to gratify a whim, perhaps a curiosity about the destructive capacity of one's weapon. A young man riding in Washington, D.C. motor traffic decided he wanted to kill someone, anyone. He fatally shot a young woman, a complete stranger to him, in another car. According to a *Washington Post* news article (December 1, 1991, p.2), the killer, a nineteen year old unwed father of two children, free on bail from a previous assault case, told fellow passengers that "'he felt like busting somebody.'"

The sophistry in anti-gun control critiques of the statistics of killings by the use of guns is highly reminiscent of the tobacco interests' rebuttal to medical research tying smoking to cancer and heart disease. They attack each correlation which shows a positive relationship between homicide and guns in isolation from the others, notwithstanding that the picture yielded by all of the correlations taken together inescapably points to the deadly role of guns. As Franklin E. Zimring and Gordon Hawkins put it in their criticism of an anti-gun control tract: "Instead of grounding their attack in a coherent vision of violent assault, they put forth rival hypotheses to each strand of circumstantial evidence individually, conclude that none is strict proof of instrumentality effects by itself, and assume that the cumulative effect of multiple strands of evidence is no more persuasive than individual strands." (Zimring et al, 20)

In attempting to diminish the contribution of guns to homicide rates, critics of gun control emphasize the superior importance of sociocultural factors which predispose people to use guns. Don Kates, citing international statistics, points out that the much higher homicide rate for the United States attributed to guns is offset by low rates of suicide by shooting compared to other developed nations with low homicide rates. Combining suicide with homicide rates in making international comparisons substantially reduces the overwhelming lead of America in deaths by firearms. Undoubtedly, as Kates claims, cultural factors in the targeting of violence, whether toward the self or others, help explain the national differences in the inclination toward homicide or suicide. (Kates in Nisbet, 192) But the equating of homicide with suicide, behaviorally or morally, to make a case against gun control is an exercise in desperation since the intentions involved in the two forms of killing are quite different. Suicide is a volitional taking of one's own life by a person who wants to die; murder is the destruction of the life of one who wants to live.

Anti-gun control writers attempt to separate the availability of guns from the use of guns in criminal acts by attributing the latter solely to a criminal culture pattern of the underclass which they regard as the real menace. They attempt to prove the irrelevance of gun control laws to variations in rates of homicide by noting that that nations like Switzerland and Israel which have universal military conscription, requiring reservists to keep military weapons at hand, produce homicide rates as low as nations with highly restrictive gun laws. (Kates, in Nisbet,189) They overlook the additional facts that the Jews, who make up the bulk of Israel's population, particularly the Eastern European Jews, and the Swiss, have deeply rooted traditions opposed to physical violence in interpersonal relations and do not regard the keeping of weapons as necessary for personal fulfillment or as implements for predation. Those who wish to aggrandize themselves at the expense of their fellows have non-violent options.

The vocal minority of Americans who oppose gun controls are the inheritors of a gun symbolism of hunter, warrior, and defender of the hearth—a legacy of the frontier ethos which has filtered down historically into regional, social class, and minority subcultures. The "John Wayne" personification of the gun culture holds a powerful appeal for those who have learned to equate manly virtue with physical combativeness. The legend found on the ubiquitous bumper sticker, "God, guts and guns made America great. Let's keep it that way", epitomizes the attitude. In short, gun availability, culture, and personality do not go their separate analytical ways; there is an interaction among them that must be taken into account in explaining the peculiar patterns of American homicide.

The anti-gun control forces are not as blind to this truth as they affect to be. The more candid among them recognize the role of the racial factor in the expansion of gun ownership and its effect on the epidemic of American homicide. Their rhetoric, more powerful in its implications than its explicit language, conveys that it's not the fault of the good folk (read white people) who need guns for recreation and protection if the criminal element (read black people) threaten robbery and rape and wage what amounts to internecine drug warfare in the inner-cities of America. The proponents of this view generously concede the same need to black people who feel similarly threatened. African-Americans echo the obverse sentiment. True, they need guns for protection against other African-Americans driven to criminality by the insults and oppression of racism, but also for protection against the aroused bigotry of whites.

The argument of the futility of gun control laws resonates powerfully in the contention that an unknown but very large portion of guns used in crime are illegally obtained by the users. An exposé by the American Broadcasting Company news show *20/20* (12/11/92) documents how the illegal distribution is abetted by the opposition of anti-gun control interests to tightening the procedure for the issuance of gun dealers' licenses. Licenses can be easily obtained by people who serve the criminal market. The Bureau of Alcohol, Tobacco, and Firearms to which applications are submitted lacks the staff to investigate properly applicants' criminal records or misrepresentations. Licensees can phone in their orders to gun distributors and receive the merchandise within a day or two. Many operate out of their homes, the trunks of motor vehicles, in public places, or at guns shows. Attempts to stiffen the requirements for licenses to deal in guns are blocked in Congress by representatives who wish to preserve the Constitutional right to bear arms and cavalierly sweep away concerns that the growing volume of guns assures an increase in death and injury by shooting.

The estimate of the number of guns in circulation is so great, ranging from one hundred million to two hundred million, that for the foreseeable future anyone who wants a gun will have no difficulty getting one, legally or illegally. This gloomy forecast disregards that not all of these guns are usable or available for criminal misuse. The total number can be pared down over time by uniform national registration, the confiscation of those found illegally in possession, by a careful monitoring of the transfer of guns admitted into legal ownership, and by sharp scrutiny of applications for licenses to deal in guns.

Opponents of gun control maneuver to seize the high ground with the argument that the issue is debated less on its merits than on ideology, that it is a skirmish in the larger struggle over the nation's values. In their perception the ideological foundation of the opposition to guns emanates from the fuzzy-minded liberal, egg-head community, spoken for by social scientists who would deny the Second Amendment right to bear arms to the deeply patriotic, rural, outdoors, blue collar workers. (Tonso) In fact, the lines of partisanship are not as clearly drawn as the the pro-gun forces claim. There are plenty of ordinary folk, gun owners among them, who, public opinion polls reveal, favor some form of gun controls; and there are intellectuals, albeit a small proportion, who, if the extensive body of pro-gun literature written by them is an indication, oppose gun-controls.

The most telling criticism made by opponents of gun control charges that advocates have not been able to come up with any broadly acceptable practical proposals which offer any assurance of success. They argue that there are some twenty thousand licensing and control statutes on the books, and they don't seem to have much effect on the homicide epidemic. The gun control camp replies that these are preponderately state and local ordinances which have no effect outside of the jurisdictions to which they apply. When the

District of Columbia legislated strict limitations on gun acquisition, many residents of the District got guns in neighboring Virginia, a stone's throw across the Potomac River.

The unadopted Brady Bill, named after President Ronald Reagan's press secretary, James Brady who was shot in the attempt on the president's life by John Hinckley, is an attempt to bring about a national policy on eligibility for gun ownership. It is the first major federal legislation to screen out purchasers with histories of mental disturbance or criminal records. The original version calling for a waiting period of one week was later reduced to five days by compromise with opponents who argued, with some justification, that the Brady Bill would not hinder serious criminals from obtaining guns. At the same time they damaged their claim to be seriously concerned about the problem of the misuse of guns by their strenuous opposition to a measure as mildly inconveniencing as a week's waiting period. Their substitute proposal, which called for an instant investigative check from the gun store, reeks of cynicism since the computerization of records required for such a procedure would take several years to accomplish. The value of the Brady Bill lay mainly in its symbolism, as a means of raising the public's understanding of the problem, and as step toward more effective measures. The issue has become moot, however, since the anti-crime bill in which the gun control measure was imbedded was scrapped in March, 1992 by a lack of votes to cut off a Republican filibuster. Even if the bill had passed, it is doubtful that the the supporters could have mustered enough votes to overcome President Bush's threatened veto.

Given the ferocity of the resistance to moderate policies proposed by gun control groups, there is a powerful suspicion that the bedrock opposition lies less with supporters of Consitutional rights and individual freedom than with gun manufacturers, importers, and distributors determined to crush any attempts to diminish their revenues. Robert Sherrill's lively discussion of the gun problem in *Saturday Night Special* presents ample evidence of the financial bonanza of the American gun market. Government agency statistics of time trends in the domestic production, sales, distribution, and import of non-military handguns in the United States attest to the soaring profitability of the handgun business. From 1966 to 1980 handgun production tripled; from 1976 to 1980, handgun sales increased by 74 percent; and from 1960 to 1980 the number of handguns distributed in the United State increased by four and one-half times. The profits as of January, 1981 were spread among 176,870 federal firearms licensees—manufacturers, dealers, and importers. (Shields, 172-182) The decline in the annual sale of firearms from more than six million in 1975 to a mere four to five million, including two million handguns during the last few years, has lately prompted the National Rifle Association and gun companies to sponsor new kinds of target sports which they hope will interest people in guns and create a continuing market for new gun designs. (Eckholm) In the meantime, untold numbers of guns are diverted from legitimate channels of marketing to an illicit street trade where they fall into the hands of irresponsible people.

The symbiosis between the National Rifle Association and the gun business—manufacturers, importers, distributors, and retailers—attains the passion and fidelity of a love affair. Josh Sugarmann's exposé tells how the NRA has succeeded in protecting firearms from legislative and administrative control to a degree unenjoyed by manufacturers and distributors of other hazardous consumer products. In return gun advertising in NRA publications provides a substantial portion of the NRA's budget, $7.4 million (8 percent) in 1990. (Sugarmann, 87-105)

If the political unresponsiveness to public opinion continues, the most realistic hope for the future of the gun control imbroglio is that it will go the way of the tobacco controversy. The enlightenment that has fostered considerable withdrawal from the tobacco habit has not eliminated smoking, but has reduced the amount of tobacco-related disease and the discomfort from billows of smoke in public places. Similarly, it can be hoped that public education, accompanied by strict enforcement of existing laws will reduce the toll of mortality attributable to the efficiency of guns as killing instruments. These changes, if they do eventuate, will take years. In the meantime the carnage goes on.

A Final Word.

It is considered a sign of good scientific breeding to speak of the multiplicity of causes for any particular social problem, the more vexatious the the problem, the more complex the skein of causation. This book has aimed to show the essential unity of the impulse to kill; that all of the scientific causes, innate and environmental, relate directly or indirectly, to a deficiency in civility. I construe *civility* broadly as due regard for the rights of others, the minimum respect that we owe one another as human beings—a sentiment that rests, if not on a reverence for human life, on the self-serving recognition that only by according it to others, can we ensure it for ourselves. The social contract that works so well in other nations is badly rent in America. Too many persons are not parties to the covenant.

While the identification of the homicidal impulse may be simple enough, the cure, to instill the sentiments of compassion and civility in the groups whose members are most at risk to kill continues to defy, indeed shame, our collective will. The enigma of endemic criminality in a wealthy nation that offers the individual freedom and opportunity on a lavish scale can be traced back to the articles of American political organization, *The Constitution of the United States*. The founding fathers, themselves gentlemen of honor, proclaimed a set of freedoms which presumes a populace made up of self-controlled people of good character, like the farmers, artisans, and merchants who participated in the establishment of the nation. They could hardly foretell that events would bring to our shores millions of immigrants and slaves more or less prepared for acculturation to the value system of their new homeland. The problem persists in that millions of Americans, some whose roots in America go back generations, have not been assimilated to minimal standards of civility. Any program of crime prevention and control to be truly successful must go beyond supression to instill civility in those elements of the population in which it is lacking.

The law enforcement system, overwhelmed by the weight of numbers of violent crimes has become a part of the problem rather than the solution so many think it is. Thinking about the homicide epidemic as an organic or psychological problem has inspired all sorts of gimmickry, ranging from brain surgery to brain washing by various forms of psychotherapy. Sociologists have come closer to the crux of the problem but keep it at arm's distance by skipping from the facts of social structure and culture to the act without looking at the intervention of the self-controlling individual.

The knowledge upon which to base an integrated policy is no mystery. Media commentators, academicians, criminal justice personnel and legislators, indeed, informed people from all walks of life demonstrate a grasp of the various aspects of the problem, but not of how they fit together. Agencies of government wallow in an inertia traceable to a preference for political advantage over hard decisions. The violent proclivities of the literally millions of the underclass for whom murder is a commonplace of life cannot be significantly affected by exhortations to a higher morality or the threat of punishment. Unless we resolutely move to bring the underclass into the mainstream of social opportunity, the conditions that sustain the epidemic of violence will continue unabated. Since the people most at risk to kill or be killed are the least politically aware and able to help themselves, it is certain that without public and private help, the problem will persist. But the intervention will have to be better conceived and more inspired than the routine of administrative initiatives, legislative enactments, or appellate court decisions, which are based more on exigency and appeal to popular misconception than on a coherent vision of the problem. The crime control legislation under consideration in the early 1990s exemplifies the all too common policy of cutting off the regrowable tail, not the head, of the monster. It proposes to do a lot to stiffen the reaction of law enforcement to crime, but not enough to strengthen family and community resources to provide a safe and secure environment for growing up, learning, and making a living.

The Proposed Plan for 1993 of the Federal Office of Juvenile Justice evinces a broad grasp of what needs doing to head off violent crime at the source. Educational and care programs that serve the needs of children at risk are particularly appealing. The amount of the national funding is ridiculously low relative to the stakes. For crime and drug abuse prevention, $200,000; reaching at-risk youths in public housing, $300,000; improving literacy skills of institutionalized juvenile delinquents, $250,000. These dollar amounts would hardly suffice for the needs of one large city. To be sure, most of the programs are intended only as demonstrations or pilot studies. But given the present financial state of state and local governments, it is unlikely that they will be emulated.

To attain the desired ends requires determined informed leadership to bring about the needed coordination among policy makers, law enforcement, and social agencies to change the lives of fellow citizens adjusted to unproductive and unfulfilling social patterns. Little is gained by preaching the values we cherish as a civilization to the converted. It takes a sense of mission and the mobilization of human resources on a national and community-wide scale to do what is needed to instill them among the alienated.

References Cited

Abbott, Jack Henry, *In the Belly of the Beast*. New York: Random House, 1981
———and Naomi Zack, *My Return*. Buffalo, N.Y.: Prometheus Books, 1987
Abrahamsen, David*, Confessions of Son of Sam*, New York: Columbia University Press, 1985
———*The Murdering Mind*. New York: Harper & Row, 1973
———*The Psychology of Crime*. New York: John Wiley & Sons, Inc. Science Editions, 1962: 41
Adler, Freda, *Sisters in Crime*. NewYork: McGraw-Hill, 1975
Alexander, Shana, *Very Much a Lady: The Untold Story of Jean Harris and Dr. Herman Tarnower*. New York: Little, Brown & Co. 1983
American Psychiatric Association, *Diagnostic and Statistical Manual of Mental Disorders (Third Edition)* 1980, Washington, D.C.
Anderson, Chris, and Sharon McGehee, *Bodies of Evidence*. New York: A Lyle Stuart Book, 1991
Asch, Solomon E., *Social Psychology*. New York: Prentice-Hall, 1952
Baldwin, James, *The Evidence of Things Unseen*. New York: Holt, Rinehart and Winston, 1985
Bandura, Albert, *Aggression: A Social Learning Analysis*. Englewood Cliffs, N.J.: Prentice-Hall, Inc. 1973
Bensing, Robert C., and Oliver Schroeder, Jr., *Homicide in an Urban Community*. Springfield, Illinois: Charles C. Thomas, 1960.
Bing, Léon, *Do Or Die*. New York: Harper Collins Publishers, 1991

Blinder, Martin, *Lovers, Killers, and Husbands.* New York: St. Martin's Press, 1985

Block, Richard, Homicide in Chicago: A Nine Year Study (1965-1973), *Journal of Criminal Law and Criminology*, 314 (December, 1975: 496-510

Blumstein, Alfred, Jacqeline Cohen, and Daniel Nagin, *Deterrence and Incapacitation: Estimating the Effects of Criminal Sanctions on Crime Rates.* Washington, D.C. National Academy of Sciences, 1978

Bohannon, Paul, *African Homicide*, New York: Atheneum Press, 1967

Bonger, W.A., *Criminality and Economic Conditions.* Bloomington, Ind.: Indiana University Press, 1969

Bresler, Fenton, *Who Killed John Lennon?* New York: St. Martin's Press, 1989

Brittain, Robert, The Sadistic Murderer. *Medicine, Science, and the Law*, vol.10, no. 4, 1970, pp.198-207; cited in Masters, 246-7

Brown, Claude, *Manchild in the Promised Land.* New York: Macmillan Co.,1965.

————Manchild in Harlem. *New York Times Magazine*, Sept. 16, 1984

Browning, Christopher R., *Ordinary Men: Reserve Police Battalion 101 and the Final Solution in Poland.* New York: Aaron Asher Books/ Harper Collins Publishers, 1992

Bugliosi, Vincent, *Helter Skelter.* New York: Bantam Books, 1975

Cahill, Tim, *Buried Dreams.* New York: Bantam Books, 1987

Camus, Albert, *The Stranger.* New York: Vintage Books, 1946

Capote, Truman, *In Cold Blood.* New York: Random House, 1965

Cavan, Ruth Schonle, *Criminology.* New York: Thomas Y. Crowell Co., 1962

Center for Afroamerican and African Studies, *National Study of Black College Students,* University of Michigan, Ann Arbor

Charny, Israel, *How Can We Commit The Unthinkable?* New York: Hearst Books, 1982

Cleckley, Hervey, *The Mask of Sanity.* St. Louis: Mosby, 1955

Cloward, Richard A, and Lloyd E. Ohlin, *Delinquency and Opportunity.* New York: The Free Press, 1960

Clinard, Marshall B., *Sociology of Deviant Behavior.* New York: Holt, Rinehart and Winston, Inc. 1963

————with Richard Quinney, *Criminal Behavior Systems: A Typology*. New York: Holt, Rinehart and Winston, Inc. 1967

Cohen, Albert K., *Delinquent Boys*. New York: The Free Press, 1955.

Cohen, Morris, *Reason and Law*. Glencoe, Ill.: Free Press, 1950

Cook, Philip J., The Effect of Gun Availability on Violent Crime Patterns, in Lee Nisbet, editor, *The Gun Control Debate*. Buffalo, New York: Prometheus Books, 1990, p. 133

Coppolino, Carl A., *The Crime That Never Was*. Florida: Justice Press, Inc. 1980

Cox, Bill G. et al, *Crimes of the Twentieth Century*. New York: Crescent Books, 1991

Cressey, Donald R., Role Theory, Differential Association and Compulsive Crimes, in Donald R. Cressey and David A. Ward, *Delinquency, Crime and Social Process*. New York: Harper & Row, 1969,

Cressey, Paul G., The Motion Picture Experience as Modified by Social Background and Personality. *American Sociological Review*, 3:516-25, 1938

Dalgard, Odd Steffen and Einar Kringlen, Criminal Behavior in Twins, in Leonard D. Savitz and Norman Johnston, *Crime in Society*. New York: John Wiley & Sons. Source: A Norwegian Twin Study of Criminality, *The British Journal of Criminology* (July, 1976)

Daly, Martin, and Margo Wilson, *Homicide*. New York: Aldine DeGruyter.1988

Damore, Leo, *In His Garden: The Anatomy of A Murderer*. New York: Arbor House, 1981

Davis, Don, *The Milwaukee Murders*. New York: St. Martin's Paperback Edition, 1991

Dear, William C. and Carlton Stowers, *"Please Don't Kill Me"* Boston: Houghton Mifflin Company, 1989

Del Giudice, Marguerite, and Philip Leonetti: The Mobster Who Could Bring Down The Mob. *New York Times Magazine,* June 2, 1991

Dershowitz, Alan M. *Reversal Of Fortune: Inside The Von Bulow Case*. New York: Random House, 1986

Driver, Edwin D., Interaction and Criminal Homicide in India, *Social Forces*, 40 (December, 1961)

Dugdale, R.L., *"The Jukes" : A Study in Crime, Pauperism, Disease and Heredity*. New York: Putnam, 1895

Durkheim, Emile, *Suicide*. New York: The Free Press, 1951.

Eckholm, Erik, Gun Industry Aiming to Improve Its Sales, New York Times News Service, *Sarasota Herald Tribune*, March 8, 1992

Eisenstein, James, and Herbert Jacob, *Felony Justice*. Boston: Little, Brown and Co. 1977

Eysenck, H.J. *Crime and Personality*. Boston: Houghton Mifflin Co. 1964

Feshbach, Seymour, The Function of Aggression and the Regulation of Aggressive Drive. *Psychological Review* 71(1964) 257-272

Fishbein, Martin, and Icek, Ajzen, *Belief, Attitude, Intention And Behavior*. Reading, Mass.: Addison-Wesley Pub. Co. 1975

Fleming, Jacqeline, *Blacks in College*. San Francisco: Jossey-Bass Publishers, 1985

Fox, Richard G., The XYZ Offender: A Modern Myth? *Journal of Criminal Law, Criminology and police Science* 62 , March 1971

Frank Gerold, *The Boston Strangler*. New York: The New American Library, 1966

Frondorf, Shirley, *Death of a "Jewish-American Princess" : The True Story of a Victim on Trial*. New York: Villard Books, 1988

Gaylin, Willard, *The Killing of Bonnie Garland*. New York: Penguin Books, 1982

Gibbons, Don C., *Society, Crime and Criminal Careers*. Englewood Cliffs, N.J.: Prentice-Hall, Inc., 1973

Ginzburg, Ralph, *100 Years of Lynchings*. Baltimore: Black Classics Press, 1988

Glueck, Sheldon and Eleanor, *Unraveling Juvenile Delinquency*. New York: The Commonwealth Fund, 1950

———*Physique and Delinquency*. New York: Harper & Row, 1956

Goddard, Henry H., *The Kallikak Family: A Study in the Heredity of Feeble-mindedness*. New York: Macmillan, 1912

Goldstein, Abraham, Testimony of, in *Attorney General' s Task Force on Violent Crime*, Hearings, Atlanta, Ga., May 20, 1981. quoted in Thomas Maeder, *Crime And Madness*. New York: Harper & Row, 1985, 158

Goodall, Jane, Life and Death at Gombe, *National Geographic*, May 1979, 592-621

Goring, Charles, *The English Convict*. London: His Majesty's
 Stationery Office, 1913
Gottfredson, Michael R., and Hirschi, Travis, *A General Theory of
 Crime*. Stanford, California: Stanford University Press, 1990
Green, Edward, Race, Social Status and Criminal Arrest. *American
 Sociological Review*, 35: 476-490, 1970
—— with Russell Wakefield, Patterns of Middle and Upper Class
 Homicide, *Journal of Criminal Law and Criminology* 70 (June
 1979)
Goulett, Harlan M. *The Insanity Defense in Criminal Trials*. St.
 Paul, Minnesota: West Publishing Co. 1965
Guttmacher, Manfred, *The Mind of The Murderer*. New York:
 Grove Press, 1962.
Harris, Jean, *Stranger in Two Worlds*. New York: Macmillan
 Publishing Co. 1986.
Hinckley, Jack, and Jo Ann, *Breaking Points*. New York: Berkley
 Publishing Co. 1986
Hirschi, Travis, *Causes of Delinquency*. Berkeley: University of
 California Press, 1969
Hoffer, Abram, *Orthomolecular Medicine For Physicians*. New
 Canaan, Conn.: Keats Publ. Co., 1989
Hooton, Ernest, *Crime and the Man*. Cambridge, Mass.: Harvard
 University Press, 1939
Howard, Clark, *Zebra*. New York: Richard Marek, Publishers, 1979
Ingleby, David, *Critical Psychiatry: The Politics of Mental Health*.
 New York: Pantheon Books, 1980
Jeffrey, Clarence Ray, Criminal Behavior and Learning Theory,
 Journal of Criminal law, Criminology and Police Science, 56
 (Septenber 1965) 294-300
"Joey," with Dave Fisher, *Killer: Autobiography of a Mafia Hit
 Man*. New York: Pocketbook Edition, 1974
Johnson, Ray, *Too Dangerous To be At Large*. New York:
 Quadrangle-New York Times Book Co., 1975
Jones, Ann, *Everyday Death*. New York: Holt, Rinehart and
 Winston, 1985
Joselson, M., Prison Education, A Major Reason for Its Impotence,
 Corrective Psychiatry and Journal of Social Therapy, 17(2,
 1971)
Kahaner, Larry, *Cults That Kill*. New York: Warner Books. 1988

Kahn, Marvin W., A Comparison of Personality, Intelligence, and Social History of Two Criminal Groups, *The Journal of Social Psychology* (49) 1959, 33-40

Kalven, Harry, Jr. and Hans Zeisel, *The American Jury*. Boston: Little, Brown and Co. 1966

Kaminsky, Alice R., *The Victim's Song*. Buffalo, New York: Prometheus Books, 1985

Karnow, Stanley, review of Haruko Taya Cook and Theodore F. Cook, *Japan At War: An Oral History*. New York: The New Press, 1992, in *The New York Times Book Review Section*, 11/22/92

Kates, Don, Guns, Murder, and the Constitution: A Realistic Assessment of Gun Control, *Pacific Research Institute for Public Policy*, 1990, pp. 36-43. In Lee Nisbet, *The Gun Control Debate*. Buffalo, N.Y.: 1990, 187-194)

Katz, Jack, *Seductions of Crime*. New York: Basic Books, Inc. 1988

Kearney, James J., *Clark and Marshall: A Treatise on the Law of Crimes*. Chicago: Callaghan & Co.,1952

Kinder, Gary,*Victim.: The Other Side of Murder*, New York: Dell Publishing Co. 1982

Kinzer, Stephen, *N.Y. Times*, July 27, 1991, p.4, col. 5

Kinsey, Alfred C., Wardell B. Pomeroy, and Clyde E. Martin, *Sexual Behavior in the Human Male*. Philadelphia: W.B. Saunders Co., 1948

Klawans, Harold L., *Trials of an Expert Witness*. Boston: Little, Brown and Company, 1991

Krafft-Ebing, Richard von, *Psychopathis Sexualis*. New York: G.P. Putnam's Sons, 1965

Kuper, Leo, *Genocide: Its Political Use in the Twentieth Century*. New Haven and London: Yale University Press, 1982

Landau, Simha F., Israel Drapkin, and Shlomo Arad, Homicide Victims and Offenders: An Israeli Study. *Journal of Criminal Law and Criminology*, 65 (September, 1975) 390-396

Langevin, Ron, Mark Ben-Aron, George Wortzman, Robert Dickey, and Lorraine Handy, Brain Damage, Diagnosis and Substance Abuse among Violent Offenders. *Behavioral Sciences and the Law*, Vol. 5, No. 1, 1987

Larsen, Richard W., *Bundy: The Deliberate Stranger*. Englewood Cliffs, New Jersey: Prentice-Hall, Inc. 1980

Lasch, Christopher, *The Culture of Narcissism*. New York: Warner Books, 1979

Lester, David, The Relationship between Suicide and Homicide. *Corrective & Social Psychiatry, & Journal of Behavior Technology, Methods & Therapy*, 23 (1977)

Leyton, Elliot, *Hunting Humans*. New York: Pocket Books, 1988

Levin, Jack and James Alan Fox, *Mass Murder*. New York: Plenum Press, 1985

Levy, Ronald, *The New Language of Psychiatry, Learning and Using DSM-III*, Boston: Little Brown and Company, 1982

Lewis, Craig A., *Blood Evidence*. Little Rock, Arkansas: August House, Inc. 1990

Lieber, Arnold L., And Carolyn R. Sherin, Lunar Cycles and Homicides, in Leonard D. Savitz and Norman Johnston, *Crime in Society*, New York: John Wiley & Sons ,1978, pp.353-358. Source: Homicides and the Lunar Cycles: Toward a Theory of Lunar Influence on Human Emotional Disturbance, *The American Journal of Psychiatry* (July, 1972) 129:101-106

Lindsey, Robert, *A Gathering of Saints*. New York: Simon and Schuster, 1988

Linton, Ralph, Universal Ethical Principles, in Walter Goldschmidt, *Exploring the Ways of Mankind*. New York: Holt, Rinehart and Winston, 1960, 534-44

Lorenz, Konrad, *On Aggression*. New York: Bantam Books, 1966

Maeder, Thomas, *Crime and Madness*. New York: Harper & Row, 1985

———*The Unspeakable Crimes of Dr. Petiot*. Boston: Little Brown and Co. 1980

Mailer, Norman, *The Executioner's Song*. Boston: Little Brown & Co., 1979

Malcolm, Janet, *The Journalist and the Murderer*. New York: Alfred Knopf, 1990

Maquet, Albert, *Albert Camus: The Invincible Summer*. New York: George Braziller, Inc. P.59

Martin, John Bartlow. *Why Did They Kill?* (New York: Bantam Books, 1966

Masters, Brian, *Killing For Company*. New York: Stein and Day, 1985

———Dahmer's Inferno, *Vanity Fair*, November 1991

McClintock, F.H., *Crimes of Violence*. London: Macmillan & Co. Ltd. 1963

McCord, William, and Joan McCord, *The Psychopath: An Essay on the Criminal Mind*. Princeton, N.J.: D. Van Nostrand Co. Inc. 1964

McCormick, Charles T., *Handbook of the Law of Evidence*. St. Paul, Minnesota: West Publishing Co. 1954

McGinniss, Joe, *Fatal Vision*. New York: G.P. Putnam's Sons, 1983
——*Blind Faith*. New York: G.P. Putnam's Sons, 1989
——*Cruel Doubt*. New York: Simon & Schuster, 1991

Nader, Ralph, *Unsafe At Any Speed*. New York: Bantam Books, 1973

McNulty, Faith, *The Flaming Bed*. New York: Bantam Books, 1981

Martinson, Robert, What Works? Questions and Answers about Prison Reform, *The Public Interest* 35 (1974)

Mednick, Sarnoff A., Vicki Pollock, Jan Volovka, and F. Gabriella, Biology and Violence , in Marvin E. Wolfgang and Neil Weiner, *Criminal Violence*. Beverly Hills, California: Sage Publishing Co. 1982

Megargee, Edwin I., "The Role of Inhibition in the Assessment and Understanding of Violence," in Jerome L. Singer, ed., *The Control of Aggression and Violence: Cognitive and Physiological Factors*. New York: The Academic Press, 1971
——and G.A. Mendelsohn, A Cross Validation of Twelve MMPI Indices of Hostility and Control, *Journal of Abnormal and Social Psychology*, 65 (1962)

Merton, Robert K., (*Social Theory and Social Structure,* The Free Press, Glencoe, Ill., 1968)

Meyer, Peter, *The Yale Murder*. New York: Empire Books, 1982

Michaud, Stephen G. and Hugh Aynesworth,*The Only Living Witness*. New York: Linden Press, Simon & Schuster, 1983
——*Ted Bundy: Conversations with a Killer*. New York: Signet Books, New American Library, 1989

Milgram, Stanley, *Obedience to Authority: An Experimental View*. New York: Harper Row, 1974

Miller, Walter B., Lower Class Culture as a Generating Milieu of Gang Delinquency, *Journal of Social Issues* 14:5-19 (1958)

Mokhiber, Russell, *Corporate Crime and Violence*. San Francisco: Sierra Club Books, 1988

Joel Norris, *Serial Killers: The Growing Menace*. New York: Doubleday, 1988, 182

———*Jeffrey Dahmer*. New York: Pinnacle Books, Windsor Publishing Corp. 1992

Packer, Ira K., Homicide and the Insanity Defense: A Comparison of Sane and Insane Murderers. *Behavioral Sciences & the Law*, Vol. 5, No. 1, 1987

Pallone, Nathaniel J., and James J. Hennessy, *Criminal Behavior: A Process Psychology Analysis*. New Brunswick, N.J.: Transaction Publishers, 1992

Palmer, Stuart A., *A Study of Murder*. New York: Thomas Y. Crowell Co., 1962

Parwatikar, S.D., W.R. Holcomb, & K.A. Menninger, The Detection of Malingered Amnesia in Accused Murderers, *Bulletin of the American Academy of Psychiatry and the Law*, 13, 1985

Petersilia, Joan, Peter Greenwood, and Marvin Lavin, *Criminal Careers Of Habitual Felons*. Santa Monica, California: The Rand Corp. 1977

Pittman, David J. and William Handy, Patterns in Criminal and Aggravated Assault, *Journal of Criminal law, Criminology, and Police Science*, 55 (December, 1964)

Pokorny, Alex D., A Comparison of Homicide in Two Cities, *Journal of Criminal Law, Criminology and Police Science*, 56 December, 1965).

Pollak, Otto, *The Criminality of Women*. Philadelphia: The University of Pennsylvania Press, 1950

President's Commission on Law Enforcement and Administration of Justice, *Task Force Report: Science and Technology*. Washington: U.S. Government Printing Office, 1967

Quinney, Richard, *Criminology*. Boston: Little, Brown & Co. 1975

Rainwater, Lee, Crucible of Identity: The Negro Lower Class Family, *Daedalus* 95 (Winter 1966) 172

———*Behind Ghetto Walls: Black Families in a Federal Slum*. Chicago: Aldine Publ. Co. 1967

Reckless, Walter C., Simon Dinitz, and Ellen Murray, Self Concept as an Insulator Against Delinquency, *American Sociological Review* 21: 744-756 (Dec. 1956)

Reiss, Albert J., Jr. and Jeffrey A. Roth, Editors, *Understanding and Preventing Violence*. Washington, D.C.: National Academy Press, 1993

Rensberger, Boyce, King of the Myths, *New York Times Magazine,* October 14, 1973, 121

Reston, James, Jr. *The Innocence of Joan Little.* New York: Times Books, 1977

Richard, Suzanne, and Carl Tillman, Murder and Suicide as Defense Against Schizophrenic Psychoses, *J. Clinical Psychopathology,* XI, 1950, 149.

Roche, Phillip, *The Criminal Mind.* New York: Grove Press, 1958

Roebuck, Julian, *Criminal Typology.* Springfield, Ill.: Charles C. Thomas, 1967

Rubinsky, Elizabeth W., and Jason Brandt, Amnesia and Criminal Law: A Clinical Overview, *Behavioral Sciences and Law,* Vol. 4, No. 1, Winter, 1986

Rubinstein, Frankie, *A Dictionary of Shakespeare's Sexual Puns and Their Significance.* London: Macmillan Press, 1984

Rule, Ann, *The Stranger Beside Me.* New York: W.W. Norton & Co. 1980

———*Small Sacrifices.* New York: New American Library, 1987

———*Lust Killer.* New York: New American Library, 1988

———*If You Really Loved Me.* New York: Simon & Schuster,1991

Ruotolo, Andrew Keogh, *Once Upon a Murder.* New York: Grosset & Dunlap, 1978

Ryzuk, Mary S., *Thou Shalt Not Kill.* New York: Popular Library, 1990

Samenow, Stanton E., *Inside the Criminal Mind.* New York: Times Books, 1984

Sandiford, Kay, and Allen Burgess, *Shattered Night.* New York: Warner Books, 1984

Satten, Joseph, Karl Menninger, Irwin Rosen, and Martin Mayman, Murder Without Apparent Motive, 1960, *American Journal of Psychiatry* 117: 48-53

Schacter, Daniel L., On the Relation between Genuine and Simulated Amnesia, *Behavioral Sciences and the Law*, 4:47-64,1986

Schwartz, Anne E., *The Man Who Could Not Kill Enough.* New York: Carol Publishing Co. 1992

Scott, D. D., Battered Wives, *British Journal of Psychiatry,* 12 (1974) 433-441

Sellin, Thorsten , *Culture Conflict and Crime.* New York: Social Science Research Council, 1938.

————*The Death Penalty*. Philadelphia: The American Law Institute, 1959

————and Marvin E. Wolfgang, *The Measurement of Delinquency*. New York: John Wiley, 1964

Sharansky, Natan, *Fear No Evil*. New York: Random House, 1990

Sheldon, William H., *Varieties of Delinquent Youth: An Introduction to Constitutional Psychiatry*. New York: Harper, 1949

Sherif, Muzafer, and Carl I. Hovland. *Social Judgment*. Yale University Press, 1961

Shields, Pete, *Guns Don't Die—People Do*. New York: Arbor House, 1981

Silverman, Milton J., and Ron Winslow, *Open and Shut*. New York: W.W. Norton, 1981

Solomon, George F., Psychodynamic Aspects of Aggression, Hostility, and Violence. In David N. Daniels, Marshall F. Gilula, and Frank M. Ochberg, *Violence and the Struggle for Existence*. Boston: Little Brown and Co., 1970

Solzhenitsyn, Alexander, *Cancer Ward*. New York: Random House, 1984

————*The Gulag Archipelago*. New York: Harper/Collins, 1985

Speiser, Stuart M., *Lawsuit*. New York: Horizon Press, 1980.

Stevens, William Randolph, *Deadly Intentions*. New York: New American Library Signet Book, 1983

Straus, Murray A., State and Regional Differences in U.S. Infant Homicide Rates in Relation to the Sociocultural Characteristics of the States, *Behavioral Sciences & The Law*, Vol. 5, No. 1, 1987

Strean, Herbert, and Lucy Freeman, *Our Wish To Kill: The Murder in All Our Hearts*. New York: St. Martin's Press, 1991

Sugarmann, Josh, *National Rifle Association: Money, Firepower & Fear*. Washington, D.C.: National Press Books, 1992

Sutherland, Edwin H., and Donald R Cressey, *Criminology*. Tenth Edition. Philadelphia: J.B. Lippincott, 1978)

————*The Professional Thief*. Chicago: The University of Chicago Press, 1937

Sutton, Willie, with Edward Linn, *Where The Money Was*. New York: Viking Press, 1976

Sykes, Gresham M. and David Matza, Techniques of Neutralization: A Theory of Delinquency, *American Sociological Review,* December, 1957, 22: 664-670

Szasz, Thomas S., *The Myth of Mental Illness.* New York: Harper & Row, 1961

Scott, P. D., Battered Wives, *British Journal of Psychiatry,* 125 (1974) 433-441

Sherill, Robert, *The Saturday Night Special.* New York: Charterhouse, 1973

Tierney, Patrick, *The Highest Altar.* New York: Penguin Books, 1989

Tonso, William R., Social Problems and Sagecraft: Gun Control as a case in Point, in Don B. Kates, Jr. ed. *Firearms and Violence: Issues of Public Policy.* 1984. Also in Lee Nisbet, 1990

Treen, Joe and Constance Richards, A Monster Caged At Last, *People,* 10/19/92

Trilling, Diana, *Mrs. Harris: The Death of the Scarsdale Diet Doctor.* New York: Penguin Books, 1982

Van Dine, Stephan, Simon Dinitz, and John Conrad, The Incapacitation of the Dangerous Offender: A Statistical Experiment, *Journal of Resarch in Crime and Delinquency,* 14:22-34

Voss, Harwin L. and John R. Hepburn, Patterns in Criminal Homicide in Chicago, *Journal of Criminal Law, Criminology and Police Science,* 59 (1968)

Waldo, Gordon P. The "Criminality Level" of Incarcerated Murderers and Non-Murderers, *Journal of Criminal Law, Criminology and Police Science,* 61(March 1970)

Walker, Samuel, *Sense and Nonsense About Crime.* Monterey, California: Brooks/Cole Publishing Co. 1985

Webb, Eugene, J., Donald T. Campbell, Richard D. Schwartz, and Lee Sechrest, *Unobtrusive Measures: Nonreactive Research in the Social Sciences.* Chicago: Rand McNally & Co. 1966

Weiss, James M., Joseph W. Lamberti, and Nathan Blackman, The Sudden Murderer: A Comparative Analysis, *Archives of General Psychology,* 1960: 674)

Wenk, Ernest A., and Robert L. Emrich, Assaultive Youth: An

Exploratory Study of the Assaultive Experience and Assaultive Potential of California Youth Authority Wards, *Journal of Research in Crime and Delinquency*, 9 (2, 1972)

Wertham, Frederic, The Catathymic Crisis, *Archives of Neurology and Psychiatry*, 37 (1937) 974-978

———*A Sign For Cain.* New York: The Macmillan Co. 1966

———*Dark Legend.* New York: Doubleday & Co. Inc. 1949

Wilson, James Q. and Richard J. Herrnstein, *Crime & Human Nature.* New York: Simon & Schuster, 1985

Wilson, John P. and Sheldon D. Zigelbaum, The Viet Nam Veterans on Trial: The Relation of Post Traumatic Stress Disorder to Criminal Behavior, *Behavioral Sciences & The Law,* Vol. I, No. 3, Summer, 1983

Wishman, Seymour, *Confessions of a Criminal Lawyer.* New York: Penguin Books, 1982

Wolfgang, Marvin E., *Patterns in Criminal Homicide*, Philadelphia: University of Pennsylvania Press, 1958

———and Franco Ferracuti, *The Subculture of Violence.* London: Tavistock Publications Ltd. 1967

———Suicide by Means of Victim-Precipitated Homicide, *Jl. Clinical and Experimental Psychopathology & Q. Rev. Psych & Neurology* 335 (1959)

Wright, Theon, *Rape in Paradise.* New York: Hawthorn Books, Inc. 1966

Wyden, Peter, *The Hired Killers.* New York: Bantam Books 1964

Yochelson, Samuel, and Stanton E. Samenow, *The Criminal Personality.* New York: Jason Aronson, 1976

Zimring, Franklin E. and Gordon Hawkins, *The Citizen's Guide to Gun Control.* New York: Macmillan Publishing Co.1987

Ziskin, Jay, *Coping With Psychiatric And Psychological Testimony,* Second Edition. Marina Del Rey, California: Law And Psychiatry Press, 1970

Name Index

Subject Index